The Undefeated

The
Undefeated

GEORGE PALOCZI-HORVATH

ELAND

London

First published in England by Secker & Warburg in 1959

First published by Eland in 1993

This paperback edition published in
the United Kingdom by Eland Publishing Ltd
61 Exmouth Market, London EC1R 4QL in 2011

ISBN 978 1 906011 18 5

Cover shows a detail from *Fallen Worker* © 2011 Sylvia Plachy

**Printed and bound in Great Britain
by Clays Ltd, Elcograf S.p.A.**

For Georgie

Foreword

WE LIVED AT THAT TIME in a sort of catacomb like the early Christians and we talked about salvation. Our physical survival seemed quite hopeless. We were prisoners of an evil system bent on our destruction. But some of us in that prison cellar and in similar catacombs all over the country were in fact doubly imprisoned; our minds were in chains. The obsession which helped to build up the evil system still held some of us in its grip. That obsession – a curious sort of controlled schizophrenia – made the life of its victims difficult even under 'normal circumstances'; it turned jail existence into an unbearable nightmare.

And then some of us were saved; our minds were liberated by the relentless shock treatment.

My salvation came in 1951, when I had already spent two years in jail. I was feverish for days. I went through a crisis very near to a nervous breakdown. Then I slowly recovered and began to appreciate my return to the normal world of common sense and common decency.

We still sat in the very same catacombs; we were still emaciated convicts, the lowest of the low. No old and sick beggar in his senses would have changed places with us, but we – the freshly saved ones – were intensely happy. After years or even decades of mental strait jackets it was wonderful to be free within our skulls. We watched shyly and humbly the re-emergence of our consciences, the restoration of freedom within us.

My cellmates of that period were not all pessimists. There was a grey-haired man who believed that in ten or fifteen years we might be released. Knowing the story of my life, he said that the greatest responsibility in our group was mine.

The Undefeated

'You are a writer and intellectual, Sixteen (we called each other by our bunk number). You know both worlds. You have to write everything down when you are released into the greater prison. You must get a room for yourself all alone. You must write at nights, for years, and when you have written down the truth you must make several copies, somehow get aluminum containers, place a copy in each, and at various points in the country dig holes and put them away for the future.'

He liked to talk about all the details of this task and mused with quiet satisfaction about the time when my manuscript would be found and the truth known. He was sorry that our country had no seashore. What a wonderful thing it would be if we could put our messages in bottles and let the waves carry them to the shores of free countries!

In time things took an unexpected turn. After three more years we were released into the 'greater prison' as we called our country. Then the nation started to sizzle with revolt. We attacked the dangerous obsession and the evil system which had the powerful backing of a huge empire. We revolted and fought, and for a few glorious and crazy days we even thought that we were victorious. But the gigantic empire sent its armour and fire against us and our country was turned into the graveyard of a revolution. After the holocaust a great exodus started and on a stormy winter night I too struggled through the swamps on the frontier of my country to safety on foreign soil. As I lay at the foot of a haystack next to my wife and baby son, I thought of my grey-haired friend and his aluminum containers. What unshakable belief he had in the power of truth!

Now as I write I am thinking of messages in bottles, carried by the waves, carried on the ocean of time. I must try to report the facts. After an infinity in solitary confinement I see most things in a different light. Like many others I am a Rip van Winkle of the mid-twentieth century. Many Western intellectuals have fallen prey to the obsession; many learned to know intimately the evil system. Many went through tortures, brain-washing and solitary confinement. Many took part in revolts and many escaped. The world in my time is full of survivors, prison graduates and liberated minds. Their reports are conditioned by their intellectual tools and by their approach. Mine is that of a writer who has a background of social anthropology and of history.

There was a time not very long ago when the art of remembering became of vital importance for me. I spent more than a year alone in a humid, cold cellar cubicle, without anything to read. Some eighteen waking hours day after day, month after month in a cubicle three yards by four, with a wooden plank for a bed, four unlovely walls, a very bright naked electric light glaring mercilessly day and night – an ocean of time and a human being utterly dependent on his brain as mainstay, as entertainment – and as defense against madness!

I tried to defend myself by reliving my past. I searched all over my memory, I ferreted out tiny bits of my past, concentrating alternatively on various periods of my life. Most of us prison graduates with long solitary-confinement records have good memories. After our terrible periods of loneliness we were thrown into larger cells, and there we compared notes with others. It turned out that in trying to fill out the millions of empty seconds, most of us had evolved similar systems. Most of us were aware that through our repeated struggles in trying to remember everything, our memories improved. The mental muscles, it seems, grow stronger with exercise – and exercise they certainly had in our case.

The days had to be partitioned into various mental activities in order to avoid the despair of 'nothingness'. You lectured to yourself, you did mental translation exercises; some people even played chess in their heads with imaginary opponents.

The most dangerous times came in the evenings when one was tired but was forbidden to lie down and sleep. It took effort to occupy oneself, to forget one's situation. In the evenings I permitted myself the luxury of reliving my travels. It was great luck that I have been in some forty countries and could occupy myself with reviving some of my journeys. And again this reliving of the past strengthened the mental muscles. I first noticed this in reviving in detail the trip between Cairo and Istanbul. Actually I made that trip eleven times during the Second World War. The Haifa-Beirut-Tripoli railway was not built then, and the journey in reality took nearly five days. When I first tried to revive it in memory it took only two hours. (One could tell the time by prison routine.) Some two weeks later I let my mind dwell again on the Cairo-Istanbul trip and I did not get through it in my head in one evening. And at the end of my solitary-confinement period it took three whole evenings, because I not only remembered hundreds of details of the journey, the faces of the sleeping-car attendants on the Cairo-Haifa run and on the Taurus express, but also the various people to whom I talked on the trips and my moods and thoughts at various stages of the journey.

Another pastime was trying to remember the names and faces of all the people I had met in Tehran or Cape Town, Stockholm or Paris, and all the other cities I had visited in my life. I counted the remembered names and it turned out that my memory contained thousands of them.

But all this is only the superficial upper level of one's memory. Going deeper, one has questionable experiences.

In the cellar cubicle I dwelt patiently and calmly on my early childhood. And even amidst such singularly advantageous laboratory conditions when there was nothing to divert my attention, and concentration was often not work but luxury – even amid such conditions very little trustworthy material came back to me of my earliest childhood.

From my fifth year the bits of the past started to multiply. But were those bits virgin memories – pure recollections uninfluenced by outside sources? I had reasons to doubt it. By digging to the sources I often found that I have talked to somebody about those bits of my childhood. So, for instance, I remember very well a scene in the garden of my grandparents' estate when I was three. A naked little boy running towards a huge wooden tub filled with water. For many years I believed that I remembered this scene not only with my brain but also with my skin – and it was only as a millionaire of time during my cellar existence that I found out the contrary. It was not firsthand memory; what I actually remembered was only a snapshot of the scene.

Another frequent pastime in solitary confinement is passing judgment on one's past actions and behaviour. There is a chance to face oneself squarely, to sum up and to judge. Doing so, one comes face to face with the problems of 'personality'. Even the best of memory is not a quite trustworthy guide to one's past; the thing would be, perhaps, to find the general and prevailing tendencies – in other words, to trace the development of one's self. The difficulty in describing and dissecting your own past is the difficulty of a microscope's viewing itself, a dissecting knife's dissecting itself. In an autobiography you cannot help but use your own intellectual, emotional and moral tools – tools which are suspect even if you can attain a great degree of objectivity.

Common sense and common decency – these are in most cases the most reliable test of the story of a single human life.

About eighteen months after I 'saw the light', our prison conditions underwent an amazing change for the better; I was given a typewriter in my cell and managed to write nearly twenty thousand words of my autobiography, writing in English so that if the guard came in suddenly I could tell him I was doing a translation. When I was transferred to another jail I left a copy with my cellmate, Paul Ignotus, and when we were released we both succeeded in smuggling out our copies. What follows is much altered and expanded from that earlier version. But it is written with the same intellectual tools that were sharpened by solitary confinement, and based on standards of truth and objectivity I set myself when there seemed little chance of my memories being reduced to the printed word and when the act of remembering was a way of staying alive.

Chapter One

I WAS BORN IN 1908 IN BUDAPEST, the second city of the Austro-Hungarian Empire. Francis Joseph the First, with his ruddy cheeks and enormous cotton-wool whiskers, was to be for a further eight years Kaiser of this strange anachronism. In the Balkans the Austro-Hungarian troops were occupying a Turkish province called Bosnia, French troops arrived in Morocco, and up north the tall and lean tennis-playing king of Sweden handed the Nobel Prize to scientists for discoveries with questionable consequences. Rutherford was already at work and Lenin visited daily the library of the British Museum in London.

Some people contend that the nineteenth century really came to a close in 1914. If so I could say that I was born into several centuries. The twentieth was beginning to show its nightmarish outlines; yet Budapest was still a replica of Paris of the Second Empire, and my family was top-heavy with representatives of the old feudal times. They lived on their estates without really being aware of the liberation of serfs, the elderly uncles still talked more Latin than Hungarian and regarded the non-nobles as a kind of subspecies of humanity. If our age is really a gigantic watershed between quite different historical periods, those of my generation can rightly say that they witnessed a dynamic change similar to the transition from the Middle Ages to the Renaissance. By a social accident I knew intimately some very intensively living relics of feudalism: huge red-faced gentlemen with Gargantuan appetites, thin-lipped matrons who always walked beneath nonexistent baldachins, or fussy old bachelors who preferred the company of bees, hounds, or game to humans. Later on, during various turns of the twentieth century I saw them peering into the bewildering, strange world in which they were as out of place as a huge molten gold watch limply hanging on a treetop in a Salvador Dali picture. Aunt Isabella, who taught me table manners according to the Spanish etiquette, once remarked that there is some consolation even in a piece of bad luck. The fact that I had broken my right arm and consequently my left was stronger was positively a good thing: it was easier for me to learn to hold the knife in my left hand as you must when you eat at court. She cold-shouldered the machine age and stuck to her carriage with – now very modestly – two horses, nor would she use those contraptions called elevators or lifts. She was killed by the slow blast of a Thermit bomb.

Uncle Arpad read only Horace and Virgil. In his youth when the family wanted to visit some relatives on a distant estate during the winter, they traveled by ox cart because the roads were impassable for horse-drawn carriages. When crossed, he boxed the ears of his peasants and he would not receive the Lord-Lieutenant of the county who had married outside of nobility. Human beings for him began with 'chamberlains'; that is, people who can prove on both sides sixteen noble ancestors. A merciful stroke took him away before his estates in Transylvania were lost; otherwise he would have starved, for a nobleman does not work.

These elders longed for the time when our kind had still the right to behead people, and they treasured family diaries for items like this: 'This Monday morning my lord Szemere visited me to sue for the hand of my good daughter Anne for his good son Geyza; after breakfast I heard the case of three villains and had two of them beheaded. My lord Szemere said those cursed Germans are to be blamed for all this villainy.' They despised the so-called counts and barons elevated in return for treason by the Hapsburgs – damn their eyes – barely a century or two ago. The hurricane-like changes in the last decades of the sleepy Austro-Hungarian monarchy made them dizzy and distempered; they had to forget and drink. They drank a lot. Then they disappeared into family crypts, or eked out a bare existence in genteel civil service, or occasionally emigrated to the Americas, where surprisingly enough they adapted and became useful twentieth-century citizens, as did my two maternal uncles Miklos and Sandor. Within three years of coming of age, they 'liquefied' my grandfather's estate of some five thousand acres; that is, they changed the land into card losses, wine, women and gypsy music and then went out penniless to South America, where one became a prosperous hotel owner in São Paulo, the other a successful railway contractor in the Argentine. My grandfather after paying their 'debts of honour' was left very poor. With the remnants of his fortune he bought a few hundred acres near Budapest at Imrehaza, with a small manorhouse where he never could entertain more than twenty people.

My mother came from a Transylvanian Calvinist family, the Kovacsy's of Hadad. When she was sixteen her family arranged her marriage to a man of twenty-eight, Zoltan Paloczi-Horvath, a barrister who belonged to another old Calvinist clan. The chief factor in the alliance was that the male descendants of the union would all be royal chamberlains, able to prove sixteen noble ancestors on both sides. My mother, still half a child, was simply told she was to be married – that was that. She knew more about her future husband's lineage than she did of him.

In the fourteenth century the Paloczi's were oligarchs in northeastern Hungary, and one of them became Prince Primate of Hungary. Both the Paloczi's and the Hadadi-Kovacsy's belonged to that group of 'rebel lords' who turned Protestant when the Protestant revolution reached Hungary, a conversion which was due in many cases to political reasons. The anti-Hapsburg and anti-German nobility embraced Calvinism, the 'Hungarian Religion' or Lutheranism, the others remained Roman Catholics and were rewarded by the Hapsburg Kaisers with titles. Old Michael Karolyi used to tell us that his great ancestor was raised to earldom for treason.

This Calvinist nobility was proud of having a 'longer ancestry' than most of the Roman Catholic dukes, counts and barons. Till the turn of the twentieth century many families of this middle nobility – that is, those with no title – still had very large estates. But the liberation of the serfs in 1848 set the landowning aristocracy on a downward path. They began to lose their estates, now managed for them by dishonest bailiffs, and the one feature of modern capitalist society they did find useful was the banking system; they borrowed heavily, and when they could not pay their mortgages, bit by bit the estates were sold.

The Paloczi-Horvath's had large estates in northern Hungary and in Transdanubia, and in the middle of the last century still owned some fifty thousand acres. The famous Calvinist College of Sarospatak was founded by two ladies: Susanna Lorantffy, the wife of George Rakoczi, and Maria Paloczi-Horvath, who gave seven thousand acres to the newly founded college. By the time I was born, my paternal grandfather had managed to lose all his land and only my grand-uncle Istvan was left with a large estate. So my father had to read law, which, apart from a commission in a crack hussar regiment, was then considered to be the only profession fit for a gentleman, if he must work at all. My father was a hussar officer in reserve and gave his name to a law firm in which his partners did most of the work and he most of the spending.

He must have been a rather heedless, superficial young man, something of a roué, with his side whiskers and enormous moustache, and his conviction that his name must secure for him a pleasant existence.

His name certainly did secure a suitable match and a very easy time indeed as long as the marriage lasted. His wife's parents paid all his household expenses, and at dawn every Monday morning a cartload of the best their estate could offer in food and wine left Imrehaza for Budapest and the newly married couple.

The marriage was no success. They were married in 1896, in the year of the 'millennium', when Hungary celebrated her thousandth year as a sovereign nation. My mother was almost a child when her first child, my sister Margot, was born; she had grown up in a large and complicated household of which she was supposed to be the showpiece. Now she saw her husband when they gave dinner parties or went out together, but most evenings she spent alone while he disappeared into his man's world of night clubs and all-night card parties. During her pregnancies she almost never saw him. In her loneliness she escaped into a world of books and music. But after nearly twelve years of marriage, in 1908, a few months after I was born, she came to know of a particularly sordid affair of my father's and not long afterwards she herself fell in love with a young bourgeois, the deputy director of a small bank. She braved the inevitable scandal, was divorced, and marrying out of her class, entered a different, kinder and more sympathetic world.

My mother's second husband lived comparatively modestly; they could afford only two servants and they lived in a small five-room flat. My stepfather was a liberal-minded, ambitious bank employee, who soon became a director and later founded his own firm of chartered accountants. He traveled a great deal in Europe and entertained all sorts of foreign financiers, manufacturers and engineers. While in my father's class people spoke Latin and German, and comparatively rarely, French, in my stepfather's circle almost everybody spoke French, German and English, and often two or three other European languages as well. In my father's feudal world they lived in the past and were conscious of their decline; in my stepfather's bourgeois world they lived in the future and looked confidently forward to an ever-expanding European existence.

My mother soon found herself at home here, for her own family was relatively unconventional. Her younger sister became a painter and her brothers, as I have said, turned into successful businessmen in the Argentine and Brazil. She traveled constantly with her second husband and enjoyed their full life together, their common interests in music, theatres and art, and his wide circle of friends beyond the world of bankers and businessmen.

I grew up in my stepfather's household and my first memories are associated with a big flat on the fourth floor of a house in Felso-Erdosor Street. As I grew old enough to take stock of my surroundings I learned that I had two fathers, 'Daddy' and a 'Sunday Father', whom my nurse took me to visit every Sunday. I did not like him. I kissed him because my mother told me to, but I hated doing it. 'Daddy' I loved because my mother loved him and because he was handsome and good; 'Zoltan-Papa' was not bad-looking either, but I did not like his looks. Somehow I guessed that he had been unkind to my mother, though she always spoke nicely about him. And there was a subtler reason for my dislike: the unconscious hatred I felt towards my beloved 'Daddy' for not being my real father was transferred to 'Zoltan-Papa' and grew into an intense bodily revulsion. Not only did I hate kissing him; I even took care not to eat in an even rhythm with him, feeling that if my soup spoon were to touch my lips when his spoon touched his there would be bodily contact. I avoided it.

I envied boys who only had one father and never talked to my school friends about the two-fathers situation, and when my younger brother Tomi was born I envied him; Daddy was his real father and he had no Zoltan-Papa to visit on Sundays.

The summer after my sixth birthday, war broke out, and I had to pay a farewell visit to Zoltan-Papa, and liked him better because of his splendid hussar uniform, his helmet with white horsehair wound about it, his long sword and handsome shining riding boots with their clashing spurs.

Of all the games I played, my favorite was 'playing in my head'. My German governess, Miene, became quite worried when she observed how I used to sit for hours on end in the nursery, staring vacantly into space, doing nothing. I never explained, when she scolded me, how busy I was 'just sitting there and not playing'. I didn't mind being called stupid; I enjoyed sitting quietly and letting things happen in my head.

This is how it is done: you sit still and colours and smells happen in your head and body – a colour, perhaps, that makes me feel sore-throat hotness or Balaton coolness, or makes me feel forbidden-good. You can feel with your whole body things which are not there; yet no one knows you are doing it, no one calls you a liar, as Margot did when I told her about Tahiti. She herself had previously told me all about Tahiti, about its people and its coconut palms; she had shown me pictures. For whole afternoons I played Tahiti, bathed in its warm blue seas, crunched raw coconut between my teeth. Naturally I now knew more about it than she did – but when I described it to her she said I was lying.

This intense, compulsive daydreaming stood me in good stead in prison. Once while I was a prisoner I was given a handful of plums. They were deep blue, and some of them still carried on their skin that thin layer of wax which makes them seem light blue while they are still on the tree. I absently rubbed the wax of one plum and *my hand remembered a former self* – the little boy who discovered this plum-wax for the first time. I was walking with mother in the huge orchard at Imrehaza, and she reached up and picked me a plum. The afternoon, mother's lovely gesture as she reached up into the leaves, the smooth roundness of her arm and the quivering summer air made the plum a royal present. I rubbed off the newly discovered plum wax, my fingers delighted in the sun-kissed warmth of its skin and my heart overflowed with happiness to have such a beautiful mother.

I see that summer afternoon through the haze of four decades in a light soiled by the scum of the boiling times. During an eclipse we once watched the sun through country-style dark glass, a piece of glass covered with a thin film of candle smoke. And now the years between cover my vision with their smoke, everything in my childhood seems darkened. But in my cell, as I fingered the plum, that summer afternoon unfolded all its splendours and showered happiness on me. My mother was humming a tune, little lights whirled in her hazel eyes, her bronze-auburn hair reflected sunrays that stole through the leaves; and her figure swayed slightly. I knew then that I wanted to be my mother's child. Soon afterwards I was to hope fervently that my body was flesh out of my mother's flesh, that there was nothing in me of my father. Soon I was to search myself, my skin and bones, the way my hair grew, for signs of my father – happy, always, to find nothing of him. Later on this manhunt changed into a fight against a whole set of ancestors lurking in my bones. But that is another story.

The summer days at Imrehaza are coupled for me with mother's singing voice, with mother's piano sending out to me in the garden waves of music that fade quickly on the afternoon air, an old tune that I still love. This was goodness, this was safety: I played in the garden, she played her piano in the big cool room and at any time I could run into the house and stand close to her, and watch her long, flowerlike fingers dance on the white and black keys.

I developed slowly in my first five years – all my life I have had periods of stagnation followed by sudden unexplained flowerings. I began to be enchanted by the world of colour, smell and sound, the sweet sensation of taste and touch; life soon became the theatre of my five senses. Then came books. Through them I began to guzzle up half the world. I read novels when I was eight, by ten I was a voracious reader.

The Undefeated

Mother was worried by this at first; she did not relish the idea of a poor little wonder-child; but when she found I was racing through books looking for facts – facts about people, colours and scents, landscapes and events, facts about the world – in the same way that other little boys collect stamps or tin soldiers, she saw there was no harm in my reading. So I went on, tearing through travel diaries, historical novels, everything I could lay my hands on. Certain books were kept locked away; I pinched the key of course, and soon found out for myself how dull those books were, mostly about a lot of uninteresting 'he and she' business. I remember reading Zola's *L'Argent* – the only thing that interested me in it was a description of Mount Carmel in Palestine.

I soon developed the habit of cramming as much as possible into my day, a habit which never left me – even under jail conditions I managed to lead a crowded life. By eleven my day was divided into several equally busy sections. I threw myself into my school life, read a lot, and devoted part of every day to furthering various 'aims'. One of these 'aims' was to become captain of a bunch of kids I played with during the afternoon in the big playground of our city park. They were quite different from my schoolmates and I was different when I was with them. In school I was quiet, studious, reserved. On the playground I became a roaring tough. But most of all I looked forward to a half an hour or so of intensive daydreaming in the evenings. If, as captain-candidate, I happened to hear something which caught my imagination, I went on fighting and throwing my weight about, but filed away what I had heard as material for my evening pursuit.

One afternoon while we were playing handball, a big freckled boy – the captain I was planning to oust – was stopped by a girl of about ten. She wanted him to come and eat a sandwich; he said he was not hungry, and she shrugged her shoulders so that her blond curls danced as she turned away.

'Who is that?' I asked.

'My sister Herta – a silly kid who makes up poems in her head.'

I was still bedazzled by her golden locks. 'Herta who makes up poems in her head' was collected for my daydreaming. The ball came flying towards me; I smacked it back, meanwhile making a delicious private rendezvous for the evening with Herta. Private, yet not private. I certainly did not want anyone in the real world outside myself to know about my daydreams; all the same I had my audience. I had developed strict rules for the game: my fantasies had to be rounded-out stories, acceptable not only to me but to 'everybody'. I always imagined an audience of strangers, and while daydreaming, I had to take into account their imagined tastes, opinions, sensibilities. In addition, my fantasies were much more than verbal expressions; my audience saw the same images, shared the same bodily sensations, felt the same feelings that I conjured up in myself, and if I did not feel intensely and accurately while imagining my story I would fail to please and entertain them. The private theatre of my skull contained playwright, manager, actors, critics and audience.

All the details of my imagined story had to reach a high degree of realism, and on the 'Herta' occasion, I had to make up real poems. There we were walking in Tahiti on a cliff high above the summer-evening-blue sea, among the cocoa bushes with their flaming red berries.

'Let's make a poem about the chocolate of Tahiti', I suggested. She looked at the bushes pensively. She was making up her poem and so was I. The spicy air of Tahiti was giving our cheeks butterfly kisses as we walked on in peaceful silence. And behind the scenes of my private theatre I was furiously busy, for it was evident that I should have to have poems ready for both of us. We had rather a long walk that evening in Tahiti; it went on all the time my real-life self was being compelled to eat his dinner, endure his bath, and get a good-night kiss from Mother. It was quite an ordeal to go through a normal boy's evening and at the same time compose two poems, direct a whole play and last but not least, as an 'actor-feeler' *not to have a single dissonant feeling in my body*. My audience would have been terribly shocked, if, while walking with Herta in the enchanted air of Tahiti, they had detected the sensation of nausea. *Yet the real-life boy had to eat roast liver with paprika,* he had to *smell* the sweet air of Tahiti while actually eating this revolting dish.

At last it was dark in the nursery, and the world became less complicated. As we sat watching the short tropical sunset, Herta said,

'Let me hear your poem.' I repeated it. Then she said hers. By the time the last verse, softly spoken, dropped into the sea, I was almost asleep after a very exacting experience.

After all daydreaming is common enough, and there is nothing special about daydreaming while doing something dull. What seems to me singular about my fantasy is the way in which I imagined an audience-critic for whom I had to act with all my five senses, with all my bodily feelings. Perhaps this compulsive and rather obsessional activity had its uses. Here is my only clue: my daydreaming ceased at the age of thirteen, when I began to write.

Chapter Two

M Y FATHER spent his summers 'visiting'. He started out at the end of May and went from one estate to another, one of many guests who passed their time drinking, playing cards and tennis, hunting and philandering. He did not return to Budapest until after the vintage festivals in the Tokaj district in the first week of October. After I was ten he took me for a few weeks every summer to the estate of one relative or another; so I had ample opportunity to compare the two worlds – my father's and my mother's. Not unnaturally I attributed the difference between them not to classes, but to human beings, to characters, to families. My father's world represented everything I disapproved of.

My father and his friends were impossible reactionaries. Even after the First World War they still looked upon non-nobles as cattle. They disapproved of general education, of humanitarian principles generally, and they were extremely chauvinistic. During the White Terror after the First World War and after the brief Bolshevik interlude in Hungary, there were many anti-Semitic outrages and I heard my father and his associates chuckle with pleasure when they read in the morning papers that some Jews had been lynched. The White Guardists who placed a bomb in the club of Jewish merchants in Budapest, killing many, were friends of father and of Uncle Istvan. Istvan Paloczi-Horvath, the lord of the Orkeny estate, who opened the front gates of his park only to royalty, was the first president of the Awakening Hungarians, worthy forerunners of Hitler and Belsen and Dachau. These were the people who in the nineteen-thirties went around bragging that thanks to them fascism and Nazism were really invented in Hungary.

These, then, were the people who started me on the way to *the obsession*. It was enough for my father to utter any opinion for me to embrace instantly the exact opposite. Father was reactionary, I became progressive; Father was anti-Semitic, I started to befriend Jewish boys; Father was for the Germans, against the French and British, so I naturally became anti-German, determined to speak perfect French and English. Father had a contempt for America, 'a nation of salesmen', hence when the time came, I broke with his family and went to an American college.

According to the divorce settlement I was to remain with my mother till I completed my fifteenth year. After that I was to live with my father. At the end of the school year when I was fifteen, I was transferred to my father's care and he took me to Orkeny, to my uncle's estate. There was the usual crowd of retired hussar colonels, reactionary politicians and White Guardists. I befriended a young bachelor of agriculture named Labay in the estate management office, who showed me around. Behind the huge park, beyond the estate office, behind the stables lived the estate servants in long rows of miserable huts, each containing two tiny rooms and a kitchen. Every hut was shared by two families, often by twelve to fifteen people. Till then I had had a vague idea of the picture-book peasant, the salt of the earth, the fountain of cultural rejuvenation, the backbone of the nation. I shall never forget my first visit to a peasant hut on my uncle's estate.

The air in the hut was a fog of dishwater and sour sweat and rancid fat and wet linen. Opposite the small door, by the cooking stove, two middle-aged and two old women were standing humbly to attention, greeting us with the customary 'God's welcome to your honours!' Through the damp darkness sharp sunlight projected our shadows on the wall behind the women. Several very dirty babies were playing on the muddy ground while other children stood about gaping at us. I saw as through a mist several beds piled high with pillows, heaps of rags in the corners, a fly-blown picture of Kossuth and a few cooking utensils hanging on the wall.

In a minute or two I was out again in the brilliant summer sunshine. Labay understood my hurry.

'They stink, don't they? Of course for us, used to the smell of the stables, it's not so bad. Still, I never go into a hut if I can help it – only I wanted to fix up tonight with Mary. A well-trained girl – always washes herself in my room with scented soap, before the 'darning' … Don't make such a sour face, old man. I tell you what. Let me fix you up with a girl for tonight. You can have old Jaszai's room, it's next to mine. You'll give her a few crowns, of course …?'

'You mean to say that all these girls are prostitutes? That any of you can have them for a few crowns?'

'Prostitute is a city word. Anyhow, they aren't prostitutes. It's the custom, or tradition if you like, that we landowners, estate manager, overseers, 'use' the girls. Incidentally this is their expression. When we sleep with their womenfolk, they say we "use" them.'

'And this goes on all over Hungary?'

'As far as I know, yes. Of course only on the estates. We use the girls if we feel like it and they are in no position to refuse. But we never order married women to come in. There would be trouble. And they age too quickly, anyhow. How old do you think the woman next to the stove was? … Forty-five, my foot, she is a good deal less than thirty. But then, five children, a lot of work … well, so it is.'

'How many of them live in these huts?'

'Two families. Maybe eleven or twelve people – I don't know. Why this sudden interest? What's bitten you? In a reforming mood?'

'No, I'd just like to know. How much is their pay?'

'That's not so easy to answer. They get almost no money at all, but they have free lodging, they get some wheat, barley and so on and they can keep chickens.'

'But, practically speaking, they are serfs?'

'Well, if you want to play with words … They are poor. The poor are poor. That's all. The thing is not to be poor. There are about a hundred million people now in Europe who live like your uncle's estate servants and some thousand millions who are even worse off in places like Asia. So what? Come on, the girls want to play tennis.'

'And you know all this and go on … and "use" Mary and … I think it's awful.'

'We'll talk about this, old man, some other time. Now come on or we'll be late for tennis. There is only an hour till sunset.'

The Undefeated

... That summer afternon; the little gate leading to the servants' quarters; the brilliant green grass, the red tennis court, the dazzling white dresses of my cousins, girls whom one doesn't 'use'; the big redfaced men of the family; the endless dinner in the huge dining room – rich spicy food washed down with cool, dry wine; uncle's shortclipped pronouncements, Father's long-winded political arguments and I, all the while remembering the nauseating smell of the hut, wondering what's happening now between Labay and the girl he is using and knowing that my Europe is just as lifeless and phony as Father's, that the famous human chauvinism, the intellect accepting responsibility for entire humanity lives on a small isolated park, that I am wrapped up in the cotton-wool of my class, that my entire body, my brain and my nostrils are foreigners to millions of Hungarians, millions of Europeans, that any middle-class intellectual of Asia or Africa is probably much less foreign to me than this peasant Mary or her father, less exotic than the old woman over there saying 'God's welcome to your honours', that ...

And later, walking in the dark park, flashes of summer lightning, the feeling of being alone in the world, or of being between two worlds – I had left a world behind me. Now the males of the species were gathered round a table in a kiosk at the far end of the park so as not to disturb the ladies with their roaring. The females in the manorhouse novel-reading, gossiping, divided into subspecies: my grandmother's tough uncomplicated world, the aunts' provincial world, and my cousin Rita's postwar world. Now down in the park a gypsy band warms up, plays old folk songs and fake folk songs; Uncle Geza sings in his throaty bass, beginning in a whisper and ending in a roar, the drinkers' mood swaying up and down the emotional scale from brash gaiety to patriotic melancholy, the bandleader watching the most important faces, anticipating their change of mood and changing from one tune to another.

There are hundreds of other worlds – the fat old bailiff's world, the young agriculturists and overseers, playing cards, getting drunk, 'using' girls. And vast unknown worlds – the peasants and workers here in Hungary, in other countries and continents. And the worlds inside people, the world of sex that lights up pictures in the mind of

Labay and the peasant girl, of the unknown girl he promised to get for me, a plump girl squating half-undressed on a bed, her face like the janitor's daughter in Budapest.

What happened then? I only remember standing under a tree, the glow of a cigarette end, and Labay saying 'The little bitch didn't turn up after all. Come up to my room and have a drink.'

A small white-washed room, poorly furnished with a bed and a shelf of books which I examined while Labay was getting out the wine. History, philosophy, religion. ... many of them given by a Father Toth to a Joseph Leibner.

'Who is Leibner?'

'I was. I changed my name before I went to the University. A Hungarian should have a Hungarian name ... Well, here's how.'

We drank.

'But I thought you were a Calvinist?'

'I am. But I was a Catholic before.'

'Of course! I heard you were a convert, that's why Grandmother likes you so much –'

'Drink up, old boy ... Convert my foot. I simply grew to hate the good fathers. And one's got to have some sort of religion – officially. And a Calvinist's the thing to be nowadays in Hungary, if you want to get on. Horthy's one. And Bethlen and most of the high-ups.'

'You're a cynic, aren't you?'

'Words, old boy, words. I am a realist. Come on – drink up. You're an idealist, of course. You wait – life will get you.'

'I believe your cynicism's just a pose, Joseph.'

'Clever fellow! What a discovery! ... "Pose" ... words again ... well, have it your own way. I'll tell you what your pose is – the young, clean genius, the ... Tell you what. Let's open a bottle of brandy, it'll be good after wine. I don't mind now – the little bitch not turning up. She'll come tomorrow. Nice hard breasts, beautiful white belly. Won't undress until I've turned out the light, can't see her properly unless there's moonlight. But I'll train her.'

'Does she enjoy – well – sleeping with you?'

'I don't know and couldn't care less. I like my fun. I'm not senti-mental. You know something? You're all right if you have nothing to do with the girl – nothing as far as your soul is concerned. I'm going to be bloody careful not to get involved with a girl – like Rita, for instance – that I might lose my head over and spoil my career. Not till I can get married. I mean to marry well, some day. I shall be fairly important myself … let's drink to the future!'

The rain was falling in torrents. Labay drank a lot and I finally made him angry by trying to get under his defensive armour, uncover some past injury, make him admit he was not indifferent to the sufferings of the estate servants.

At last he burst out, 'Now listen, little brother, I know all about you. Your old man bores us to tears talking about you when you're not around. I know you guzzle up all the books you can lay your hands on. You don't make a bad use of the education your family's buying for you – that is, the education the estate servants are buying you. And when you talk about me getting hurt in the past you're damned right I was. All right – I'm cynic, a go-getter, anything you like. And why? Because of poverty.'

His father had died when he was eight years old, leaving his mother with debts and a son to educate.

'All that stuff about a mother struggling to educate her son – you've no doubt read about it in books. In reality it means a room smelling of stale cabbage, a stinking w.c. in the corridor, a tenement full of nagging women, Saturday night brawls, going to school in clothes you've outgrown, headaches and humiliations, ticked off by teacher for the books you "forgot" to buy …'

When he was fourteen his mother couldn't afford to keep him at school any longer. But he was clever and wanted to finish his education and his mother desperately wanted him to get back into his father's class, to become a gentleman. So he thought of a plan: he would tell the priest at school that he had wanted to serve Holy Church himself, but his mother had no money, so he had given up his dream and resigned himself to being apprenticed to some trade. He knew well enough that the Church would have him educated if he promised to become a priest. His mother and he had terrific rows over it, for she had high moral principles.

'But in the end she agreed that I should, so to speak, embezzle an education from Mother Church. It wasn't easy, with her principles. But of course if you're poor enough you can't afford them. I kept on telling her I'd repay them, after I'd passed my exams I'd have to tell them I'd lost my faith, but I'd work hard to become a lawyer, I'd repay them everything. After all, they couldn't take back the knowledge they bought for me, spoon by spoon from my skull.'

He'd suffered for it, too. Living a sanctimonious lie for years, keeping up the pretense of saintliness when he wanted to drink, go out and get a girl … pretending he liked the very poverty he hated like poison. He grew to hate them so much that after leaving them, after the nauseating scenes following his 'loss of faith', he became a Calvinist.

'So that's the story of my conversion. If I was a sentimentalist like you I'd say I was just an escaped prisoner of poverty. It'll never catch up with me, I promise you. I'm in my last year at the university. I've a job to keep me going. I play a part in university politics – I'm a member of the 'Awakening Hungarians'. Am I an anti-Semite? Brother, I don't believe in anything … I believe in myself … in this good brandy. No principles, no convictions – I carry no ballast! I'm as free as air. The road's clear ahead of me! You thought me the typical agronomist? Well, so I am if I want to be. Husky chap in riding boots, smelling of manure, kicking the peasants on their backsides, getting drunk when I want to …'

My head was splitting. This is awful, I thought, I must save Labay. But first I'm going to be sick. I was. Labay gave me some black coffee, then both of us dozed off. His alarm clock went off at two-thirty. 'Come on,' he said, 'you'd better start the day with me.' We ate smoked ham and black bread, drank some *sligovitz* and went out through the dark park to the cowsheds.

Labay, bad-tempered, cursed the men, kicked a cowman who was half asleep. Men groaned, got slowly onto their feet, spat, then stood at attention when they saw us, saying 'Good morning, your honours!' Others were already tending the cows, moving sluggishly in the heavy, dung-smelling air. We went into a shed where harvesters were just getting up, a single oil lamp throwing a flickering light on young boys and girls, men and women, as they dressed. The animal noises, the trampling, the human noises, broken by a polite 'Good morning, your honours,' all subdued in the soft, sleazy, half-light, gave me a dreamlike feeling. I had no right to look, I felt, as a group of them drew water from the fountain and spilled it on their heads and hands; something was going on which I had no right to see, something sweatingly naked and private; it was as though I was being forced to witness the meting out of a humiliating punishment.

As we began to do the rounds in Labay's little carriage, he said, 'We were disgustingly drunk last night and talked a lot of nonsense. But you wanted to see how they live. Now you know. They work from dawn to dusk; they haven't enough to eat; the cowhands are the worst off – they spend most of their life in the cowsheds. In four or five years they begin to spit blood. They manage to get other work, or go away, become beggars or die.'

'And you kicked one.'

'Don't be silly. They are always tired and lazy – like the cows, they wouldn't move without a kick. It's how they wake each other up. Anyhow, I'm an outsider. I behave here as I am expected to do.'

Our horse trotted briskly along the dusty road; it was dawn. Labay, who had taken a fierce dislike to me, made sure that I missed nothing of the way my uncle's estate servants were treated, the landless workers employed for harvesting, the dwarf-holders, the small tenants. By the end I had a complete picture of the lives of three or four million serfs in Central Europe who were living, with almost none of the elementary freedoms, on starvation level.

I felt a heavy sadness; and my sadness was partly for Labay who felt impelled to expose himself to me in the worst possible light, wanting to be a proud man 'without morals', wanting his revenge on humanity. Was I beginning to use the word 'humanity' too often, without really knowing what it meant? I longed to know the world, to go from caste to caste, meeting men, talking to them, eating with them, finding out what makes them tick. Books alone aren't enough. You have to get beneath the words to the meaning of *serf, estate, landworker, peasant*. Is Labay an unusual person or are there hundreds like him? Clever, knowing how to use his good brain, but without morals, without beliefs ... They could be a terrible danger. In their hands all knowledge, all our human heritage would be a weapon to be used for their own ends.

By seven that morning I was back in bed, but I couldn't sleep. I had to do something about the estate servants, about Labay. From that moment the humanity pain started; I felt it always, sometimes numb, sometimes unbearably sharp; I acted for it or against it, but I could never be neutral towards it.

Chapter Three

THAT SUMMER DAY in Orkeny I reviewed my experiences in the light of all the imagination and moral indignation of which a fifteen-year-old boy is capable. My father and his friends were committing a monstrous crime against millions of human beings and I was ashamed of my family name; the physical revulsion which had made me avoid eating soup in rhythm with my father was now transferred to the class he represented.

That night at dinner I revolted. There were some thirty people sitting down the long table at whose head my uncle presided, or rather, held court. No one, except for a few important guests, ever spoke until my uncle had first addressed them. Children, of course, were expected to keep silent. Unfortunately a certain Mr. Piroska, afterwards one of the vilest White Guard thugs, so bragged about his exploits that I forgot myself and made a few naïve remarks about humanism and the rights of the people. I was at once banished from the table, and next morning from the estate. Father was furious: I had forfeited my inheritance, lost forever the thousands of acres from which he had hoped in time to draw a generous allowance. He did not at all mind when I asked for permission to spend the rest of my vacation with my mother at Lake Balaton.

In September I went up to the college of Sarospatak. Walking through the park from the station with my suitcase I passed a statue of Simon Paloczi-Horvath, one of the college benefactors; and two bas-reliefs flanked the gate of the huge squat main building, one of Susanna Lorantffy, one of Maria Paloczi-Horvath. The clerk in the office where I handed in my birth certificate and other documents raised an eyebrow when I registered my name as 'George Horvath'. (Horvath alone is a common name in Hungary.) But it was a liberal college and to the end I was called plain Horvath, though everyone knew my real name.

In Sarospatak my rebellious mood quickly passed. I felt free; I would have nothing more to do with my father's family and I would eventually go abroad. Since my father and his friends paid so much lip service to patriotism I thought of myself as a 'European', a disillusioned man who was above feelings of narrow patriotism. This was my violent *Sturm und Drang* period. I read greedily and published my first short story – a Kafka-esque tale, though I had never read Kafka – in the college magazine, and followed it with more stories, iconoclastic allegorical fantasies with titles like 'Zoo for Humans' and 'The Naughty Little God'. My literary idols were Anatole France and Bernard Shaw, and I read the Greek philosophers, particularly the sceptics and cynics, with my best friend Pippa. We were equally enchanted by the natural sciences and the humanities and produced plenty of poems, stories, philosophical essays, worldly-wise epigrams and plans for modern Utopias. We looked down on our professors with tolerant contempt; we read too much and were far too intense. It was Pippa who first read Schopenhauer's famous essay on indeterminism. At two o'clock in the morning he rushed round to my house and woke me up with the horrifying news that *there is no free will.* By six o'clock he had convinced me and together we discussed the consequences of our terrible discovery. *Our whole world seemed about to collapse about our ears.* But after a good breakfast I found two ways out of our dilemma: first, I suggested that though from the perspective of absolute truth everything might be determined by the chain of causation, in everyday life there is free will nevertheless; and secondly, only art and literature count anyway.

We were both just seventeen when we decided that we were *potential* geniuses, and spent much time looking through the histories of science, literature, music and the fine arts to find people who definitely *became* geniuses by the time they were eighteen. At this time we called ourselves 'philosopher-athletes', and before long we had decided that if a genius is to develop his faculties to the full he must remain chaste;

for the creative minority, we felt, sex is the great troublemaker, love a dangerous obsession. Now we searched history for proofs of the talent-destroying effect of sex and love. My pet *mot* was that most great writers should have dedicated their books to their wives or sweethearts thus: 'To So-and-so, without whom this book would have been written much sooner and better.' We pledged eternal chastity, were very intensive in our athletic training and smiled indulgently on the adolescent frolics of our fellow-students, those good average people, as they fell in and out of love. But after three or four months being a chaste philosopher-athlete seemed rather dull, even a shade ridiculous. Pippa fell in love with a bosomy bar-girl and I wrote a play about some students of both sexes who formed a society of 'Pure Ones' and subsequently became Pan-worshipers. Needless to say it was a very bad play, and before the third act was written I fell in love with a nice local girl with plenty of soul.

The College of Sarospatak was not a college in the usual sense of the word; it consisted of a 'gymnasium', or secondary school for classical studies, and a theological seminary. In the gymnasium we were taught Latin, and later on, Greek, as well as Hungarian and world history, German language and literature, and a fair amount of mathematics and physics. As Latin, Greek and German were compulsory we soon got the knack of studying languages. In addition to these compulsory subjects most of us took tutoring in French or English and I chose English as my first private language. Having learned German from my governesses, I was able to spend most of my German classes preparing for the English ones.

Though Sarostapak was a Calvinist institution, one of the strongholds of the Hungarian Reformed Church, there was very little religious indoctrination. Calvinism, as practiced at the college, was a *Weltanschauung*, a world-view blessedly free from the intolerance of closed systems of thought. Most of us grew up in Calvinist households, taking for granted the basic tenet of Calvinism: predestination. For us students this was not a cruelly fatalistic belief; all our thoughts, attitudes, and feelings were permeated by the comfortable feeling that as long as we do our duty, everything in our life was wisely fore-ordained. If fate seemed to be unkind to us we could be sure our adversity was well-deserved. Predestination made us feel that we were entirely responsible for ourselves; it was a simple, gentle philosophy of life, easy to embrace and next to impossible to escape from. Of all this we were barely conscious.

Sarostapak was one of the few Calvinist colleges to retain the old institution of *legatio*, of sending out students as legates of the Church. There tended to be more churches than there were pastors, so during Christmas, Easter and Whitsun, when two daily services were held, students from the gymnasium and the seminary helped out.

I was sixteen when I volunteered to go on my first *legatio*. A week or so before the Easter holidays we had to learn sermons and deliver them before an instructor, and later we were allowed to choose our towns or villages. Those who were the first to choose, the final-year seminary students, naturally chose the biggest towns; we of the gymnasium were left with the villages, where earnings were less. To me, however, this was an advantage, as I wanted to study the life of the peasants. Each legate took with him a small boy of ten or eleven called a 'mendicant'. A week before Easter I found myself with a little, bullet-headed peasant boy journeying by train to a small village in north-eastern Hungary and then on foot to the largest of three tiny villages in the mountains where I was to preach. Here I stayed with their pastor. Our first duty was to visit every family in the congregation. Everywhere we were offered wine and something to eat, and after the mendicant had recited some verses the head of the family gave him money for both of us. In this way the mendicant earned enough, during the three great holidays, to buy himself a pair of shoes and a suit. The legate received proportionately more. Thus, through the system of *legatio* the Calvinist community helped in the education of Calvinist students. During Easter I had to get up very early and walk to the next village to conduct an early service, then to the next for a noon service, and repeat the performance in the afternoon. The pastor and I held twelve services during the two Easter days.

I found preaching delightful. My instructor was wise enough to let me improvise a sermon rather than repeat one that I had learned, and when I went up into the pulpit and studied their up-turned faces I tried to tell them something to make their hard life more bearable. I told them the story of Leonardo da Vinci's 'Last Supper', how the artist found a model for Christ, and how, years later, when he was looking for a Judas, the man he chose as a typical Judas turned out to be the same man he had painted as Christ. So, I said, it is up to us what we make of ourselves.

During my three years at Sarospatak I was a legate six times, walking the countryside with my little mendicant, visiting hundreds of peasant homes, and increasingly appalled by their poverty and ignorance. To a boy brought up in Budapest these holiday expeditions were like explorations into a strange and primitive land. Whenever I returned to Sarostapak I felt rebellious for a week or two till I could ease myself back into the world of science and literature. In this different kind of exploration I was fortunate enough to be encouraged, in my final year, by our professor of Hungarian Literature, Professor Novak. I had become one of the boarders he took in to round out his meagre income, and the mellowing influence of his tolerant and perceptive sense of humour was just what I needed to help me see my impossibly arrogant superiority for what it was. In preaching the golden mean, our good professor was expressing the spirit of Sarostapak itself, whose liberal humanity was a permanent influence on our young, impressionable minds. In that small town we were part of the community; 'everyone' came to our festivals, our balls and amateur theatricals, and we ourselves, by the time we were seventeen, were used to taking part in the life of the town.

One way and another my superiority complex was considerably eroded, if not actually crumbling, by the time I got back to my mother's flat after matriculating. My sister Margot was able to admit at the end of our first long conversation, 'Thank God – you are almost human!'

Chapter Four

IN 1926, when I was just eighteen, I went with my mother and my younger brother to Austria. We were the paying guests of Count Heussenstamms, who had lost most of his property except a large manorhouse in the Wachau Valley of the Danube. Countess Heussenstamm was the daughter of a former United States Ambassador in Vienna, and she had collected quite an international crowd. A French family, a Polish lady with her two sons, a Czech manufacturer with his family, two society girls from Baltimore with their prim English governess, a Swedish minor authoress and an American journalist made up the 'guests' that summer. It was a treat to meet foreigners, to be at large in their strange atmosphere, so much freer than our own.

The two Baltimore girls were very pretty, and having lived in Europe with their British governess for the last three years, had become quite 'continental'. Being tall and well developed, I managed to seem older than I was and soon began flirting with the older of the Baltimore girls, who was twenty-three, and called Kate.

After dinner we went for a stroll in the park. I walked with Kate and put up some intellectual fireworks to impress her. At the end of my second or third brilliant monologue she asked me about my age. I told her in a crestfallen voice. She kissed me lightly on the cheek and told me there was nothing shameful about being eighteen.

I mused on my fate. How many worlds I had learned to know already! Father's stick-in-the-mud-gentry world, the bustling cosmopolitan world of my stepfather, the world of the estate servants, the world of Budapest and the country, Sarospatak with its peasant boys and landowners' sons, and now my new friends.

The summer passed quickly, with dances in the manorhouse and the neighboring estates, outings to various places in the Wachau Valley, tennis and riding and the quarreling and making up with Kate. I could never forgive her for two faults, for being five years older and being rich.

At the summer's end I had to decide on my profession. I wanted to be a writer. Father wanted me to read law and take over his firm, which was managed by his partner; my stepfather wanted me to learn banking; Mother took no part in the debate. The easiest way out was to accept my stepfather's offer. Go to Vienna, he said, and attend the Handels-Akademie as well as the University of Vienna. In that way I could learn about banking and could study what I wanted to at the university. I was helped by the fact that I had won a free scholarship from the College of Sarospatak which would provide me with a yearly stipend as long as I studied at a foreign university. So in September, having finally broken with my father, I went to Vienna to pursue my dual studies at the commercial academy and at the university. The result – not surprising – was that I learned next to nothing at the commercial academy and used the university lectures for a series of intellectual adventures. I attended anatomy classes with the medical students, sat through lectures on psychology and anthropology and others on the history of French literature. But mostly I sat in my room writing.

I finished several short stories and a short novel which I wrote and rewrote, never being entirely satisfied with any of them, too proud and too shy to submit them to publishers.

My brooding became acute during the second half of the month. In the first half I usually spent most of my money and in the second lived on tea and bread and butter which the landlady was willing to let me have on credit. The last week was naturally the bleakest. I stayed home and read, wrote melancholy poems and thought of the girls I could have taken out if I had had the money.

I know that I had too many interests; one cannot concentrate on philosophy, history, science, literature and the fine arts all at once. I remembered uneasily how enthusiastic I had been about sculpture for a period at Sarospatak, spending several hours a day in the studio of the only sculptor in our small town, or wrestling at home with clay. This was brought to an end by my realizing that I did not know enough about the human body – I ought to study anatomy. Then there were those two months during which, in order to understand Einstein's relativity theory, I pestered our mathematics teacher to give me special instruction in higher mathematics and astronomy.

I mused about the only paternal ancestor of whom I generally approved. He was Adam Paloczi-Horvath, a poet-scientist-rebel and a contemporary of the Empress Maria Theresa. He wrote four very long and rather dull epic poems, was doctor of law, master of art and held a degree in civil engineering. He lived at a time when gentlemen still wrote in Latin in Hungary, and he had the distinction of having written the first Hungarian language textbooks on such widely different subjects as astronomy, psychology and statistics. He was quite a successful landowner. He married his fourth wife – a sixteen-year-old Kazinczy girl – when fifty-five, and got in trouble with the Hapsburg court for writing naughty limericks about the Empress Maria Theresa. He was a roaring old man, dynamic and many-sided, but after all there were only some fifteen lines about him in the encyclopedias; and in the histories of Hungarian literature he was mentioned among the minor poets. Would this be my fate too?

Then when the long-awaited money order arrived I rushed out for a meal in one of the fashionable restaurants, called up my girls and various friends, and happily re-entered my world of music and literature.

Towards the end of this Vienna period I became increasingly dissatisfied with myself and the aimlessness of my life. I had a craving for some strong foundation, for some firm hold, for a real father. I toyed with the idea that I should embrace a cause, join some movement, give myself to something wholeheartedly.

In such a mood I joined Coundenhove-Calergi's famous Pan-Europe movement. Here was a cause I could really believe in; my dearest ambition was to become a real European. For years I had thought of Europe as a wonderful place to explore, in which to make my home. I was convinced that only European values could help humanity to a better future. How I listened to the erudite and fervent speeches, to political plans and learned analyses of the situation – and yet the thing somehow seemed slightly ludicrous. Politics failed to give me that strong foundation, that father-image I was looking for.

My life in Vienna seemed to be leading nowhere; the best way out was escape. And escape I did. At the end of the Vienna year, with Mother's help, I got my stepfather's backing to my American plans. My stepfather's younger brother, who ran a Hungarian language daily, *Szabadsag*, in Cleveland, Ohio, invited me over and promised to send me to college.

In June, 1927, I left for America. I spent a week or ten days in Paris first, falling, of course, hopelessly in love with the city. For an entire afternoon I toyed with the idea of selling my ship ticket and staying in Paris. At the end I decided reluctantly to go, but promised myself years of Paris in times to come.

Chapter Five

IN THE EARLY SUMMER OF 1927 I left Cherbourg on board the S.S. *Majestic*, then the biggest ship in the world. I was nineteen and felt grateful to be alive. My student's visa gave a promise to a brand-new world; I had in my suitcase the poems of Walt Whitman, many of which I knew by heart, and I spent the five days of the voyage talking to as many Americans as were willing to hold long conversations with an eager young man from Central Europe. At night I lay in my bunk reading American periodicals and newspapers, too excited to sleep.

We arrived in New York on a brilliant summer afternoon. I took a room in a small hotel and rushed out in breathless haste to see everything at once. I travelled on the subway, boarded buses, rode on the elevated, walked – getting more and more enchanted, frightened and puzzled. It was too gigantic, too strange, too roaring, too rushing.

The general impression in Manhattan was of immaculately dressed men with clear-cut profiles, shining faces and shining shoes, ever alert for the unexpected. The girls and young women on Broadway and on Fifth Avenue, with their sexy dresses and erotic gait, were very attractive, very sure of themselves, and wore their pretty breasts and behinds proudly, as if they were medals for valour. By nightfall I had lost some of my cocksureness; I became a shy little greenhorn, overwhelmed by it all and feeling that America altogether too fast and too expensive for me.

For the next two years I 'learned' America in all-night sessions with Greenwich Village intellectuals; I worked as a house-to-house salesman for a Negro phonograph company; as chauffeur for a prosperous advertising salesman whose beat was Ohio, Michigan and Pennsylvania; as a crime reporter for the *Cleveland Hungarian Daily;* teaching Hungarian in a summer school; acting minor foreign roles in a small-town stock company; concentrating hard on my studies at Franklin and Marshall College; hitchhiking with my college friends and working in the university restaurant; falling in and out of love with a series of American girls; reading omnivorously in one of the great public libraries. I saw the end of the Coolidge prosperity and the beginning of the Hoover era, mainly through the eyes of Henry Mencken and his then excellent *American Mercury.* That bulky monthly with its dark green cover was my principal guide to American life and letters. My cicerones and masters in Americanology were Mencken, Eugene O'Neill, John Dos Passos, Carl Sandburg, Sinclair Lewis and Joseph Hergesheimer.

Whether in Cleveland, Lancaster or New York, I managed to get into intellectual circles and had a much higher opinion of American culture than the average European visitor at that time. At college I got the impression that the American social sciences were run on a very high scientific level combined with daring imagination. I had a very poor opinion of those continental visitors who pretended to exist in a constant state of cultural starvation. The concerts and art exhibitions, the art theatre movement, the leading American novelists, poets, playwrights and philosophers seemed to me part of a cultural renaissance. At the same time I felt that the cultured American was in some sense an exile in the America of Coolidge and Hoover.

Listening to Hoover's election campaign speeches, I longed for this great captain of industry with his political naïveté to be defeated. (In the summer of 1930, back in Hungary, I read that a delegation had visited Hoover to urge an expansion of federal public works. His reply was, 'Gentlemen, you have come sixty days too late. The depression is over.') My step-uncle was a successful American businessman, with a wide circle of banker and industrialist friends who were mostly genial. Some of them were self-made men who had succeeded in building up huge factories, millionaire concerns; yet their political thinking seemed to be unbelievably primitive. It was a shock to learn that some of these friendly big businessmen had close connections with shady political machines, that some political bosses and captains of industry were tied up with gangs. The America I got to know was that of the Prohibition era, an America of speakeasies, of bootleggers, of gang warfare, an America which had just got over the scandals of the Harding administration, whose politics then were not only primitive but corrupt. All this made me even more contemptuous of politics, but I did not attach undue importance to it. America for me was the country of Walt Whitman and Eugene O'Neill, of Professors Boas and Millikan, of the Middlewest farmers who gave lodging to the hitchhiking students, of all the kindly nonpolitical people.

At Franklin and Marshall College in Lancaster, Pennsylvania, I was accepted as a 'junior'. F & M, founded by Benjamin Franklin and first Chief Justice of the United States Marshall, was a Calvinist institution and remarkably progressive and tolerant. I had to take on more subjects than usual, because I had to pass exams in most of the English courses and, naturally, in American history. In addition I studied philosophy, esthetics, sociology, and social anthropology. Compared to similar European institutions the requirements were not too exacting and I managed to get an 'A' in most subjects. What with having to earn most of my living and taking so many courses, the first half year at F & M was hard work. I never went out with girls, or for outings, and I slept very little.

During the Christmas holidays of 1927 I had the curious experience of being a Calvinist legate again, this time in East and West Buffalo, and also in Tonawanda near Niagara Falls. Faithful to the *legatio* tradition, I visited the homes of many American-Hungarian families of the congregation during the Christmas festival. From greater Hungary nearly a million peasants emigrated to America before the First World War, driven out by poverty, by my own class, and settled in Cleveland, Pittsburgh and in the Pennsylvanian mining towns. I was astonished by the physical difference between the first and the second generations. Father and mother were generally 'typical' Hungarian peasants, short, thick-set, thick-boned, with big hands and feet. Their sons and daughters were on the whole tall and slender, with fine limbs. When I made a remark about this difference, the mothers said something like this: 'Yes, yes. You see *they* had plenty of milk and fruit when they were little and *they* never worked from dawn to dusk in the fields.' Or, 'Of course my pets are tall, they get proper food here.' This was a long time before Boyd-Orr and MacAllister published their findings about the influence of food on the physical characteristics of nations.

I studied the difference between first and second generation immigrants, but later it turned into a kind of torment. The first generation immigrants, even after years in America, were curiously humble. They still respected 'gentlemen', they 'knew their place' too well for my liking. The second generation was self-assured and had nothing but contempt for Hungary where the gendarmes slap the villagers' faces. Till now I had always thought of the Hungarian peasant as a different species from the upper classes, who were tall and on the whole fine-featured while the peasants were short and thick-set. Now I realized that these were not unchangeable characteristics; given proper food, a healthy atmosphere and less drudgery, the second generation was altogether a finer specimen of humanity. And for scores of generations my people had made it impossible for the peasants to develop their full potential. I suffered again when I thought of all the guilty ancestors lurking in my bones. That day in Orkeny when I first visited an estate servant's hut was again vivid in my memory and in a curious way I felt guilty for all the crimes which generations of noble landowners had committed against their peasants.

Back at college after Christmas a new experience awaited me. One day while we were boxing, the manager of the local stock company came in and chose three of us to play small parts in his Somerset Maugham's *Rain*; he needed three South Sea island natives. The company played seven nights a week with two matinees. I lost a lot of sleep but got to know a little of the theatre. In the next play, *What Price Glory?*, I had two small parts – a French innkeeper and a supercilious Prussian captain. Later I played several other minor roles where foreign accents were required. I enjoyed acting immensely. The director even suggested that with my looks I might consider acting as a profession. But I never thought seriously about it; I liked going out with the actors after the show and listening to their egotistic talk as I liked flirting with the young actresses, but I remained uninfected by the drug of the stage.

In my studies I did quite well according to general standards. From my own point of view they were unsatisfactory, for I still recoiled from specilization. Yet it was in the college atmosphere that I began discovering Europe for myself. The more I studied America, the more European I became. For days and weeks on end I was reading Thomas Mann and Proust and Jane Austen, and books on the histories of Paris and London, and on Italian and Spanish art. I hitchhiked frequently to Philadelphia, to Pittsburgh or even to New York in order to see a Pirandello play, or spend hours in one of the museums of fine arts or galleries. At the same time that I was up to my neck in the American tumult, I swallowed large gulps of Europe.

In 1929, when the time came to return home, I was grateful to America, even a little sad at leaving it, but I looked forward to stepping ashore in France and starting my European *Wanderjahre*.

Chapter Six

WHEN THE TRAIN pulled in to the Hungarian frontier station the first person I saw was a red-faced, overfed Hungarian policeman in his coarse blue uniform, his huge hands bursting out of his white cotton gloves. Here we are again, I thought. The Hungarian customs people came in, being very polite to foreigners and speaking in a superior tone to the Hungarians, the 'subjects'. I traveled third class, so I received a third-class treatment; the obsequiousness I met with when I travelled first class was equally sickening.

After America, after crossing half of Europe, this homecoming seemed to plunge me again into the world of my red-faced uncles, of the great landowners and the estate servants, of girls 'used' and stable-boys kicked. Of course, visiting foreigners only saw Budapest with its theatres, sophisticated cabarets, first-class concerts and interesting intellectuals, or at most they visited an estate or two where they were charmed by the hunting, bridge-playing gentry or by the cosmopolitan culture of these good-looking people. No foreigner ever saw – at least, so I thought – what went on beyond the stables. No foreigners saw the fourteenth century behind the twentieth, the 'darkest Hungary' on which all the splendours were based.

My task was simple: I had to help those who wanted to pull all Hungary up to the level of the twentieth century.

After the train left the frontier and the Transdanubian countryside rolled by, my mood changed. I was happy to be home again, eager to arrive, to see Mother, to talk about my experiences. I saw myself as the much-traveled young man with an aura of success. I had saved some money in America and came back with a wardrobe trunk full of clothes, several cratefuls of books, and plenty of notes for articles and short stories.

I had only the vaguest plans as to my future and I wanted to spend some weeks with my family before deciding. But knowing that in a day or two they would begin to ask me about my plans, I decided to get a job so as to be independent, preferably on a morning daily paper which would leave time for writing. At the next station I bought all the morning dailies. The choice was quite large: there were fifteen. By the time the train reached the outskirts of Budapest, I had read the lot and chosen the *Pesti Naplo,* a liberal paper founded in 1851. It was an open forum, politicians and publicists of all political parties wrote for it; and it published the work of the best writers.

My brother Tommy and my stepfather were at the station. Mother had stayed behind to supervise the homecoming dinner. In the car it was good to feel that my stepfather treated me as a grown-up man. Mother's hair was white and she wept when she took me in her arms. There was a questioning look in her eyes all through dinner; she was trying to see from my face whether I really wanted to stay at home now or not.

Late at night, after long hours of excited talk, she found some pre-text to come into my room and sat on the edge of my bed, fidgeting with the bedclothes. Did I, she asked, want to stay at home? I knew that it would not be enough if I simply said that I wanted to be with my family. So I talked about Hungary needing men who knew the world, about my ties with the Hungarian language, about belonging to the country of Petöfi. The more I talked, the more I believed every-thing I said. When she kissed me good night, Mother was at peace with the world. I gazed for a long time into the darkness, not quite under-standing myself. How is it with the great decisions in one's life? Have I decided? Will I give up Europe for Hungary? Am I weak? A hypocrite? Did I mean everything I said? Why can't one have several lives?

The following afternoon at five I went to the *Pesti Naplo* and asked to see the editor, Dr. Michael Foldi, a former psychiatrist, well-known novelist and the most successful editor in the country. I surprised myself by giving him my full name: George Paloczi-Horvath. This was a result of my American experience. I knew I had a greater chance of being taken on as a member of a historic family. Dr. Foldi was sympathetic. He asked me about my travels, my academic interests and knowledge of languages. I told him quite frankly about my prolif- erating interests and that I was not sure whether I wanted to choose journalism as my profession. At the end of an hour I was taken on for a trial period of two months, without salary. In two weeks they gave me a contract and I remained on the staff of *Pesti Naplo* for nearly ten years, till the day the Hungarian government suppressed the paper for good at the request of the Hitler government.

Pesti Naplo became my real university. The chief sub-editor was Geza Laczko, novelist and man of letters, a former university professor of French literature. His assistant, the diplomatic correspondent, was Dr. Rudolf Szanto, a fascinating Faustian intellectual, doctor of philosophy and doctor of medicine, a master of all the necessary and unnecessary sciences. The two of them took me in hand.

I reported at the office at four every afternoon and till five I had to get a general impression of the world press and the Hungarian press. The members of the inner staff sat at a very long desk, reading the *New York* and London and *Cape* and *India Times, Le Temps, Die Vossische Zeitung, Corrierè della Sera* and scores of other papers.

At half past six there was the editorial conference during which all the department heads informed us about what had been happening on their news 'front'. The whole conference lasted barely twenty minutes. Everyone seemed to use a shorthand sign language which I found hard to follow at first.

From four in the afternoon till half past one at night, with a short break for supper, I was kept busy translating foreign articles, rewriting agency messages, rushing out to interview people or report on some minor event. For weeks Dr. Laczko tore up the first and second or sometimes even the third version of anything I wrote. The third or fourth version he accepted, made enormous cuts in it with his soft black pencil, changed a word or two and sent it to the Linotype room. He made me furious, disheartened, rebellious. I often decided never to go back.

Dr. Szanto was kinder, but at night, during the half-hour before deadline when there was very little to do, he would call me into the big room which he shared with Foldi and Laczko, and question me in front of the others. He made me feel terribly ignorant and foolish.

After a month or so, Laczko asked me to have a drink with him. With Szanto we went to the most fashionable night club, Laczko ordered champagne and drank *pertu* with me. This meant that he accepted me as a friend, I had the right to speak to him with the familiar 'thou'. Szanto laughed and said, 'All right, your initiation period is over!' Laczko just smiled and explained that a good journalist has to rise above his material. Writing is a craft. One has to learn to rewrite, to mold and remold, to wrestle with the material.

From then on we became friends. They wanted to train me for editorship. For the next few years I took turns in being a crime reporter, in working for the financial editor or the theatrical editor, being general reporter, assistant sub-editor, foreign correspondent. My only failure was as a parliamentary reporter. The first day I was sent to attend parliament, the principal political correspondent took me to the press gallery and said, 'We get the stenographic report of everything, of course. You just listen and make a note when something significant is being said.'

There was an eight-hour session and I did not make a single note. Back at the office, when I told my superiors that nothing significant had been said, they roared with laughter. Szanto played with the idea of throwing out the parliamentary report and just printing a notice in small type: 'Parliament had an eight-hour session. Nothing significant was said.'

Pesti Naplo was an exciting place to work. One had the feeling of being at the very centre of events and of knowing most of the behind-the-scenes occurrences. In the *Pesti Naplo* offices I got acquainted with almost everybody in Hungarian literary life. Poets, novelists, playwrights, whose very names had made me excited before, sat around the tables, brought in their material, waited for an advance.

For nearly a year I was a police reporter. The crime reporters formed cartles to beat each other to scoops at which I would have been lost if the *doyen* of the crime reporters had not taken me under his wing and made me his 'partner'. 'It should be easy for you to write everything in two versions. I will tell you how to arrange the material.

Sometimes you will use more of the stuff, sometimes I.' Uncle Noldi had spent all his life at Budapest Police Headquarters. He knew every police officer, every investigating judge, all the coroners. He knew the underworld inside out, he was *persona grata* in the vilest gangster districts, and as his partner, I had a sort of safe-conduct.

This kind of life pleased me immensely for a while. One night I sat in Dr. Szanto's enormous study talking French literature till dawn, the next I would sit with Uncle Noldi in a gangster district called 'Csikago', in a cellar café with confidence men, prostitutes, pimps, 'bears' (safe-specialists), smugglers and dope-peddlers. Uncle Noldi always told them what he wanted and never argued if they refused some information. There we would sit discussing horse races, famous card games and the events of the underworld.

Later I spent months working for the finance editor, getting inside glimpses of the world of high finance and industry.

After a few years of this kind of life one had the feeling of knowing what makes the world tick.

But the *Pesti Naplo* was only the most important of many activities. Thanks to James Joyce I soon became the correspondent of a chain of American newspapers. Mr. Whit Burnett, of the *New York Sun* Foreign Service, came over to hire a Budapest correspondent. Every journalist in the city who knew English went along to his hotel, including newspapermen of great repute. To my surprise, I was among the ten men he asked to stay on after the party. I said very little until the talk came round to literature and Burnett mentioned James Joyce. Everybody, it seemed, had read *Ulysses*. My heart sank. When my turn came I admitted that I had only read about two hundred pages, but managed to say something about the treble symbolism of the book which interested Burnett sufficiently for him to question me further. Next day he called me up and offered me the job, in spite of my pointing out how inexperienced I was. After I had worked for him for a year he told me why: I was the only one who had told the truth; obviously no one else had read *Ulysses* at all.

The *New York Sun* Foreign Service was an ambitious venture; hundreds of American afternoon dailies used its service. They paid extremely well and were most exacting. Now I really had to get to know the Hungarian political situation; they expected the utmost objectivity. In the summer of 1931 they asked me to report on the general economic situation of Hungary. Count Bethlen's government was at that time trying to negotiate a large American loan. I telephoned a long report, and learned a week later that more than a hundred American afternoon papers had printed my report under the headline given in New York: hungary nearing bankruptcy. Government papers in Hungary called me a traitor. A few weeks later all our banks were closed, Count Bethlen resigned his premiership and the great depression reached Hungary.

Although I was not aware when I made it that my factual and objective report proclaimed the bankruptcy of the country, I was glad that Count Bethlen did not get his loan, and when I came to write my first book in English I exposed the Bethlen regime with all its official racketeering and embezzlement. (The book, tainted already by my growing obsession with communism, was published by Victor Gollancz in 1944 under the title, *In Darkest Hungary*.)

One day a distant relative, a hussar colonel who worked in the War Office, asked for my help in exposing a huge fraud that was being hatched there. It concerned a large and quite useless deal with government contractors, involving an enormous sum of money. He brought me documents to prove it and we kept up the campaign for three days. On the fourth the Minister of War and his Under-Secretary of State resigned. But I was not very much liked after that by the authorities.

About this time our greatest novelist, Zsigmond Moricz, wrote a novel called *Rokonok* (Relatives), which told the story of an imaginary Hungarian city where the lord mayor puts his relatives in key positions and they systematically embezzle the municipal funds. Soon after publication, Moricz was sued for libel by a real lord mayor. This was serious because, according to the law, if two witnesses were to state under oath that they recognized the man who was being fictitiously slandered, the case was proven. A few days later, however, the second lord mayor of a town sued for libel, and before the month was out, six more libel suits were filed. In all, eight mayors were sufficiently guilty to feel Moricz's novel applied to them. Of course, all the suits were dismissed.

The Undefeated

To be an opposition journalist in such circumstances you did not need an ideology or even a party allegiance. *Pesti Naplo* was on the whole a liberal paper, in a country where the liberal party was unimportant. It was a national paper in the first sense of the word, one of the three dailies which everyone who wanted to be informed had to read. *Pesti Naplo* belonged to the powerful and mildly progressive *Az Est* – Athenaeum group – owned by the 'Hungarian Hearst', Andrew Miklos. Athenaeum was the largest publishing house in the country. *Az Est* was a noon tabloid, with the largest circulation in the country. The other sister daily, *Magyarorszag* was an evening paper. *Pesti Naplo* kept scrupulously to being an open forum. In a single issue Count Bethlen would write about his government's policy, to be attacked on another page by the leader of one of the opposition parties. The Sunday issues (the national dailies had large Sunday editions but did not appear on Mondays) generally contained articles by representatives of most or all political parties and shades of opinion. Conservative-Royalists, Horthyites, Social-Democrats, Radicals, Right-Wing Christians and Communist sympathizers wrote for the paper, which in its leading articles kept to its liberal tradition.

In this atmosphere I remained still somewhat contemptuous of politics and vaguely leftish in my views.

A part of my work at *Pesti Naplo* was interviewing 'important' or interesting foreigners. Being a highbrow paper, the interviews published were a mixture of an essay and a proper newspaper interview. Through the years this work brought me in touch with statesmen, famous writers, financiers, millionaire playboys, Nobel Prize winning scientists and other front-page names. Of all the great ones I interviewed in my time, only a few left lasting impressions on me. These were Thomas Mann, Sir Arthur Eddington, Max Planck, Aristide Briand, Arturo Toscanini, Pablo Casals and Moissi, the actor.

For four years after I got back from America, the 'humanity pain' was mostly only latent in my consciousness. I lived as intensely as ever, and my private life became complicated, which pushed politics into the background. From the *New York Sun* colleagues I caught the 'objectivity infection', the 'outsider complex' of a certain type of journalist. Human affairs, politics and all, was a game, like a sporting event which one reports truthfully from the press box. We were not in the game, but knew what went on behind the scenes, had very few illusions, and our only loyalty was to the public. They should be told everything: then it was up to them, not to us. The world for us was divided into two uneven groups, the majority being the suckers, and us – 'the boys', newspapermen, a fraternity of convinced outsiders. My latent Calvinist attitude left my conscience at peace as long as I did my duty: truthful reporting.

Our odd working hours meant that we saw very little of anyone except each other. We were working at a time when other people enjoyed their private lives. Hence most of my colleagues either married early, or had their private lives between two and six in the morning, with actresses, night-club girls or women of the demimonde.

For a while I was a night-club habitué. As soon as we put the paper to bed I joined some young colleagues in the Parisien Grill. Budapest had at that time scores of night clubs, from those on the cosmopolitan level down to those of the 'Csikago'. Every night club kept a special journalists' table. Night-club owners liked keeping in touch with journalists and we were allowed to buy food and drink at cost prices as we sat around arguing, swapping stories, or flirting with the hostesses when they were not engaged. After closing time at five in the morning we used to go with some of the girls to an early morning coffeehouse, where we had an enormous breakfast, read through the morning papers and retired to bed at about seven. Naturally it was nearly four in the afternoon before we got up, so our life was spent entirely at the office and in night clubs. For some months I went every night to the Parisien Grill. It would have been unthinkable to stay away. Then one evening I had something urgent to write and missed a night. From then on I never went to a night club on my own initiative, and to this day find them rather dull places.

It was soon after the end of the Grill period that I met Tinty. She worked as a photographer's apprentice in the Mayfair of Budapest, and had a widowed mother and an elder sister who worked at a milliner's. They were poor and lived on a dark side street in one of the tenement districts, in a one-room-kitchen 'flat', with the kitchen tap for a bathroom and one w.c. in the corridor for four 'flats'. Tinty, who was extremely beautiful, had no money for bus or tramway and walked a good mile and a half four times a day because they had a long lunchtime break. She had very little schooling but a delightful sense of humour and a most exciting way of walking and holding herself. It was the usual love-at-first-sight affair; I used to see her two or three times a day, waiting for her at the beginning of her lunchtime break or taking her home by bus, often managing a further meeting during my dinner break. We began an affair without ever having the chance to get to know one another properly. Her mother was not supposed to be aware of what was going on, as she was rightly anxious to keep her far too attractive eighteen-year-old daughter from going out too often with young gentlemen. I decided to marry her, if the word 'decide' adequately describes a mental state in which one is taken completely by surprise by one's own actions.

I had to tell my family about the proposed marriage. Father was naturally violently against it, thereby making my decision really firm. Mother met Tinty one Sunday afternoon and was very sweet to her, but late that night she came and sat on the edge of my bed and spoke her mind. We two made a handsome pair, she said. But she was a bit worried for Tinty. I had become so intensely intellectual. All sorts of foreign friends would turn up in my home. Tinty would feel out of it, and would be bound to be unhappy. 'You know,' she said, 'that I am not worried by her family. It is the individual that counts. But she, poor darling, has very little music, she's had nothing to do with literature, pictures, the great world. Don't forget, marriage is mostly conversation. You must enjoy talking to each other, discussing your mutual problems.'

I had my answer ready: I shall build her up. She will stop working, be at home, have time to read, learn languages. I will make the most of her. I will transform her ... and so on.

'This is life, you know,' Mother said as she got up. 'Life, and not a novel. But you know best. One should never interfere in other people's lives.' She kissed me and was gone.

Father tried to get me fired from the *Pesti Naplo* in order to stop my getting married. Of course they didn't fire me, but this was what finally made my mind up. I saw my marriage, my plan 'to build Tinty up', as a splendid way of defeating him.

So married we were. I left Mother's home, took an expensive flat in Buda, had 'hyper-modern' furniture made, all stainless steel and glass and plastic, which cost money; but I was getting a good salary from the *New York Sun* and would be able to pay off the installments soon. Then in 1932, because of the Depression in America, the *New York Sun* wound up its expensive foreign service and I lost the job. My *Pesti Naplo* salary was barely enough for our household, not to speak of all the installments on the furniture. If up till then I had been working hard (and so seeing very little of Tinty) now I had to work furiously to pay off what I owed. Unfortunately I was sued and legal costs were added to my debts. I wrote ten detective novels straight off, under various pen names, two children's books under my own name, and began translating novels for the Athenaeum. All this meant very little sleep and the kind of life in which I could not afford even a quarter of an hour to be idle, to be a private person.

So I could not even try to 'build up' Tinty. She gave me breakfast and lunch and dinner; at night we made love. There was no conversation in our marriage. And it was not really a marriage, for in fact I abandoned her completely. I got her press tickets for the theatre and cinema, to which she went and returned home alone. Naturally enough she began to have affairs. I had not the faintest idea about all this; I was in love with Tinty and was faithful to her. When I found out I was badly shaken; I felt humiliated, soiled; my male vanity was terribly hurt. Here I was, a healthy young man, 'the frightfully handsome Paloczi', betrayed several times over by his wife. I divorced her, taking the blame on myself and making an overgenerous settlement.

Two months later, when I had got over the shock, I started to have my 'revenge' on women: for nearly two years I led the life of a Budapest man-about-town, enjoying change and variety. Looking back on it now, I realize it was one of the bleakest periods of my life. One night I remember almost with physical intensity.

... Summer night in the early thirties, the terrace of Café Japan on the wide pavement of Andrassy Avenue in Budapest. It's just past eleven; the city is very much alive. People dine on the terrace, shielded from the other half of the busy pavement by a stone balustrade with flower pots. The bright electric bulbs throw their light up to the heavy green foliage of the pavement trees. Cars swish by on the smooth wooden blocks of the avenue, bright blue buses sail along, streetwalkers flutter past. The Philistines dine in the shop-window-like terrace while inside … inside there is everybody, if by 'everybody' we mean those actors, playwrights, playboys, journalists with their females, and hangers-on who are just below real success, just a step from stardom, just not quite in the big money. Here is Madame Nusi, a huge pink woman of uncertain age with several of her wide-eyed and vermilion-mouthed young 'girl-friends' who at the moment are somewhat exasperated by editor Jarmay, a tall individual whose long black-coated arms hover about the table. Below the whirling mist of cigar and cigarette smoke people play cards, argue about Picasso and tomorrow's horse races and Hieronymus Bosch and Freud and the newest discoveries of Madame Nusi. Everybody dashes from table to table always in the way of perspiring waiters sailing by with big trays and flopping frock-coat wings. At one end two girls from the nearby night club are having champagne with a couple of dyspeptic-looking individuals, the silver and golden lamé evening frocks of the girls are reflected in the mirror walls and mirror columns. Veronica the lean Lesbian slaps her fins screaming with laughter at a joke told by a sad-faced bald man. Two tall young men arrive and sit down in one of the niches, order coffee and ham sandwiches from the flat-footed waiter who has melancholy eyes and very big ears and whom they address as 'Little Angel'. Then the newspaper boy in his soiled brown uniform appears with stacks of illustrated foreign magazines. The two young men consume their meal, looking through the magazines, then light cigarettes and talk.

'The trouble is,' says the older of the two, 'that all this has been written before. Here it's called Café Japan instead of Rotonde or Capoulade, but it all has been written up, these good people don't realize that what they are living is plagiarism, the slightly repetitive existence of people who originally weren't so hot either. In London it's Bloomsbury; in New York, Greenwich Village. Every big city has these places and these people – these lovers, lounge-lizards, intellectual pimps and pimpish intellectuals. The whole lot is second or third edition.'

'Yes,' says the younger of the two, 'all this has been written up before, so have you been, the frustrated young man who is suffocated in his particular aquarium, who'd like to go to foreign parts, who feels he could do so much if only he could get out of this stifling atmosphere. This place is all right. What we need is a little more will power. We should work a bit harder.'

'But how can you? How can you sit down and write when you have to chase money, you have to look out always for the next twenty pengős, so you dash off half-baked articles and sell next year's fortune for the porridge of a short story paid for next week. All of us live on advances and then ...'

'Then we come to the Café Japan instead of sitting on our behinds at a typewriter and doing some real work.'

'Well, why are *you* here?'

'You know I don't come often. I am a visiting member. I don't belong.'

Now he dislikes me, thinks the younger of the two. He dislikes me because there is some truth in it, because he feels that I am different and it's a crime to be different.

'Yes, I know,' says the older one. 'You frequent the Café Central too and the Hangli. Quite an intellectual and a politician ... Want a game of rummy? No? Well, then, I am off, I'll find somebody. Will you come over later to the Moulin? Good. Then at the Moulin. Hey, Little Angel, bill please, unless you want to charge it.'

Little Angel doesn't want to charge it. The older one pays and is off. The younger one sits alone and gazes at the interior of Café Japan, he is somewhat self-conscious, after all he is not quite at home here. Lately he has a funny feeling when among people, a feeling of being insufficiently dressed or something like it. The truth is, of course, that he is vexed by the fact that he doesn't amount to more, he isn't an editor yet, he hasn't written really good things. This is gnawing at him, this feeling of not being more ... more what? 'Promising young man?' Yes, he promised himself and all the others that he'd do something extraordinarily good and great and ... the other day in the Hangli the boys all getting bright-eyed and eager because Labay came in, now almost corpulently successful as prominent M.P. of the government party and head of a law firm and owner of a political weekly. Labay had changed a lot since the Orkeny days. He was well dressed and oozed success. And called him 'little brother' saying, 'I liked your clever little piece in the *Naplo* on behaviorism and politics, but all you young geniuses should get into a more constructive and practical mood of nation-building,' the silly fool making electioneering speeches at them, and then the patronizing way he said, 'I am sure, little brother, my sub-editor would like to print some of your stuff.' Doesn't Labay realize that he is a Marxist or does he just want to get back his own for having been a poor boy working on uncle's estate? After Labay left the boys pulled his leg and said they didn't know that he had a fascist friend, and Sanyi who was two years in jail for communism said that Labay was in Germany last month and visited the Brown House. Silly fool – as if that Hitler had a future in Germany. There will be a revolution against them soon, the whole damned place is ripe for a revolution. If the thing starts in Germany maybe these swine here can be kicked out, too.

Today at the newspaper office he had had a lot of fan mail about his Sunday article, 'Dinner Jackets and Human Beings'. The only really interesting one was anonymous, signed by 'Realist'. The young man sitting alone in the Café Japan takes out everything from his various pockets, letters from creditors, three ten-pengö notes, the draft of his next Sunday article, two dirty cards full of phone numbers, clippings, and between the free pass for the municipal tramways and his journalist card, the letter of 'Realist': 'And may I ask what the hell you are doing, you young fool? Denouncing yourself to the political police as a Communist? Or sabotaging the morale of the young generation by promising your leftish readers that revolution is at the gate? Writing in bourgeois papers, eruditely preaching revolution, do you really think this is your duty?' Who can 'Realist' be? It's funny with one's fan mail. On the next page 'Realist' explains that there won't be revolutions in this century, it will be the century of fascism and monopoly-capitalism. The only solution is to go completely underground, take everything underground, Marxism-Leninism, everything lock, stock and barrel, and go on with science, not phony sciences like psychology and sociology but with the real stuff, natural science and logic, just to keep the flames burning. 'Educate, young fool, educate first of all yourself, and then the others, and leave this revolution-prophesying alone.'

It would be interesting to meet 'Realist', maybe he'll advertise in the paper. 'Will "Realist" get in touch with me, and so forth.' Anna will be back next week, sunburned and eager, Anna the sexy madonna. Four free nights yet, he really ought to do something – could drop in the Moulin, that redhead there, Bela, said she likes only very athletic men, but not too many muscles, well, maybe she won't mind some muscles, but, of course, she might want to place it on a sucker basis, couldn't afford, would be better to rush home now and spend the free nights writing on the 'Unhappy Society'. *Atlas* would give an advance for half of the manuscript.

Of course, he ought to write a play. That's where the real money is. Well, another cigarette and then home. He might look into Café Central on the way, Deutsch might give him a book to review, fifteen pengös, how will the rent be paid next month? If only the paper would agree to that North-European tour, he might spend two days in each Baltic state, travel third class and sell the series to Swiss and American papers. But even without them, one could save five hundred on the tour. And one spent too much time sitting in one place. Nerves need change. Maybe it would be better to have less vitality. Burning too fast. Such summer nights are hell, girls bulge in their silk frocks, that plump night-club girl in Belgrade who said she feels like a klaxon, a pneumatic one, men want to squeeze her. Pretty good picture, must write for once an honest-to-goodness prostitute story, with strong words smelling of life, complete with social background. Now come, come, it's not necessary to mix Marxism into this. Anyhow, who is a Marxist? A would-be one.

How can one check up on whether one's life is worth while? By having a good time? Of course, in company I always have a good time – Julia says I have a radiant personality, so eager and cheerful and erudite. Of course, all of us become *causeurs*. Budapest, a city of ten thousand 'interesting intellectuals'. That American publisher said he envies us all, we seem to be so fully alive. Of course, if it were only a question of enjoying yourself, this place would be marvellous.

The Undefeated

Ambition. My feeling of not being more. You've got to have a shirt and necktie on, and you have to wear a new success, an editorship or authorship or bank directorship, or whatever you crave. Then the real ambition to write something really worthwhile, to create books or movements, to make *coups d'état* and things. Funny, this 'common people' business is getting to be something sacred for me, in me, even now I am somewhat reluctant to think of it. Is it true perhaps that one's ideologies are decided by one's surroundings and climate, by one's geographical position? But my surroundings? Family: conservative, feudal, semi-fascist; surroundings: capitalist upper-middle classes; position: middle-class intellectual; circle of friends: Bohemians, journalists, cranks. So why my ideology? Or am I just contrary? Julia is becoming leftish because of me. Can we be trusted, we 'leftish' people? Of course not, though we yearn to place all our life in the service, to be monks and dervishes and fighters for the cause, we would love to plunge into it. But *it* is at present a lot of hairsplitting talk, tedious leaflet distribution, danger without excitement. Must go home to write, just the proper tension, God must she come now?

The young man who feels like swimming out to Andrassy Avenue is collared by the corpulent salmon, Mrs. Bergman, the feminist. Promises to give that lecture Friday two weeks, pays Little Angel and rushes out, sliding along underneath the theatrically illuminated green trees, his body exposed to a lot of feminine fluttering. He thinks that if he had an endocrinological detector in his body as he walks through the summer night, this yet nonexistent apparatus could record how certain female forms cause his glands to send drunken warm mists up to his brain, the waves of desire rising and falling, almost pulling him up at times. What the hell is this? Rutting heat or what? The riots of his body are countered by the revolt of his will, he hails a taxi, rushes home and while he waits for the janitor to open the gate he thinks: Anyhow what the hell do I complain of? This is nothing but the world-famous Youth. Youth can be cured. It's the most easily curable malady. *Dementia juvenilis.*

At home he lights a cigarette, looks at Anna's picture on his desk, pulls out his typewriter and writes an article which later he'll 'rather like'. The title is 'Youth – A Curable Malady'.

Chapter Seven

IN THE AUTUMN OF 1932 my mother died. In her I lost my best friend. She had cancer. I saw her waste away in three months. She lost half her normal weight and her lovely face shrank and shrank.

She died when Europe still seemed to be Europe and the sinister potentialities in men had not yet become monstrous realities.

My mother's death came at a time when I was struggling to pay off my debts, when I had to suffer doubly for having no time to mourn her properly. Only very late at night, when I dropped into bed, was I choked by the feeling of being abandoned, completely alone in the world.

In 1934, my stepfather died. He was the last remnant of mother's world. I became an adult.

From 1933 onwards the objective journalist in me was swiftly turned into an engaged publicist. Hitler's seizure of power, the Reichstag fire, the February revolt in Vienna in 1934, the Dollfuss murder, the 'sanctions without teeth' of the Abyssinian war, not to speak of events inside Hungary, made it increasingly more difficult to remain a neutral onlooker.

As principal foreign correspondent and later as Foreign Editor of *Pesti Naplo* I witnessed the rape of Austria, the famous *Anschluss*, the occupation of Sudetenland, of Prague and Memel; in Austria during the February revolt I saw the workers' homes destroyed by gunfire, I learned the vile behind-the-scenes story of Dollfuss's murder; I looked on while Poland had her last few weeks of peace; in the Baltic and the Balkans, in Germany and Western Europe I participated in the death struggles of our unhappy continent. How could one stay neutral while mass murders were being committed, and murderous thugs planned to overrun Europe? And in Hungary itself 'fascism' was not the remote foreign charade it still seemed in some western countries; a large section of the government camp split off and became openly fascist.

By that time the Communists were interested in me. In 1934 the illegal 'Communist party in Hungary' (it was not yet known as the Hungarian CP) started a monthly called *Gondolat*. It was a 'People's Front' periodical, containing literature, sociology and politics, run by Communists, but by no means all written by them. They got together good 'names', liberals, Peasant party people, Social-Democrats and many people who were vaguely leftish. The type of young writers whom Virginia Woolf called 'Leaning Tower Intellectuals' were all invited to contribute. There were the representatives of the 'March Front', harking back to the 1848 March revolution, all practicing sociologists, who were often referred to as the 'village explorers'. They studied various districts of the country, reporting on the lives of estate servants, landless landworkers, small peasants and other country folk, and their revelations in the mid-nineteen-thirties shook the country. This group was for a while a fourth force. In Hungary at that time opinion was divided between the camp of the Westerners, that of the Establishment, the fascists, and lastly this 'March Front'. I belonged to none of these factions but was nearer in my sympathies to the 'peasant writers'.

And we all wrote for *Gondolat*.

I find it difficult not to seem muscle-bound when trying to give a truthful account of the subject 'Marxism and Myself, 1934–1935'. In Sarospatak, in Vienna, in Paris and America, and later as a newspaperman in Budapest, I met many Marxists off and on. I did not much like their cocksure manner and their clichés. My impression was they were cranks with a superiority complex, totally lacking in humour. I had read some Marx, which rather bored me, and Lenin, who was far too rude in his writing. But I had a certain respect for Marxism. While I was in America I had read Engels' *The Origin of the Family, Private Property and the State*. This book was based on the work of an eminent American social anthropologist, Lewis Henry Morgan. In fact Engels quotes whole chapters from Morgan's *Ancient Society*. But Engels put forward in this book the Marxian theory on the development of social forms. This theory purports to explain the development from primitive communism, through slaveholding society to feudalism, capitalism, and as the final peak, to socialism. I had a healthy suspicion of all closed systems, mainly because of my debates with orthodox Freudians. As a social anthropologist I found ridiculous the monopolist claim of the Freudians that their school is the science to end and embrace all the sciences. The Marxists made a similar claim, therefore they too were suspect in my eyes.

But in 1934 I began to see them as practical politicians, as fighters against the common enemy, fascism. I knew how courageous the members of the illegal Communist party in many countries were, I did not hear of corruption within Marxists and was sceptical about attacks against the Soviet Union, which always seemed to be made by the wrong sort of people. The 'People's Front' idea appealed to me. Occasional visits to my father, who by then had given up all pretence of working and lived with my sister, drove me nearer to the Communist camp. Father thought rather well of Hitler and Mussolini. He agreed with our Regent Horthy; what a pity that Hitler was only a corporal! It rather harmed the prestige of anti-Semitism.

I began to read Marxism again, not as one of the scientific theories on economics and human society, but as a handbook for political fighters against fascism. And I found much Marxist writing at that time a good guide for our common fight. When I read Marxist philosophy I did not stop to think how much its dialectics owed to Hegel; it was an intellectual adventure, a revelation. The picture of the world and human society as a dynamic process, ever on the move, driven on by inherent contradictions; the change of quantity into quality; the interpenetrating influences and contradictions shaping human affairs; the fighting quality of the whole world-view appealed to me. I had always been interested in philosophy and by 1935 I had reached a point at which, though I did not want to accept party discipline, I embraced much of Marxist philosophy.

The Communists whom I met at the *Gondolat* office were friendly and tolerant and frequently assured us non-Communists what good democrats we were!

And then came the Spanish Civil War. By that time I was one of the influential publicists of the Western camp in Hungary. *Pesti Naplo* gave me freedom to write as I pleased and my somewhat too intellectual and too subjective style, coupled with my daring in attacking the other side, made my writing popular in our camp. The 'Invisible Front' of the Hungarian Hitlerites in an anonymous letter threatened to kill me. The next Sunday I gave my answer in a leading article, stating that our fight would go on.

The tragedy of Western nonintervention, the plight of the Spanish people, the massacre at Guernica, the intervention of Mussolini's divisions and of Hitler's air force – all this was not a distant drama for us. We felt that the fighters on the Madrid or Andalusian fronts defended our liberty. We of the Western democratic camp felt in a way responsible for whatever 'the West', meaning Great Britain, France and America, did. We knew how most of the British and French peoples felt during this period. Europe was divided into two camps, and we were by now heart and soul in the 'People's Front'.

I paid a horrible price for 'the obsession'. I lost many of the best years of my life, I went through the nightmares of the streamlined Security Police inferno, the writer in me was nearly lost, the obsession hurled my country into a terrible tragedy – and yet I would lie to the reader and to myself if I wrote that I am ashamed of my 1933–1945 period. Being a writer, a publicist, I had to take sides. The choice was then either fascism or anti-fascism. I had to choose the latter.

My life, however, was by no means that of an obsessed anti-fascist. I kept up my omnivorous reading, I traveled a lot as principal foreign correspondent, went regularly to the Opera and to concerts and plays, led some social life, and enjoyed swimming and playing tennis. From May to October there was barely a day when I didn't go for at least an hour to one of the many beaches and swimming pools of Budapest. Although alcohol was never a problem in my life and I can do without it for months, like most Hungarians of my social stratum I enjoyed and still enjoy good wine and brandy and attach considerable importance to delightful food. My health and vitality never allowed fanticism to suppress my sensual artistic side.

True enough, as a foreign correspondent rushing about in cars, express trains and planes in Europe, I witnessed the various initial stages of the oncoming catastrophe. But whether in Riga, Stockholm or Paris, in Vienna, Rome or London, I took time off to explore the non-political human world and enjoy new encounters.

In the spring of 1937 I married for the second time. I was twenty-nine, Marthe eighteen. She was the daughter of a well-to-do business-man, tall and slender, with enormous black eyes in her puckishly pretty face. She was cultured and impulsive and had been educated in German, Swiss and English schools. By this time I was well over the bankruptcy of my first marriage and had grown tired of meaningless affairs. I had a craving for a real home, I wanted to 'solve' my private life, to be able to write in peace. We soon fell in love. I was glad to see that Marthe needed no 'building up'. Although in many ways refresh-ingly childish and naïve, she had a strong personality of her own. In March, 1937, we went on a long Italian honeymoon and afterwards settled down in a fashionable flat in the Buda district. We entertained and were entertained as popular members of the 'smart set' in the Western camp.

Marthe was a delightful child-wife, if somewhat over-possessive. I still spent the afternoon and half the night at the *Pesti Naplo* several times a week, was still very busy writing short stories and literary arti-cles, translating novels, lecturing to the 'progressive' literary societies. Marthe, who never went out without me, took as big a part in my life as she could. But this was increasingly less; my journalistic travels grew more and more frequent as I had to go on long journeys for my paper to get a proper idea of the situation in the Balkans, in Western or Northern Europe. We drifted apart.

Because of our exceedingly active life and my many travels Marthe sensed only in the second half of 1939 that our marriage had somehow gone wrong. But we were such good friends, and there was such a 'before-the-catastrophe' atmosphere, that we did not really part until 1941, when I escaped from Hungary.

I had visas for all European countries and because of foreign exchange controls *Pesti Naplo* deposited money in my name in all the capital cities. One was forever being alerted to witness a new triumph for the dictators. Always the Soviet Union seemed the country, wronged by the rest, which was on our side. Litvinov made speeches in the League of Nations which made good reading for anti-fascists everywhere.

In 1938 when Hitler invaded Austria I covered the *Anschluss* story with journalists from many countries. Vienna, one of the most attractive centres of European culture, was violated by the uncouth Brown Shirts, by SS brigands and the Hitlerite rabble. Before Hitler made his great speech on the Ring, the foreign correspondents who had gathered at the Ballhaus (the Foreign Office) to get their passes were forcibly detained until Hitler finished his speech. This did not worry me; my concern was with how the Nazis incorporated Austria, how they staged their man hunts. I saw how the cultured Viennese Jews became hunted animals at anyone's mercy. As I walked one day in the Jewish quarter on the Tabor Strasse I overheard a white-bearded Jew saying to his wife: 'They are happy, there is no Jew among them.' He was pointing at two mongrels playing at the curb.

In the Bond Street of Vienna, the splendid Kaertner Strasse, the Nazis worked to tar shop windows with the words 'Jewish shop'. Three days later when the shops were taken over by 'Aryans', the tar letters had to be scraped off. It was the middle of March and rather cold. A red-headed Jewish boy of about thirteen was working on one of the shop windows. He scraped away and cried. A crowd stood around jeering.

Since that time, all through the epoch of Himmlers and Berias, I saw horrors which I do not care to describe ever. But the eyes of that ugly little boy in the Kaertner Strasse still look at me from time to time with the timid question: 'How can you do this to me?' That unimportant little scene filled me with dark forebodings.

Back in Hungary the situation was very bleak. A few days after the *Anschluss*, Regent Horthy – without consulting his government – broadcasted a touching but futile funeral oration, over the Austria which he loved, having spent many years there as one of the aides of Emperor Francis Joseph. Next day this simple, weak-willed naval officer, in the hands of his political advisers, approved of a new propaganda drive which was to convince the world, but mainly the Italian and German fascists, that fascism was in fact invented by the Horthy-

Bethlen set. The government press informed their readers that the political principles of fascism were framed by them as long ago as 1919 in the city of Szeged, and pointed out with some pride that the first modern anti-Jewish law in Europe was passed by this 'pure fascist' regime in 1920 – this was the *'numerus clausus* law' limiting the number of Jewish university students to six per cent of the Christian students. Ever since then the regime had been inspired by fascist principles. The Hungarian extreme right – even more extreme than the Horthy-Bethlen set – naturally gained by this policy; the latter, afraid of having power snatched from them, *promptly adopted the extremists' political line*, countering the demands of various Arrow Cross and Nazi parties for a more determined anti-democratic policy by more stringent anti-Jewish legislation and increased co-operation with the Axis. In Hungary the Arrow Cross groups represented the Nazis and the Horthy set the Papen-Hindenburg-Hugenberg group; but the Hungarians had no chance to stage a revolution, for the Hungarian Papen (Bethlen) and the Hungarian Hindenburg (Horthy) swiftly and effectively out-Nazied the Nazis.

A number of the regime's aristocratic and middle-class adherents were disturbed by these developments; their leaders damped down their fears by persuading them that 'We must have humane, decent anti-Jewish laws, then the Hitlerites won't bother us.'

The Western-democratic camp did what it could. Nearly two-thirds of the Budapest press was against these developments and we writers – as we usually do – came out with our protests. Then Istvan Hertelendi, a young writer-colleague of mine, and I organized a large-scale protest against the intended outrage. Hertelendi, like myself, possessed a 'historic' name; no one could say that we were not 'real Hungarians'. Our plan was to have our protest signed by all the great artists, writers, and scientists of the country who could not be attacked on any racial basis; most of them were either of noble origin or pure peasant stock. The first man we visited was Béla Bartók, the great composer. After strengthening the text of the protest, he signed at once. Zoltan Kodaly, the other famous composer, Istvan Csok and Karoly Kernstock, the great painters, then a galaxy of other artists, writers and scientists signed. With the exception of Jews, the best representatives of Hungarian culture signed the protest against an anti-Jewish law which was published by all the newspapers and periodicals of our camp. And the other camp got the law passed.

Nineteen thirty-eight was the bleak year when Chamberlain's umbrella hovered over Europe like the sword of Damocles; the year of Berchtesgaden and Godesberg talks, of the Munich conference and the occupation of the Sudeten district.

Having travelled a lot in Germany between the wars, I felt close to the tragedy that was enfolding the German people, and had a foreboding that their fate would soon be ours.

The German people tried by every means – smuggled letters, the books of exiled people, the witness of those who escaped from concentration camps – to inform the world that peace would be Hitler's next victim. They cried for help and pointed out that the rule of the Gestapo would make them entirely helpless, that if appeasement went on they would become utterly helpless tools of Hitler.

Hundreds of books and thousands of articles were written by Germans to convince the world that in a country ruled by efficient, ruthless and unscrupulous gangsters it would be impossible for the people to find a way to defend themselves; that such gangsterism might be thoroughly unpopular and universally hated, but at the same time perfectly secure.

And the Great Powers entered into diplomatic relations with Hitler.

Before the war, the Italian people lived for more than ten years, and the German people for seven years, under such a tyranny, and got no help from outside. They asked for help. People escaped and cried aloud to the world about the horrors inside Germany and about the future, when Hitler would let those horrors loose on the world. A huge library could be filled with articles, speeches and books uttering such warnings. And nothing happened.

We watched all this and got more worried every day. The White Terrorists appeared again in Hungary. Their actions showed us clearly when the people's cause suffered a defeat anywhere. Was Mussolini permitted to massacre the Abyssinians? Next day Jewish students were beaten up in Budapest University. Did Hitler march into the

Rhineland or Austria? Next day the village White Terrorists tortured the leaders of the land-workers.

Each victory of the Nazi and Fascist militarists in Spain, in Munich, in Prague, made the White Terrorists bolder. They now adopted the catchword 'Arrow Cross' – i.e. they became Hungarian Nazis. They boasted that the rich Jewish financiers had been frightened into financing them, and that the Fascists in Spain, Germany and Italy received loans from France, England and America.

We watched with cold fear in our hearts. Would the people of France, Britain and America let their appeasers permit the Nazi-Fascists to be helped to complete victory?*

All this time I was vaguely pro-Soviet and pro-American; my contact with the Communists was broken in 1937 when the editor of *Gondolat* was jailed and the monthly banned. My leaning towards Marxism became less marked. The enemy was Hitler, and in the fight against him the Communists represented only one group of allies among many others. But politics permeated my personality more and more.

In February and March 1939 I witnessed the break-up of Czecho-slovakia, the birth of the puppet state of Slovakia and on the morning of March 15 I stood in the huge St. Wenceslas Square in Prague when Hitler's tanks rolled in, fouling the virginal white snow of the square. The Czechs spat into the faces of the SS troops; they cried and shouted. I described these scenes truthfully in *Az Est* and in *Pesti Naplo*.

Thus the nightmare started. People leaped to their death from the windows of tall buildings; Black Marias worked overtime taking victims off to the swiftly opened concentration camps. In the Ambassador Hotel I found an elderly man standing trembling in the corridor; he had rushed in, seeking a place to hide, only to find himself in a hotel requisitioned for German officers. Only we foreign journalists had been allowed to stay on. He was a Jewish professor of pre-history and with some journalist friends we managed to smuggle him and a few others like him out of the country. But thousands were killed, jailed, hunted down.

---

* *In Darkest Hungary*. London: Victor Gollancz, 1944.

The Undefeated

There was a very strict curfew in the city. In the cellar of the Ambassador Hotel there was a fashionable nightclub called the Embassy. The manager got in touch with the German officers and the foreign journalists, offering to keep his establishment open if we would promise him our custom. This we did. The Embassy bar was indeed a strange place at that time. British, American, French, Argentinian, Danish and other journalists sat around the little tables, drinking, flirting with the hostesses, and eying each other curiously. I was sitting with two British friends at a table when a bullet-headed German General Staff major got into conversation with us. Soon other General Staff officers joined us. Speaking of Czechoslovakia, they told us how ashamed they felt at having to take part in Hitler's breach of faith; had he not said he had no more territorial ambitions?

When we asked them why they didn't do something about it they said they would try; but later the major, a little drunk, burst out, 'All right, you fine critics, do you know what it means to live under terrorism? Do you know what it feels like to live in a police state? You are kids – you don't know the half of it. In terrorism, in a police state, it's not only a question of courage. Most action of resistance leads to sudden arrest. To resist is generally nothing but committing an isolated suicide.' We said we understood, or would try to understand. He made us promise never to mistake Hitler for Germany.

The atmosphere in the Embassy bar was sometimes like that of a second-rate Hollywood thriller with a dashing romantic foreign correspondent as the hero. The main ambition of the elegant German General Staff officers was to convince us of their anti-Hitler sentiments. A few days after the occupation of Prague one of them drew me aside and earnestly warned me that Hungary might very well be the next victim, and that very night a young Danish colleague suggested that we should make a bilateral maintenance pact: if Hitler occupied Copenhagen he would come to Hungary where I would support him; it would be the other way round if they went for Budapest. An old French newspaperman listening to us asked:

'And what if he occupies both?'

The Gestapo and the SS helped by the local Nazis, the followers of Herr Henlein, had made most careful preparations for *der Tag*. Seeing that I could not cope alone with the flood of news, I organized a team of ten taxi-drivers. They reported to me every morning at eight and till six in the evening they were out gathering news for me. It was their task to visit all the clinics and hospitals and cemeteries to find out about suicides; they got details of arrests from Czech policemen and they naturally reported everything else they heard during the day. For all this I had to pay only what the taximeter showed and give them a normal tip. They were enthusiastic and conscientious reporters. I telephoned my material. Our three newspapers *Az Est* at noon, *Magyarorszag* in the evening and *Pesti Naplo* in the morning were able to print a running account of Czechoslovakia's crucifixion. When the time came to leave Prague, I gave a farewell party to my taxi-driver friends, who had spent the last week helping me and other colleagues to arrange the escape of some Czech intellectuals. I was in a melancholy mood. They told me not to worry. 'We Czechs' – one of them said – 'are great survivors. We are going to survive this too. Don't you worry.'

I spent three weeks in Prague, then rushed home and wrote a book about the past two years entitled *Chamberlain Is Responsible*. It was published on August 25, 1939, and was an immediate best-seller, selling about two thousand copies a day, and it was still going strong when Britain declared war on Germany on September 3. But then I withdrew it from circulation and cancelled the new edition: if Britain was at war with Germany, no book of mine should attack their Prime Minister. I only hoped they might get another one before long.

That summer I made several trips to the Balkans, to Poland and the Baltic states. In Danzig the Nazis kept me in jail for two days because someone denounced me as an anti-Nazi.

A day after France and Britain declared war on Germany, I was sent to Rome; the Italian authorities had expelled our former correspondent. The Hitler authorities cut off telephone communications between Hungary and Western Europe, and I had to get French and English news by calling up London and Paris from Rome and by reading the French and British press. In fact I had to report not only on

Italy but the whole of Western Europe from Rome. With a spinsterish old secretary, a former admirer of Mussolini, I settled down to work in a penthouse room in a hotel on the wonderful Via Veneto. My journalistic work didn't begin till midday; I got up at six every morning and sat on the flat roof in brilliant sunlight, high above the chestnut trees of the Veneto, typing away furiously at a new novel called *Farewell to Europe*.

Writing a novel then and there was pure escapism. I drugged myself with writing, with occupying all my waking hours, not to be tormented by the 'humanity pain'.

How well we knew that this was *it!* The Second World War had begun. We – the fraternity of foreign correspondents – gathered night after night in the Stampa Estera, drank cognac and barked at each other in our shorthand language. We had watched Europe drifting towards war; we knew by heart most of Churchill's warnings. It was the most easily avoidable war in human history. Hitler could have been stopped easily when he reoccupied the Rhineland. A year later it would still have been easy; it could have been done over Austria – even up till a week or so before the Munich conference in 1938. Instead Europe gave away Austria, then the Czech armament industry and the frightened support of south-eastern Europe. And now it had begun, now his strength was built up and we sat around in our clubs and Press Associations reading in impotent rage the tragic news of the ticker tape: *Blitzkrieg*. Poland swiftly trampled down, Polish cities bombed to smithereens, Polish divisions encircled and annihilated – how prudent it was to warn the Poles against rounding up the Nazis living in Poland; what brilliant diplomacy it was to manoeuver Hitler and Stalin into their pact!

All of us – newsmongers and wholesale merchants of news, experts and high priests of international affairs – what a sad and futile lot we were! Oh yes, we'd always sounded our warnings. I thought of my friends in Poland, in Austria, in Czechoslovakia, of the hundreds and thousands of Germans in concentration camps. Below me lay Rome – hopeful Rome, hopeful Italy – still hoping Mussolini would be clever, would stay out of the war. Listening to their talk I felt sadly how little chance they had. They would have to fight side by side with the Nazis.

I saw ruins everywhere. Rome and Florence, and Paris and London, all the cities of Europe in ruins.

The alarm clock woke me at six in the morning and I went on writing my farewell to Europe.

At noon every day I rushed into my newspaper work. There were cables and confidential letters from Budapest. But I got letters from the West too. A French friend of mine, a young essayist, was called up. He wrote me a subdued letter: 'I go into this war as into a monastery, with no feeling of elation. It had to come. Let's try to get it over.'

The 'humanity pain' ... So little left to believe. The Soviet Union pouncing on Poland. The 'Socialist Sixth of the Earth' the principal ally of the Nazis. It must be curious for Dimitrov, sitting in Moscow, to witness the sudden outburst of love between Stalin and Hitler, Göring and the rest; the Nazi press writing about the 'alliance of young proletarian nations'; the Budapest hooligans discovering their sympathy for the Communists. What would Marx and Lenin say to this? Or had I misread them?

And the West was at last at war with Hitler. But what a strange war, declared but not yet begun.

The novel was less and less effective as a drug. Before I had finished it a sudden blow fell: early in November I was recalled to Budapest. 'They' had expropriated the company which owned *Pesti Naplo* because the owner was a Jew. My Jewish colleagues were all fired, but this did not satisfy the Nazis. They demanded that the government of Count Paul Teleki suppress *Pesti Naplo* for good. I was called back to try and save the paper. All my efforts were in vain. The newspaper which was founded in the dark days after our 1848–1849 war of liberty, in 1851, was to close down for ever. Dr. Foldi, a Jew, ceased to be editor; Laczko had gone to work for another paper. So my dream of becoming *the* editor was fulfilled, for three whole days. I thought a lot then of that nineteenth-century novelist, Count Zsigmond Kemeny, who had founded the paper with such forebodings, not expecting it to last. But the paper went on for eighty-eight years, true to the dreams and aims of 1848, preaching a tolerant liberalism to a world which was by no means liberal and became less and less tolerant.

The Undefeated

I wrote no leading article in the last issue announcing the death of the paper. I brought out a normal issue, attacking Hitler Germany and our government for backing it. Among the small news items there was a notice. It just said: *Pesti Naplo will not be published tomorrow. The paper was twice suppressed during its history. Once in the last century, upon the demand of the Czar Nicholas of Russia, and in 1919 by the Bolsheviks.*

When I had put the paper to bed for the last time, I went over to the printers to shake hands with them. They gave me the copper die with which they had printed for so many years along the top of the front page: *Pesti Naplo.*

Chapter Eight

NOVEMBER AND DECEMBER OF 1939. Chaos in Europe, chaos in Hungary, chaos in our hearts. Some people still believed that Hungary could stay out of the war, but most of us were haunted by the nightmare that very soon we should be forced into uniform to fight for Hitler against the West.

The pro-Nazi, anti-Semitic propaganda had its effect, as I saw in the army. After I did my basic training in the Hungarian equivalent of the territorials in 1935 I was called up twice for summer manoeuvers, and in the autumn of 1938, when, as a consequence of the Munich agreement, Hungary received a strip of Czechoslovakian territory, I found myself in uniform again. By that time I was a lance corporal in the machine-gunners, wearing on my sleeve the so-called 'cadet stripe' which showed that even if you were in the ranks you belonged to the officer class.

The commander of the company, a member of the Arrow Cross party, ordered that the company should have three 'Aryan' platoons and that all the Jews should go into the fourth. One November day, as we started on our ten miles back to the barracks – three abreast – our commander ordered us to sing a vile anti-Jewish song. As the tallest man in the company I was at the head of the column and it was my duty to begin the song. I refused. The outcome was that no one sang it. Next day I was sentenced to a fortnight's 'hard solitary confinement', meaning a day of complete darkness plus bread and water in a stone-floored cell without blankets, followed by a day with no darkness but no bread and water. Naturally I ate my fill before my sentence began! The sergeant of the barracks prison, an L-shaped building, escorted me to the very end of the corridor; my name and rank were pasted on the last but one door. 'This will be your official cell,' he said, 'but in fact you will stay here.'

The last cell of all was furnished with a camp bed and candlesticks. There was a table piled with food, cigarettes, newspapers and magazines, and a large Thermos flask filled with tea and rum. As I looked round in amazement, he went on: 'Listen carefully, now. There'll be a guard posted outside this cell. When there's an inspection we shall make a lot of noise at the outer door, the guard will wake you up and you can slip into the cell next door and look properly miserable. Forget it,' he said when I tried to thank him. 'When the battalion heard about this filthy business all the non-Jews decided to do the best we could for you. No decent Hungarian will stand for this Nazi filth ... now eat!'

In spite of having already stuffed myself I had to eat again, not to disappoint the good sergeant, who was a reservist like myself and a peasant from the green belt around Budapest.

I stretched myself out on the bed and began to read a copy of *Time*. After a bit there was a rumpus outside, the guard knocked, and I was locked into my official cell. A minute or two later, a first lieutenant stood in the doorway, dismissed the guard and stepped inside.

'Hello, old chap. My name is Dr. Kepessy.' He offered his hand and smiled. 'Decent thing you did. Er ... I brought you something to eat and drink.'

My heart sank as I saw the huge goose-liver and chicken sandwiches. But I had to eat them. He waited while I drank some cognac from his his flask and smoked two cigarettes.

It went on like this for the whole fortnight. The rankers – peasants and workers – kept me going with enormous meals and lots of wine, while the reservist officers used every pretext to inspect the jail and shower me with sandwiches, brandy and cigarettes. When I eventually reported to my Nazi commander I was bursting out of my uniform. He eyed me suspiciously. Was it possible, he was overheard saying in the officer's mess, that there was something about 'hard' confinement that could cause a glandular upset?

This incident illustrates my point. In 1938 the average reservist battalion disliked the Nazis and made it a point of honor to declare its solidarity with the anti-Nazis and the Jews. I served again in the same battalion and the same company for two months in the summer of 1940. By that time the mood had changed! Some of the officers and men had become pro-Nazis, the majority 'neutral', and only a small minority stuck to its former attitude.

At the end of summer 1940 the 'Viennese award' took place – Ribbentrop and Count Ciano awarded a part of Transylvania to Hungary. A week before the occupation, the 'unreliable' elements were demobilized. To my great pleasure our Nazi commander found me unreliable too.

Many of the General Staff officers in Hungary were the sons or grandsons of the Austro-Hapsburg civil and military service men who ruled Hungary after 1849. These with other officers of German origin became more Nazi than the Hitlerites, and more German than the Austrians. In 1939 and in 1940 they applied for permission to revive their old German family names. My company commander was christened Kurt Schreiner when he was born; before entering the Budapest military academy he took on a very Hungarian-sounding name and became Karoly Bordas to further his career. In 1940 he became Kurt Schreiner again. Lieutenant-Colonel Regos, our battalion commander, became Hermann Raith in 1940. Some of these officers and civil servants revived family names which their forefathers dropped five generations ago. The thing was to be a Nazi. A still better thing was to be a *German* Nazi, so they reverted to Hermanns and Kurts, and longed for the day when they would fight as allies of the Hitlerite armies.

The anti-Jewish laws created golden opportunities for 'Aryan' middle-class and petty-bourgeois people. The Jews had to give up their shops, companies, factories and various enterprises, and by 1939 every private firm was forbidden to retain more than six per cent Jews. The outcome was that any limited company, shop, factory or other enterprise still in Jewish hands had an 'Aryan front' figurehead, a good Christian with a well-sounding Hungarian – or, even better, German – name, while the Jewish owner managed things from behind the scenes. Rakes and scroungers who had for long been skeletons in various family cupboards now became 'Aryan fronts', Christian 'percentage correctors', parasites nourished by the anti-Jewish laws. This situation spelled doom for the poor Jews and meant extra expenditure for the rich ones.

Hungary was not a nice place to live in. The peasants and workers were as powerless against this trend as the intellectuals of the Western-democratic camp.

The first few months of the Second World War made a far less phony impression on us, east of Germany, than on the people of the West. Although we were disgusted and disheartened by the Hitler-Stalin pact in August, 1939, many were convinced that Hitler would attack the Soviet Union and that Hungary would sooner or later enter the war. Rather than fight for the Nazis, some of us tried to find out from the French and British legations whether we could enlist in their armies. The answer was that it could not be done from Budapest.

The government of Count Paul Teleki did everything to persuade the public that Hungary had a chance to stay out of the war. There was talk of a neutral Central European-Balkan block formed by Turkey, Greece, Bulgaria, Yugoslavia, Romania and Hungary. This 'neutral' block would furnish food and raw materials to Hitler at the price of avoiding the war. Mussolini was still waiting with 'arms at rest', to see which way events would turn. It was a period of hopeless compromise for the small nations abandoned by the West. The swift and cruel way Poland was smitten down by Hitler's and Stalin's armies frightened governments and peoples alike.

After the death of *Pesti Naplo* I thought I would give up journalism. My novel, *Farewell to Europe*, was due to be published soon and I had planned a new one. Then in December 1939 an anti-Nazi politician, Bajcsy-Zsilinszky, founded a new weekly called *Independent Hungary* and asked me to become foreign editor. I gladly accepted.

The two sister newspapers of the *Pesti Naplo* were taken over by the government. One of them, the evening paper *Magyarorszag*, became the Prime Minister's personal newspaper and was augmented by a morning edition. To my surprise the Premier wanted me to stay on as foreign editor. Whereas in internal politics we might disagree, he felt we should see eye to eye in foreign policy. He assured me that he was doing his best to stem the Nazi flood in Hungary and was determined to keep her out of the war. 'We will not become the accomplices of Hitler' (*Nem leszunk Hitler cinkosai*), he told me very firmly.

Count Paul Teleki, half Transylvanian, half Greek, was a professor of political geography. While his friends in the leadership of the regime drifted steadily towards the extreme right, he became more liberal. He had many friends in the democratic camp. The Horthy-Bethlen set did not want to relinquish all power to Hitler's envoys. As the Hungarian General Staff was flirting with the extreme right and there was a danger that they might stage a *coup d'état*, the regime countered by giving more freedom to the legal democratic opposition. In this struggle the Western-democratic opposition kept the balance for the Horthy-Bethlen set.

I agreed to stay on as foreign editor provided I could do the job on the weekly, *Independent Hungary*. This condition was accepted. So early in 1940 I became foreign editor of a paper which was the personal mouthpiece of the Prime Minister, and at the same time I wrote on foreign affairs in the most prominent anti-Nazi weekly of the country.

At first I was hopeful. I did not foresee that after twenty years of a neo-fascist regime Count Teleki alone could not turn the tide.

Teleki worked for a series of pacts with Yugoslavia, Bulgaria, Turkey and Greece. Early in 1940 I was present at the conference of the Balkan Entente in Belgrade, then went over to Sofia to interview the Bulgarian Premier Popov about the possibility of a Southeast-European neutral block. In April I was sent on a Balkan tour again to sound out the possibilities of neutrality in Athens, Ankara, Sofia and Belgrade.

I was staying in the Park Oteli in Istanbul when the night porter awakened me one night with the news that Hitler had occupied my country. I soon found that he had misheard the broadcast: it was Denmark that Hitler had occupied this time, not Hungary. I thought of the Danish colleague I had concluded the bilateral maintenance pact with the year before in Prague. Knowing how prudently Denmark had tried to avoid being swamped, I foresaw the futility of Count Teleki's attempts.

The Undefeated

My room overlooked the Bosporus. It was a dark night; a few lights quivered on the Asiatic side, the street lamps of Üsküdar and Haidar-Pasha. Then faint greenish streaks appeared on the horizon. The minarets and mosques were gradually silhouetted against the deep blue sky. I sat there at one edge of the Continent and thought about Copenhagen on the other. Copenhagen, whose intriguing atmosphere I had tried so many times to describe without success. Now it was no longer a question of how and in what peculiar variation Copenhagen distilled the essence of Europeanism. The lovely city was to undergo a nightmare of brutal reality, a nightmare of Gestapo lorries filled with deathly white faces; a life from which common sense and common decency would be summarily expelled.

Now it was Denmark, tomorrow or the next week or month it would be Norway, Sweden, then the East or the West. The Nazi monster would swallow country after country and there would be no more Europe.

When I awoke, there was sunshine, the golden tops of the minarets were glistening with dew. A mixture of small and big boats were busily crawling about on the Bosporus; an airplane was flying smoothly towards Asia. The waiter knocked with my breakfast and a pile of newspapers. The breakfast was good. The newspapers had nothing new to say. The 'phony war' went on. It seemed my fight was still at home. My fight was our little conspiracy, our leaflets and propaganda manoeuvers. I went home.

Since my return from Rome in November, 1939, my life had become more and more complicated. Apart from my two foreign editorships, my own writing and what private life I had, there was also my illegal work, which determined my fate for many years to come.

In Budapest, in November, 1939, Sidney Morrell, the *Daily Express* correspondent, who had seen me working in Prague, had introduced me to a friend of his, Basil Davidson, a journalist freshly arrived from London. We met off and on, talked a lot of politics and soon became friends. In 1940 Davidson tried to set up a Budapest office for the Brita-Nova news agency, a wartime venture to counterbalance Nazi propaganda, for which the dignified semiofficial Reuter's was no match. After some wire-pulling, the concession was given, Brita-Nova started to function and furnish anti-Nazi news for the newspapers of the Western-democratic camp.

I soon had a feeling that Basil was on a special mission and it turned out that I was right. Knowing me to be one of the most conspicuous anti-Nazi publicists in Hungary, with a great many friends on the intellectual left, Basil guessed that I had some part in the various illegal anti-Nazi leaflet campaigns which were going on at that time. One day in December, 1939, he told me that he had 'some influential friends in London' who could help us in our anti-Nazi work. I told him I was not interested in who his friends were, but was willing to do anything against the Hitlerites. It was some time before I found out who his 'influential friends' were.

He himself was already working on a plan for a large-scale leaflet campaign against the Nazis and their Hungarian friends; my task would be to write the text.

The reaction of the government soon showed how effective those leaflets were. They were distributed all over Hungary and exposed many of the machinations of the pro-Nazi wing of the regime. I helped Basil with many other legal and semilegal propaganda activities and with his Brita-Nova work. Basil, an excellent newspaperman, had worked previously for the London *Economist* and had travelled a lot in Europe. As the Budapest office of Brita-Nova was not able to be in constant contact with the London head office, he and I wrote a large proportion of the news items and the Washington, Paris and London commentaries. I was the Washington political expert and wrote a series of articles on the coming American presidential elections, while Basil was in turn Buenos Aires, London or Paris commentator. We listened in every night to news broadcasts from the European capitals and put out just those news items which were most likely to get the Hitlerites in Hungary on the raw. The Budapest representative of the Transocean Press complained that it was next to impossible to beat the 'huge apparatus' of Brita-Nova. Our commentaries generally turned out right.

That year I wrote a short book under the title *America at the Crossroads*, written and published before the presidential candidates were chosen. I picked Wendell Willkie for Republican candidate and asserted that Roosevelt was going to be elected again.

Our Western-democratic camp was diminishing. In the past, politicians, journalists and intellectuals used to turn out in great numbers for the regular cocktail parties given at the British and French legations in Budapest. After the fall of Paris, only five of us attended the next French party, only seven the British.

The Arrow Cross and other extreme right-wing fascist parties talked openly of taking over power soon. The six hundred thousand strong German minority furnished some two hundred thousand members to the Nazi party in Hungary and more people discovered their Aryan origin in the army and the civil service.

Hungary was now surrounded on three sides by Hitler's empire, not to speak of the short Hungarian-Soviet frontier in the northeast. The only free frontier was the southern one with Yugoslavia. Those fortunate ones who went from Hungary to the States had to circle the globe: they went to Yugoslavia first, then Bulgaria, Turkey and Iraq to the Persian Gulf and from there via Japan to America.

Each time I went to the Balkans I had more difficulty in getting exit visas from Hungary. On every occasion the Prime Minister's office had to intervene. Many years later, when I was in jail, I found out that the political police had wanted to arrest me in the summer of 1940, but Count Teleki intervened personally to save me from arrest. It had already begun to be dangerous to have Westerners as friends or to visit the American, British and French legations.

Count Teleki was still optimistic, working harder than ever for the Southeast-European neutral bloc plan. And he had some success. In Belgrade, early in 1941 I witnessed the signing of the Hungarian-Yugoslav pact of eternal friendship, which was regarded as an anti-Hitler diplomatic victory. The Western-democratic camp in Hungary revived a little; people were hopeful. I was not. After the signature of the pact I again went on the tour of the Balkans and on my return took six weeks to write another of my short political books, *The Balkans in the Storm*.

Basil spoke more and more frequently of the coming Nazi invasion. It was obvious that I should have to escape: if I stayed I should be lucky, considering my activities, if I spent the duration of the war in prison.

On the thirtieth of March, 1941, there was a *coup d'état* in Yugoslavia. The regime of compromise was ousted and a pronouncedly anti-Nazi group took over. By that time the Nazis had a foothold in Bulgaria.

From the beginning of March some of us had a hunch that all was not well with the Hitler-Stalin friendship. There were indications of an impending German attack on Russia. In the weekly, *Independent Hungary,* I even dared to hint at such a possibility. The Belgrade coup provoked the Hitlerites to white-hot anger. Their plan to secure their flank was torpedoed. There were troop movements in Austria.

Then a blow fell. I was awakened at dawn on April 4 by a friend who told me that the Prime Minister, Count Teleki, had shot himself in the night. It turned out that without consulting him Regent Horthy and the chief of the General Staff had given permission to the Hitler army to attack Yugoslavia through Hungary. The Prime Minister wrote a letter of protest to Horthy, a farewell letter to his friends, and blew his brains out.

I called up Basil. He said he was leaving that night and urged that I do the same.

Budapest was bewildered; people in the trams and buses wept; most of the city was mourning. On my way to the Foreign Office on the Buda Castle Hill, I went over one of the Danube bridges. On the Buda side of the embankment huge German military lorries, tanks, *Panzer* cars, all kinds of military vehicles were rolling southward. They were on the move against Yugoslavia.

In the Foreign Office I called on my friends who belonged to Count Teleki's entourage. We drank black coffee and looked out of the window. Down below, the grey stream moved on.

First the government tried to hush up the suicide. Later it was published, but no mention was made of the letter of protest sent to the Regent. It would have been most embarrassing to admit that before the ink was dry on the Hungarian-Yugoslav pact of eternal friendship, the Regent and the General Staff, without even bothering to tell the Prime Minister, had given permission for a Hitlerite attack against the 'eternal' friend from Hungarian territory.

We walked up and down the large room talking of the Teleki family. Political suicide was not uncommon with the Telekis. The Prime Minister's great-uncle, Count Laszlo Teleki, had shot himself in 1867 as a protest against the Hapsburg Emperor. We – young and maybe foolish men – deplored the suicide. Why had not Paul Teleki taken us into his confidence? Why didn't he appeal to the nation, to the Hungarians in the Hungarian army? We could have armed the peasants and workers, we could have … 'If only …' 'We could …'

'Could you get me an exit permit?' I asked a friend.

'Now that the old man shot himself? Out of the question. Princess Odeschalchi was refused yesterday. She appealed to the Regent. Now the War Office reigns supreme. Go over to them.'

I went. The section chief who had been so polite to me before, did not even get up now to shake my hand. He simply asked:

'What do you want?'

'An exit permit. I want to go to Belgrade for the paper.'

'Nothing doing, young man. You stay at home. No more travelling for you.'

I called up Kaya Odeschalchi and met her in a café. She was the famous 'pink princess'; her sister, Countess Katinka Andrassy, was married to Count Michael Karolyi, the former President of the Hungarian Republic after World War I and she was an important member of the Western-democratic camp. She had just seen Regent Horthy and told him point-blank, 'I want to leave the country at once. I cannot live in a Nazi country.' The weak-willed old man, courteous and most susceptible to lovely women, gave her a safe-conduct.

'You must leave with us,' Kaya told me. 'A diplomat friend of mine will drive me over to Belgrade tomorrow. Try to get some documents.'

All through the day I rushed about trying to arrange my escape. I wasn't successful. Shortly before midnight I went to the blacked-out crowded Western Station to see Basil off. Many Western journalists and diplomats' wives and families were leaving for Belgrade. I listened wistfully to the Oxford accents, Yorkshire accents, American sing-song, quick Parisian patter. Would I ever hear it again?

I promised Basil to try everything to get to Belgrade in a day or two. Next morning I visited W., an old friend in the Yugoslav Legation who was going to make everything easy for me from the Yugoslavian side. But I still had no documents.

In the morning I saw Kaya Odeschalchi off. She was brisk and optimistic.

Just before noon something happened; with the help of friends I got a document making me out to be George Peter Howard of Quebec, Canada. As with most such documents, it was very, very good as long as it went unchallenged. But during the past two years I had crossed the Hungarian-Yugoslav frontier at least a dozen times; if someone recognized me – and this was likely – I would be lost.

I called up my flat. The previous night a friend had put me up, because I thought it wiser not to sleep at home. The maid told me that I had been called up into the army by telegram. So if they caught me, I would be a deserter from the army.

I took a taxi to the famous open-air restaurant in the city park, managed by that renowned Professor of Gastronomy, Charles Gundel, where I had arranged to lunch with F., and waited for her in the empty restaurant.

So this was it. Either I got out, or went to prison. A curious thing, I thought. My most ardent hope is to leave my identity, my friends, the unfinished manuscript of a long historical novel, my large library built up during the last fifteen years – everything. My most ardent hope was to leave F., whom I loved. F., who had worked with me on many illegal sorties.

I remembered a day last winter when I had to meet her after delivering to Basil the draft of a particular leaflet preaching sedition against the pro-Nazis on our General Staff. If I was caught with it, it would not just be prison. Basil was waiting for me in the Brita-Nova office. As I hurriedly opened the door someone stopped me. A detective. Fortunately he was not exactly a Poirot type, because he told me in a stentorian voice, 'You can't go in! There is a police search on!' I saw my only chance and took it: I pretended to be very aggressive and insisted on going in. He threw me out.

That day the political police searched fourteen premises as well as Basil's office, trying to find the leaflet-producing group.

I left the house, went to a café and almost collapsed, now that the danger was over. Had that detective not been so stupid, had he detained and searched me, I should have been shot.

At the time, when I told F. about it, she simply said, 'Of course you got through, you are a lucky type.'

Today, after she arrived, Professor Gundel conferred with us for a while, then disappeared to compose one of his unforgettable lunches.

I told her about the situation. She told me that her father heard from his best friend, General T., that the Nazi army would attack Yugoslavia at dawn.

I grew optimistic. The train for Belgrade left before midnight. By that time the Hungarian frontier authorities would no doubt have learned about the impending attack, there would be excitement and muddle. They would not bother with careful passport control. I would take a first-class sleeper and risk it.

'Of course,' F. said. 'You can't do anything else. You have nothing to lose. It's a far greater risk to stay. But you will get through all right. You are a lucky type.'

After lunch we went around buying some suits, shoes and two sumptuous suitcases. I had to look very 'first class' on that train. Then we deposited my luggage at the station and went for a walk. My farewell walk in my home town.

It was the fifth of April, 1941. There was brilliant sunshine, and up in the Buda hills we did not meet any German military cars. It was an ordinary Saturday afternoon. An ordinary afternoon before the holocaust.

If I got through, I might probably go to Greece and broadcast to Hungary from there. I should become a political exile, that curious type of humanity which from time to time makes a nuisance of itself in various places of the globe. But this did really interest me; what would become of Hungary, of Budapest, of Europe?

We were most conscious of history that afternoon and agreed how we hated it. One would like to live in a private world. One would like to …

Then we were on the platform, waiting by an empty train. It was eleven o'clock at night. Everyone knew that Yugoslavia would be attacked in a few hours. Everyone in the station knew that this was the last train to Belgrade. F. briefly took my hands in hers and was quickly gone. I gave a heavy tip to the sleeping car attendant. I told him I wanted to sleep, could he fix it so that the frontier authorities should not bother me?

Alone in the compartment I undressed, donned my newly bought pyjamas and began Thomas Mann's *Zauberberg*, which I'd bought at the bookstall. It was not my favorite copy, on thin rice paper in black morocco binding. But it was the *Zauberberg* and I was soon carried away by the majestic sweep of the Mannian sentences. Then I got sleepy. I knew I should think about the frontier, about the possibility of being caught and shot, but ... One might as well have a good last sleep.

'Monsieur should get dressed quickly. War has broken out. The train will not go on. Monsieur has to get out.'

Monsieur looked out of the window and saw subotica.

Hurrah! The Yugoslav frontier station! While I was dressing, the good sleeping car attendant told me that there were two of us in the sleeper, a British diplomat and myself. The Hungarians did not even ask to see our papers. They were busy packing.

I got out. A few seconds later the young British diplomat emerged and I introduced myself. He was a friend of Basil and had heard from him about me. We decided to travel on together. The Yugoslav frontier authorities had instructions about me from W., my friend in their Budapest Legation. They told me the Nazis were bombing Belgrade, no trains were running. We should go to the Subotica military command, they might help. Here a new and pleasant surprise was in store for us. W. had sent word to them too and they gave us a most imposing-looking military safe-conduct, with lots of huge red seals. We persuaded a garage to let us have a car and a driver, a risk for which he demanded quite a tidy sum. We got in and started out for Belgrade. My first exile had begun.

Chapter Nine

As we drove towards Belgrade that Easter Sunday, droves of bombers passed and repassed us overhead; they were running a shuttle service between some Hungarian airport and the capital. When we reached the bridge over the Danube leading to Belgrade we stopped. A raid was going on. There were no fighters in the perfectly blue sky, no anti-aircraft guns, no defence at all. The big bombers hovered like lazy vultures methodically bombing various parts of the city. Afterwards we learned that Belgrade had been declared an open city, a declaration that Hitler disregarded; he meant to have his revenge on the Yugoslavs for turning against him.

When the bombardment was over we drove on through the debris; fires had been started among the ruins, ambulances rushed with screaming sirens through streets crowded with people trying to get out, pushing handcarts piled high with their belongings. In the Bond Street of Belgrade a bomb blast had blown out the jewels from a jeweler's window – diamonds, gold watches – nobody stopped to pick them up.

That afternoon people were offering fortunes not for diamonds but for a car that would run.

At the British Legation a janitor told us that everyone had left at dawn; at the American Embassy we found that the Minister, Mr. Lane, was evacuating the Legation staff in his own car to a place south of Belgrade. That evening he returned for a final journey, leaving last of all, like a good captain, with his wife. He brought along an American journalist, Russell Hill of the *New York Herald Tribune*, who had two places left in his big car, which already contained two British Council officials, a Greek Cabinet Minister and an Englishman who looked like an Oxford don. Driving southward in complete darkness along a road crowded with refugees, livestock, and civilian and military vehicles was no joke. Round about midnight we gave up, parked the car off the road at the bottom of a hill, barricaded ourselves into a stockade of trunks and suitcases, wrapped our heads in scarves against the chill and were soon asleep. In the grey foggy dawn we were awakened by threatening shouts and found ourselves surrounded by a Yugoslavian military patrol. What we did not know was that the hill was the rear of a military fortress. We were lucky not to be shot on sight, for word had gone out that Nazi parachutists were making contact with fifth columnists behind the line. As it was they prodded us up the steep footpath to the fort and lined us up against a wall in the barrack square and ordered us to raise our hands above our heads. One or two soldiers stared at us from a row of windows, and as we stood there with our muffler-bound heads, unshaven and shivery, we felt we must look to them very much like spies who realize that the game is up. A fat little sergeant ordered out what was obviously a firing squad. I started to shout: *'Britanski diplomat! Angielski diplomati! Oshibka, Britanski liudi!'* hoping that my basic Slav would have some effect. A soldier began to hit me with his rifle butt. I continued to shout. The Englishmen looked at me with contempt. Fortunately my shouting awakened an official who appeared at a window, ordered the men to wait, came down and looked at our passports, apologized and let us go.

Some of my British companions retained their poor opinion of me for life. Much later one of them remarked, 'No offence meant, old chap, but you certainly had the wind up badly that day in the fort!'

From then on for three days we travelled only by daylight, along congested roads constantly machine-gunned by the Nazis, making for a little summer resort called Vranika Bania to which the Yugoslavian government had transferred its seat. There, in a street full of diplomatic and General Staff cars I saw in a doorway the tall lean figure of Basil Davidson. It turned out that I had missed him in Belgrade by about an hour.

He outlined the military situation for me. Hitler was attacking from Bulgaria as well as Hungary and might cut off our retreat to Greece, where British divisions were fighting. It was possible that the Italians in Albania might be attacked from Greece and Yugoslavia; the Yugoslavs were planning to make a stand in the mountainous central region of their country. If only they could hold out things might not turn out so badly.

The head of the 'diplomatic party' was Sir George Campbell, the British Ambassador to Yugoslavia. The party was composed of many British, French, Czech, Danish and other diplomats from Belgrade, Sofia and Bucharest. To this party were attached foreigners of my type: political exiles from the countries overrun by the Nazis.

Next day it was decided that the whole party should move down to Sarajevo. Several car convoys were formed. Our convoy of seven cars was led by a military-looking Scotsman. There were few Britishers in it, the rest were Danes, Bulgars, Hungarians, Greeks, Norwegians. I sat in a car with Basil and the Greek Cabinet Minister. Our driver was Flavia Kingscott of the Zagreb British Council. In one of the next cars came Kaya Odeschalchi.

The further south we went, the worse the news became; pro-Nazi generals of the Royal Yugoslavian Army who had been against the *coup d'état* now refused to obey the new High Command. In addition to the German offensives from the north and east the Italians were attacking from the northwest along the shores of the Adriatic. In the mountains we met with heavy snow and huge bomb craters. Our nights were spent in small villages and one morning Basil and I, returning from some errand, found that the entire diplomatic party had moved off. There was nothing to do but continue on foot. We were in the Sandzhak of Novi Basar and would have had to climb two six-thousand-foot mountain ranges before we got to Sarajevo. Fortunately we got a lift on a lorry and soon rejoined our convoy, which had left us behind by mistake.

There was a night we spent on a mountain ridge in a raging snow-storm. Two bottles of whiskey kept the two of us from freezing.

At last we arrived in Sarajevo. We got rooms in the Hotel Europa and indeed almost all Europe *was* represented in the hall, in the lounges, in the bar, restaurant and café of the huge hotel.

A Berlin professor, a tall, very 'Aryan'-looking man and his Baltic baroness wife, greeted me in the café. I had met them first in Prague. The professor had written some strong articles against Hitler, Goebbels and Göring. In 1933 he escaped to Austria, in 1938 to Czechoslovakia, in 1939 to Hungary and now, in 1941, they did not exactly know where to go. The professor had a chance to get a post at Istanbul University. He wanted to know my opinion: Would Turkey be safe for the duration? I did not know. I suggested South America as a safer bet.

The café teemed with unbelievable life stories. Anti-Semitic Poles, Jewish refugees, Czech industrialists, Romanian actors, White Russians from Belgrade, sat side by side with variety artists of fifteen nations, Belgian, Dutch and French businessmen, German deserters posing as Austrian patriots, Gestapo agents, dignitaries of the Serbian Orthodox church. Outside, Bosnian Moslems and Armenian and Jewish hawkers did a brisk business. Rucksacks were the article of the day: people exchanged pigskin suitcases for them, sold their dinner jackets to buy plus fours, swapped evening gowns for skiing outfits. Sad, middle-aged Jews wore *lederhosen*, elderly Czech housewives went about in outsize skiing trousers; old-fashioned Oriental belts were bought to hold gold sovereigns and louis d'or acquired at an exorbitant price.

In the bar I made friends with a young Yugoslav infantry officer who spoke good English. We drank a lot of *rakija*. When the young captain heard that I was a writer, he came out with a story. Most stories produced for the benefit of writers are generally very bad. This was good.

It appeared that the captain's regiment was in the rear guard of the retreat on the Bulgarian front. His company was the rear guard of the battalion. They were the last Yugoslav units, with the Germans hot on their heels.

Most of the villages were deserted. Approaching another village they saw people sitting on the branches of some trees. They were old peasant men and women, with white hair and brown parchmentlike faces. They were sitting in riding position on the branches, one person to a tree, and each held an enormous shotgun, dating at least from the beginning of the nineteenth century. On the first tree a toothless old grandmother perched resolutely.

'What do you think you are doing, Granny?' the captain asked her.

'The young ones left, we are waiting for the enemy.'

'Come down, all of you. This is war. They will hang you, if they find you there. For God's sake, Granny, climb down.'

The old lady cackled with laughter:

'Of course they'll hang us, sonny,' she said. 'They are the enemy. But first we'll shoot a lot of them, because we are their enemy.'

He argued, implored, begged, threatened for some ten minutes, without success. The old ones stayed on the treetops and waited for the enemy.

'You see,' the captain said, 'the Serbian people ... The generals might give up. They never will.'

That evening during a raid I had my first hot bath for a week and later slept through two more raids.

In the morning Kaya Odeschalchi and I met in the café and had a long talk. Kaya was very realistic. I was glad that she had escaped from Hungary. With her political flair, knowledge of Hungary and the West, and her excellent command of languages, she would be a first-class ally. That evening our party sent out cars to reconnoitre possible escape routes to the coast. Kaya went with someone to Dubrovnik on the Dalmatian coast. Basil, Flavia Kingscott and I went over the mountains to Mostar to see whether our party could cross over to Croatia. We drove over a snowy mountain ridge at about ten o'clock at night and saw to our surprise that the town below was not blacked out. The well-lit streets were deserted when we entered the town. Suddenly we saw four men running towards us. Basil got out and stood in front of the car while he snatched the Union Jack off the windshield and stuffed it into his pocket. When the four men reached us, he inquired the way to Sarajevo in German. They told him. He got in and said quietly to Flavia: 'Turn around and drive like hell.'

Mostar was in the hands of pro-Nazi Croats. I had a disagreeable itching in my neck till we were out of their rifle range.

Next evening I had a horrible shock: Italian planes had bombed Dubrovnik and Kaya Odeschalchi was killed. I went out and moved blindly about in the crowded streets till late at night. I remembered her speaking at political meetings; standing by her car when I saw her off in Budapest; waving her hand as she left for Dubrovnik. At home in Hungary she had left a fourteen-year-old son. Somewhere in London the Karolyi's would mourn her. Would there be a grave in the Dubrovnik cemetery: 'Princess Odeschalchi, née Countess Kaya Andrassy, 1907–1941'?

I was still dazed by shock and grief when we learned that the Yugoslav army had surrendered. Now there was not much chance for us. We drove on, greeted everywhere with conflicting information: 'The Germans will be here in ten hours.' 'The Italians will occupy the village in six hours.'

Next evening we drove up to Cetinje, the capital of Montenegro. The good Montenegrins welcomed us with sumptuous meals and champagne and assured us that if we were cut off from the coast they would hide us in the mountains. 'How long can this damned war last? Five years, ten? It doesn't matter. There will be food, there will be wine. Our mountains are safe.'

In the morning Flavia Kingscott drove us down the twenty-five hairpin bends of the seven-thousand-foot Lovcen to the Dalmatian coast. After winter and snow, we were in the Mediterranean spring. In Herzegovina the situation was pretty grim. There was some talk of a steamer or a British submarine picking us up, but neither was there.

In one of the restaurants we met a wounded RAF officer with his arm in a plaster cast. He offered to smuggle out our messages and deliver them after the war. The snag was that all the shops were closed and none of us had paper. At last Hugh Seton-Watson turned up and gave us some of the w.c. paper he always carried in the Balkans and I borrowed some to write my farewell message on. The nearness of death doesn't improve one's style; it tends to become flamboyant. Feeling the hangman very close, one is no longer afraid of clichés.

We all gave our messages to the RAF officer. Then I walked up and down on the seashore with Basil, talking. The sea was calm. A gentle April wind brought mountain smells. I was in a theatrical mood. I could not believe that everything would soon be over. I pretended to be a man who has realized that his life is over and takes it calmly. But underneath I was optimistic.

The roar of airplane engines disturbed the quiet of the afternoon. Two huge Sunderland flying boats landed on the sea at the entrance to the gulf. Instead of the submarines, the British headquarters in Athens had sent these flying boats. Everyone gathered on the shore. In the midst of a group of diplomats stood Sir George Campbell. It was up to him to decide who should go on board. I looked on with interest, glad that most of the British diplomats would be able to leave and hoping that we others would somehow be able to escape too. Basil left me and spoke to Sir George. In a minute he was back.

'George, hurry. There's a boat. It will take you to the flying boat. Contact X. in our Athens legation.'

'And you?'

'We are not coming. Don't you worry, we shall be all right. Good-by!'

The two flying boats carried some ninety people. There were two British on board, both badly wounded. The rest of them, all the diplomats, stayed behind. We were to be first, an assortment of unimportant foreigners from various corners of Europe. As I was rowed out with an excited Czech and two Danes, I looked at the British diplomats and journalists on the shore, deeply moved. As long as I live, I shall never forget that scene, those minutes. In a world which was going down into an abyss of inhuman brutalities and vile outrages, there were these people, who thought of others first. They risked being caught by the Nazis, being interned for the duration, but they were intent on saving others whom they thought to be in greater danger.

On board young RAF boys greeted us with smiling faces. One of them offered me a Players cigarette. I lit it, inhaled deeply – that wonderful smoke is still in my nostrils – and said, 'Good-by, Hitler!'

(Sir George Campbell, and the whole party, my friends Basil Davidson and Hugh Seton-Watson included, were caught next day by the Italians. They were taken through Albania to Italy and after two months of internment were allowed to return to England.)

While we were flying towards Greece, I was thinking of Athens. I should try to get a room in the Hotel St. George, have a steaming hot bath and then go to a restaurant, drink a lot of *ouzo*, live like a civilized man.

Like a civilized man … I had left my sumptuous 'first-class' suit-cases somewhere in the Sandzhak of Novi Basar. I wore slightly burned trousers, suède shoes which were not improved by a lot of marching in the snow, an overcoat; and in my breast pocket I had a toothbrush and some dollar bills.

We landed in brilliant sunshine on the nineteenth of April in the harbor of the Piraeus, where a lorry was waiting to take us to the British Legation in Athens. On the fifth of April I had seen the German army moving through Budapest. Now, on the road from the Piraeus to Athens, there were British tanks under the olive trees. Pink-faced young British officers walked about, with their funny canes under their arms. Tommies wearing shorts were loading vehicles. Would they understand my mood? My childish pleasure at seeing them? The euphoria which made it hard for me not to grin all the time, a grin of stupid satisfaction?

At the British Legation we were told that Athens was being evacu-ated. I went out, bought some shirts, shaving kit and toilet articles, and cast a wistful glance in the direction of the St. George Hotel. That bath would have to be put off till Port Said.

In half an hour we were again on our way to the Piraeus. The harbour was in a turmoil. After the collapse of Yugoslavia the Nazis were attacking all along the Bulgarian-Greek and Yugoslav-Greek fron-tier. The British – heavily outnumbered – were evacuating Greece. In a fortnight I had to witness the collapse of two countries.

The escapees from Yugoslavia were put on board the Polish passenger steamer *Warszawa*, a ship built for Mediterranean cruises, which normally carried three hundred passengers. Now there were nine hundred. Our party occupied a bit of the upper deck, and here we slept, ate and lived for the next five days. There were Polish, Greek, French, Yugoslav, Czech, Austrian, Danish families on board. A tall, gaunt elderly gentleman turned out to be Lord Dunsany, the Irish writer. Our neighbours on the deck were Alexander Sedgwick of the *New York Times* and his Greek wife. In our party were several young British intellectuals – a type I was to meet a lot during the war – with an amazing knowledge of Central and Eastern Europe. It was hard to decide whether they were young college dons on vacation or officers in mufti. They were all discreet and seemed to know about me without asking any questions.

The *Warszawa* left the Piraeus in the evening. It was wonderful to sleep under the dark blue Mediterranean sky, knowing that we were headed towards safety. It was only next morning as we queued up for our morning wash, our cups of good strong English tea and sandwiches, that I discovered that we were in a large convoy; lean destroyers circled about us like vigilant shepherds' dogs round their flock. In the warm sunshine, the blue Mediterranean made war seem far away.

Then the Stukas came. The cruisers and destroyers opened up against them, pom-poms went off, two ships received hits, a Stuka went down in flames and the dive-bomber raid was over.

They returned at night in force. It was a devilishly beautiful spectacle. Searchlights lit up the sky, white-green and bluish flares took turns in attacking the soft and dangerous darkness. Red, blue, yellow and green tracer bullets chased towards the planes. Soon two ships were aflame, casting their red glow all over the sea. A ship went down, the Nazis flew low to machine-gun the survivors and two Stukas were shot down. Then the raid was over.

I felt too elated to get really frightened. For the first time in my life I was in the midst of a real fight between the Nazis and my side. After my long spell in our ineffective Hungarian 'Western camp' now I really was in the Western camp.

The night was again peaceful under the Mediterranean sky. I shall probably join the army, I thought, now that broadcasting from Greece is impossible. Life will be simple; I shall do my duty. My French friend who wrote to me in Rome went into the war as into a monastery. For me it seemed a grim adventure which I wouldn't like to miss.

Apart from a few more dive-bombing attacks, the second part of our journey was like a peacetime summer cruise, if one forgot about the faithful destroyers circling ceaselessly around. The girls put on summer dresses; at night there was singing. On the fifth day we saw the coast of Africa.

In the Port Said customs shed sirens screamed, German bombers flew overhead, ack-ack guns barked, and most of the bombs fell into the sea. The fat Egyptian customs official informed us proudly, 'This is the first really big raid on Port Said.'

'How nice we didn't miss it,' said someone next to me.

I had my hot bath at last, and in the evening I took an express train to Cairo.

Chapter Ten

IT TOOK ME nearly a year to get a clear picture of that organization which I joined when I told Basil Davidson that I was prepared to volunteer for anything against the Nazis.

It was a most singular organization, called Special Operations Executive, S.O.E.

The British public and the world at large learned about this organization only after the war. Many of its former officers published their war memoirs. People like Fitzroy Maclean, C. M. Woodhouse, Julian Amery, George Millar, Francis Noel-Baker, Hugh Seton-Watson, Basil Davidson, Christopher Sykes, and many others wrote about their wartime exploits. There were so many books by former S.O.E. people that in 1955 an anthology of their writing was published under the title *Special Operations*. There is even a club in London, near Knightsbridge, the Special Forces Club, whose members served in S.O.E. during the war.

S.O.E. was a wartime improvisation. The Second World War differed in two important aspects from most former wars. *It was total war and it was ideological war.* The fight between the Allies and the Axis powers was not a bit more fierce and determined than the fight between the pro-Nazis and the anti-Nazis in the countries overrun by the Axis armies. Patriots were fighting against the puppet, or collaborationist, governments of their own countries. In the Allied armies many thousands of people fought who were by birth 'enemy aliens'. A French *maquisard*, a Yugoslav or Norwegian partisan was an ally the British or French could trust absolutely.

The editor of the *Special Operations* anthology, Patrick Howarth, with whom I shared an office for a while in Cairo, gave it the following description in his introduction:

> The task of S.O.E. was to fight the enemy away from the acknowledged battlefields. Simultaneously it waged economic warfare with the war of the spirit, and its strategy was continuously offensive, rather than defensive. The modern invention which it took particular advantage of was the parachute, and in time the parachute became S.O.E.'s unofficial symbol. S.O.E. had to exploit both the ruthlessness and the weaknesses of enemy occupation, and as the grip of the enemy occupying powers was loosened, much of the organisation's activity took the form of direct support of open guerilla warfare.

S.O.E. was, in the 'most political of all wars', an irregular organ of the entire government engaged in total war. Its officers were irregular diplomats, secret propagandists, professors of sabotage and most effective politicians. It was S.O.E.'s task to get the governments or some ruling groups in the Axis orbit to change over to the Allied side. The unconditional surrender of Italy, the change over in Madagascar from Vichy France to Fighting France, the never-exploited Hungarian unconditional surrender in 1943 and other similar events were prepared, negotiated and implemented by S.O.E.

The officers I met in Cairo were the same type as the young British intellectuals I met on board ship.

It is curious that the intellectual, the 'egghead', is held to be in peacetime an ineffective, slightly ridiculous and somewhat boring individual. But those young British officers who were parachuted into France, Norway, Yugoslavia, Greece, Burma, who served as liaison officers to partisans of two dozen countries, were typical eggheads. They lived in jungles and snow-clad mountain ranges, in God-forsaken huts. They fought with knives and bombs; they operated short-wave wireless sets, taught Indonesian guerrillas the art of blowing up bridges and railway lines; they negotiated political truces between quarreling anti-Nazi groups in the Balkans. They were exceedingly brave and steadfast, and preserved their sense of humor in the deadliest of circumstances. They risked their lives behind enemy lines and in peaceful countries alike. One day I had a delightful after-dinner talk with an erudite essayist in Baghdad. Some months later he was shot by an Arab in the Grand Hotel Firdouzi in Tehran. He was S.O.E. field commander in Iraq.

The former S.O.E. officers whom I knew are now university professors, wardens of colleges, well-known novelists, Members of Parliament, directors of scientific institutions, stage designers, actors, excellent surgeons. But they all wore the parachute sign on their breasts, showing that they had been dropped behind the enemy lines.

I liked these egghead parachutists. No man in danger can have had better comrades-in-arms.

I would like to describe the impressions of a foreign member of S.O.E. I would like to write the story of my hectic war years. It would make a fair-sized book. Condensed, it would read like a mixture of a thriller and a travelogue. Of the five war years I spent one in Cairo and two in Istanbul, the rest was taken up with travels in a gigantic triangle between Tehran, Cape Town and Casablanca. I flew across Africa, in south-north and east-west direction, spent days or weeks in many African and Asian countries, visited wartime Britain and the fortress of Malta, worked for a short while in Italy.

In 1941 and for a few months in 1942 I operated from the Middle East a one-man radio station making anti-Nazi propaganda in Hungarian. I broadcast forty-minute programmes every night. These broadcasting activities infected me with the pathological obsession of political exiles and propagandists.

There are various kinds of *Dementia Emigrantis*. Comparatively simple and unambitious people, when they lead the life of a political exile, become insanely ambitious. I knew in Istanbul two Romanians, a former village teacher and a clerk in the Constanza customs. They shared a room. Once they had a fist fight. It turned out that the clerk wanted to become Prime Minister of Romania after the war and allotted the secondary role of Foreign Secretary to the village teacher. The latter wanted it the other way round. So they fought, parted company and never spoke to each other again.

Of course this mental delusion is not as strong and ridiculous in more intelligent people. But even otherwise prudent and worldlywise persons are often misled by the awakened monster of political ambition.

They feel that after their exile when the long-craved-for change of regime will take place, anything will be possible. The complicated reality of their country becomes simplified by distance, and they quite sincerely think they should get leading positions when the day comes.

Artists, scientists, writers rarely fall into this category of *dementia emigrantis*. There are other dangers in store for them. If they engage for a long period in emigrant propaganda, they are apt to develop strange obsessions. They are now in the position of speaking in the name of silenced public opinion at home. They are the 'voice of the people'. They write and speak in the name of 'our people' or probably 'my people'. As they write or speak into the microphone, they are apt to work themselves up into frenzies of brave patriotism. Full of enthusiasm, they feel that they are the wise and brave leaders of their people.

Although I had a long habit of catching myself in theatrical moods, of having a little ironical eyewitness on the upper shelves of my brain, the nightly broadcasts had an effect on me too. There I sat alone in the studio, high above Haifa, speaking into a microphone. I was reading my own text. Fiery, persuasive, fervent sentences. As the talk progressed, I had the feeling that here we were face to face, the Hungarian people and myself. I imagined that most of Hungary was listening now and was being infected with *my* enthusiasm, convinced by *my* convictions, fired by *my* emotions.

A good broadcaster resembles the good actor who does not play his role but *becomes* his role. My propaganda certainly convinced me a hundred per cent. I felt that I was the mouthpiece of 'my people', a true representative of our cause for which I had risked so much.

This mental and emotional state certainly made my broadcasts effective – insofar as they were listened to in Hungary – but did not help in my development. I was speaking against the regime which had ruled Hungary for more than twenty years, against the regime of kicked estate servants, 'used' peasant girls, against the National Park of Feudalism which so readily turned into a fascist country. I spoke against the criminal accomplices of Hitler. The emigrant malady of seeing everything in black or white got hold of me. In becoming a freedom fighter of the radio waves, I lost the most important aspect of freedom in my mentality: tolerance.

And then – when I was in such a mood – came the news of Hitler's attack against the Soviet Union.

The outbreak of the German-Soviet war made almost everybody more optimistic. While some British officers and commentators thought that the Soviet Union would not hold out more than six weeks or three months, the majority had faith in the enormous territory of the Soviet empire, two hundred million strong. More and more people became pro-Soviet. The young exiles from Europe, myself included, revised many of their former judgments. How wise it was – we thought – that Russia occupied a part of Poland. Hitler would have crushed Poland anyway, but this way at least the Soviet Union had better defences. We now approved of the Hitler-Stalin pact. Stalin bought time through this pact to prepare for the inevitable attack. How clever it was of the Soviet armies not to show their full strength and technical superiority in the Finnish campaign. Had they used their most modern weapons, they would have betrayed them to Hitler.

When Hitler announced that he would take Leningrad in a few days, I declared in my broadcast to 'the Hungarian people' that 'Leningrad will never fall. Not in a few days, not in a few months, not in a few years.' Later I kept repeating: 'This is the one hundred and forty-seventh day since Hitler declared that he would take Leningrad in a few days.'

My interest in Marxism was revived. In the secondhand bookshops of Haifa I bought scores of volumes of Marxist literature and read and reread them avidly. Now I did not mind their rigid style, the black and white world they presented. After years of suicidal muddle, they seemed to me simple and manly. In a thoroughly ill world only daring surgical operations can help. The new grand alliance made me hopeful. A lot of well-founded suspicions the Soviet people had about the West would disappear after this war. Years of comradeship-in-arms would dispel mutual suspicions. The United States would soon come into the war too, Hitler would be beaten and the globe would be a better place to live on.

There was again something to believe in.

In March, 1942, I gave over my broadcasting station to a colleague and started to do S.O.E. work proper. In September I was in Kampala,

Uganda, during a flight between Cape Town and Cairo, when a young RAF officer greeted me with triumphant smiles at the hotel bar. He opened his wallet and took out some brown w.c. paper. He was the wounded RAF man who had volunteered to smuggle out my famous last words to my family from Yugoslavia. I had last seen him in April, 1941, on the seashore in Herzegovina, with his arm in a sling, smiling shyly, because he too was convinced that I would soon be executed. Now he was on leave from Nairobi. We talked into the early hours of the morning. Without going to bed, I went straight to the flying boat. On the way to Khartoum I several times reread my 'last message', with a lot of clichés about remaining faithful to the Hungarian people to the last drop of my blood, and so forth.

After half a year of knocking about, I was transferred to Istanbul in the spring of 1943. It was obvious that the Alamein and Stalingrad victories had convinced many leading personalities of the Horthy regime, including some members of Premier Kallay's government, that the Axis defeat was not only possible but most probable. They began to show an inclination to 'jump out' – this was their expression – from the Axis cart. It was the task of S.O.E. to channel these inclinations into an unconditional surrender to the Allied powers.

Before leaving Cairo for Istanbul my *pouvoir* was defined in detail.

'You know, of course' – I was told – 'that British officials cannot talk directly to enemy representatives. They can get in touch with the enemy only in case the enemy offers unconditional surrender. Our task is to bring negotiations to that stage. Until that stage is reached you, as a free Hungarian who has contact with us, can get our advice. But nothing you say or do can mean any commitment on our part.'

My experience as a diplomatic correspondent and the two years spent in S.O.E. fortunately helped me to take a realistic view of my 'mission'. If a diplomat is a sort of glorified postman, my mission was to prepare the ground for such postmen. In this preparatory work I could only write memos to S.O.E., Cairo. If they agreed, they might pass on some of the suggestions to S.O.E., London, and maybe one or two might even get to the British Foreign Office and with luck, some policy-making official of the Foreign Office might see them. My function – if successful – would perhaps equal that of an inch of an international telephone line; yet whatever turn events took I would be criticized most severely after the war.

And then work started. The first of the Budapest gentlemen I had to deal with was a certain Dr. S., a personal representative of Count Stephen Bethlen, the former Premier and then chief adviser of Regent Horthy. Dr. S. tried to hand a long memorandum to a British diplomat through the help of a neutral diplomat, a friend of Count Bethlen. Although this neutral diplomat vouched for the authenticity of the 'offer', at first I gravely doubted the authenticity of the document. The offer purporting to come from Count Bethlen stated: 'If the British Government would guarantee:

'1. That no Hungarian territory would be bombarded during the war;

'2. No Australian, New Zealand, American coloured, Czechoslovak or Yugoslav troops would take part in Hungary's occupation after the war; and

'3. that Soviet troops would stop everywhere two hundred kilometers east and north from the Hungarian frontiers,

'then Count Stephen Bethlen would undertake to get an official guarantee from the Regent and the Government that Hungarian troops would not fight against British or American troops.'

When through the neutral diplomat in question we ascertained that this document truly came from Count Bethlen, we were flabbergasted. How could we expect any realistic steps from the Budapest government if one of the elder statesmen, the chief advisor of Regent Horthy, made such an offer?

Major M. of the Istanbul S.O.E. office was at my flat when Dr. S. called. I handed him back the document, tried to explain to him the political situation and the state of mind of the Allies. I implored him to return to Budapest and come back with a realistic offer. Dr. S. was very indignant. He clearly showed by his behavior that he regarded me as an enemy of the regime, and turning to Major M., he insisted that the full text of the offer should be cabled at once to the British Foreign Office. Major M. promised to send it on by the next diplomatic bag. Some three weeks later we received a cable through S.O.E. London from the Foreign Office. It read:

'We take a very poor view of such childish attempts.'

When Major M. read out this message in my presence to Dr. S., he was most indignant and left without a word. The very same offer was handed some months later to a British diplomat at the Vatican ...

This incident had an unfortunate effect on developments. Count Bethlen's entourage, and presumably some people working with Prime Minister Kallay, persuaded themselves that I was the villain of the piece. They seemed to be convinced that if only they could elimi-nate me, the 'British' might change their minds about Tito, the 'Amer-icans' about the agreements reached with Stalin on the Tehran Conference, and so forth. Ludicrous as it may seem, some Budapest officials firmly believed that my hostility to the regime was to be blamed for the fact that 'the British' in Istanbul insisted on uncondi-tional surrender to the Allies, and in the term 'Allies' they included the Soviet Union too ...

There were two or three similar attempts in Istanbul, but by then the Kallay group convinced themselves that the 'Istanbul channel' was hopeless because of my nefarious activities. They sent their contact men to other neutral countries with similar offers. They thought that by clever manoeuvering they could play off the Allies against each other. At times they wanted exclusive American, at times exclusive British contacts. They were firmly convinced that the Western Allies would be willing to negotiate with them behind the backs of the Russians. Lastly, they were convinced that unconditional surrender was just a propaganda slogan and that they could discuss postwar frontier corrections as a reward for any step they were prepared to take.

Our task was now to inform the young and very able men in Premier Kallay's entourage of the real situation. Our difficulty was that these advisors always believed some important secret information, some detail which 'leaked out' was reported to them. They believed everything they wanted to believe instead of seeing the simple and plain truth: Hitler was going to lose the war and if they didn't do some-thing instantly, they would lead Hungary into a catastrophic situation.

Personal intrigues and rivalries also played their part. It was not only a question of establishing contact with the Allies (preferably and understandably the *Western* Allies), but each group, sub-group and personality would have preferred to establish the contact for himself through his trusted agents. Every envoy emissary and agent coloured his report according to his own bias and policy and the bias and policy of his immediate chief. For several months we strove to convince the Kallay group how unnecessary it was to try scores of different channels. It was a question of their offer. The Allies wanted deeds and not words. And if they were offered deeds, they would enter into official high-level contact.

As the months passed and the Axis suffered defeat after defeat, our efforts in political enlightenment seemed to get some results. The emissaries by now used a more realistic language. Many of them still had some 'unimportant' conditions, say that the Allies should guarantee the present Hungarian frontiers, or that they should stop helping Tito, but some of the Budapest Foreign Office people seemed at last to know the real situation.

One of them, V., a young secretary of the Budapest Foreign Office, had lunch at my flat at the beginning of August, 1943. We were drinking black coffee when he sighed and said:

'Blast this situation. We shall not even be able to offer unconditional surrender before some Allied armies reach our frontiers.'

'Of course you could,' I said. 'There is such a thing as conspiratorial unconditional surrender.'

V. got excited. 'Are you serious? This would be wonderful!'

He was convinced that Premier Kallay would agree to the surrender. He couldn't bring himself to believe, though, that the Allies would accept it before reaching the frontiers of Hungary.

I reported the conversation. It seemed that our S.O.E. work in connection with Hungary was nearly finished. The negotiations could be carried on in the future on a diplomatic level. It was arranged that Mr. Sterndale-Bennett, Councilor of the British Embassy, should see V. and state officially that there was such a thing as secret unconditional surrender. We hoped that after this the Kallay group would see that the 'Istanbul channel' was a serious one.

V.'s doubts seemed to be dispelled and he returned in high spirits to Budapest. In the second part of August he was back again, bringing *the unconditional surrender of the Hungarian government.*

The Hungarian Minister at Lisbon made the same declaration to officials of the British Embassy there, and soon the written and properly signed declaration arrived by courier.

On the ninth of September, 1943, Sir Hugh Knatchbull-Hugeson, the British Ambassador to Turkey, came from Ankara to Istanbul. He boarded his yacht and sailed out to the Sea of Marmara. A motor launch took the Hungarian representative to the yacht after nightfall.

Sir Hugh Knatchbull-Hugeson told V. that the British government had at once informed the Allies of Great Britain about the Hungarian offer and that the Allies empowered him to make a declaration of acceptance in their name. The declaration was a *note verbale*, that is, Sir Hugh read it out to V., who took it down from the Ambassador's dictation.

According to this declaration the Hungarian surrender was to be kept secret till the time of its realization arrived. The Hungarian government had to announce and implement the surrender when the Allies instructed them to do so. Till that time the Hungarian government had to remain in constant touch with the Allies through Istanbul and the British Foreign Office. The Allies expected the Hungarian government gradually to reduce Hungary's military co-operation with Germany and to withdraw Hungarian troops from the Soviet Union. The Hungarian high command and general staff were to be reorganized in such a way that the government could use it to implement the surrender at a suitable moment. And lastly, the Hungarian government must not enter into negotiations elsewhere.

After reading out the declaration Sir Hugh told V. that the technicalities of the contact and the details of preparation for the fulfillment of the surrender would be discussed by our office.

An hour before the meeting took place the wireless stations of the world announced the *unconditional surrender of Italy*. In our S.O.E. work only top people knew about the major operations, otherwise everyone knew only as much as was absolutely necessary for his work. Till February, 1943, I only knew about a segment of the special operations dealing with Hungary. After February I had an over-all picture of our Hungarian work, and naturally nothing else. But from this work I knew very well that by the time a surrender is announced, detailed preparations must have been made to exploit all political and military possibilities of the surrender. I was convinced that northern Italian partisans working with S.O.E. liaison officers were at that very moment occupying various airports and ports and that they would try to hold them for twenty-four to seventy-two hours till British naval units, airborne and glider-borne troops took over. I knew there were only two German divisions in Italy and was hoping that with partisan attacks and parachute operations the Brenner Pass into Italy and the Franco-Italian frontier would be sealed off and the Allies would be the masters of the Italian peninsula within a week. If all this happened, the Allies could soon advance from the Trieste-Fiume region into Croatia and Hungary. And if the Bulgarian and Romanian sections of the S.O.E. worked as well as the Italian and Hungarian sections, the talks with the Bucharest and Sofia governments must be also developing satisfactorily. So this double surrender might cause a major landslide. Hungary and the Balkans might be liberated within half a year. More than fifty Hitlerite divisions might be cut off and encircled in Greece, Yugoslavia, Bulgaria, Romania and Hungary. The war might end much sooner than we thought.

That night walking up and down excitedly on my balcony overlooking the Bosporus, I understood what Churchill meant when he called Italy 'the soft underbelly of Europe'.

Then the days passed and nothing happened in Italy. I learned much later that my guess was correct. The Italian partisans occupied some airports and ports in the North, airborne and glider-borne troops were ready to go into action, naval units stood by – but the entire operation was called off. The Italian partisans held some of the strategic points for many days. Then the Gestapo arrived and liquidated them. Who called the operation off, I don't know. But I do not think that it was Winston Churchill.

I may of course be mistaken, but I am firmly convinced that with Churchill's strategy the war could have been shortened by anything between six and twelve months, and the very costly Italian campaign would not have taken place. It is a fact that on the day of the Italian surrender there were only two German divisions south of the Brenner

Pass and that Hitler sent down the bulk of the divisions which fought later in Italy only after the middle of September.

The implementation of the Hungarian surrender, which seemed to be a comparatively simple task on the ninth of September, turned into an almost impossible proposition by the twenty-ninth. The Hungarian government naturally attached a great deal of importance to the Italian surrender. At first they were optimistic and very glad that they had taken the grave step of *unconditional* surrender. But when it turned out that the Allies would not soon reach the Hungarian frontiers, they got worried and started to stall.

Our work was to maintain daily contact with Budapest and this was secured by short-wave wireless with our Istanbul office. The code we used was quite safe in those pre-electronic computer days. The transmissions were short and their time was constantly changed. We transmitted the wireless messages to London. The British Foreign Office kept Washington and Moscow informed.

We knew that the unconditional surrender was agreed to by Prime Minister Kallay's 'inner' cabinet. Those in the know were Jeno Ghiczy, Foreign Secretary; Ferenc Keresztes-Fischer, Home Secretary; and some five or six people in the Foreign Office. Regent Horthy was not informed, nor was the Minister of War or the Chief of Staff. Horthy – although well-meaning – was too easily influenced and too much of an old man of frequently changing moods. As a matter of fact, the Kallay government had not much power over the state and even less over the army.

In the middle of March, 1944, we received reports about German troop concentrations in Austria, near the Hungarian frontier. We warned the Kallay group and suggested the obvious countermeasures. Regent Horthy was at the time visiting Hitler's headquarters. On the nineteenth of March the German army moved in and occupied Hungary.

When the Kallay cabinet reported to us that the German army was moving in, there was no time to get instructions from the British Foreign Office. We in Istanbul took the responsibility on ourselves to suggest that Regent Horthy and Premier Kallay should broadcast appeals to the Hungarian people, denouncing the Hitlerite aggression and then escape by plane to Allied territory. This certainly would have had an adverse effect on Hitler's plans. A large part of the army was loyal to Horthy. Had he ordered the army to turn against Hitler, the Nazis would have been forced to occupy Hungary as an enemy country and the Hungarian army would not have been forced to fight on the side of Hitler till the very end.

There was no possibility – it seems – of persuading Horthy to such a step. But Kallay and his inner cabinet could have made such broadcasts and could have escaped – if they had made the necessary preparation. Instead the Prime Minister simply went by taxi to the Turkish Legation in Budapest and took refuge there. Of the whole group only V., the young Foreign Office secretary, escaped to Yugoslavia and thence to Italy.

The pro-Nazi General Sztojay became Prime Minister. A few units of the Hungarian army put up some resistance, thousands of anti-Nazis were arrested, three hundred thousand Jews were taken to the Nazi annihilation camps, and further Hungarian divisions were sent to the east, and the out-and-out nazification of the country began.

When we received the full story of the occupation, we understood the pathetic impossibility of the Hungarian unconditional surrender. The army was in the hands of the pro-Nazi generals; the Regent had such political advisors as Count Bethlen. The Kallay group without experience in conspiratorial methods was unable to build up an effective anti-Nazi force in Hungary. They seemed to have the feeling that by signing the first unconditional surrender in the war, they had done their duty and now it was up to the Allies to get to the Hungarian frontier. In all fairness it must be admitted that in such a case the Kallay group would probably have succeeded in implementing the surrender.

After the German occupation of Hungary we made renewed attempts to establish contact with possible focal points of resistance in Hungary, but these led us nowhere. On the fifteenth of October the Arrow Cross leader, Major Szalasi, an insane caricature of Hitler, took over. Regent Horthy now made precisely the broadcast protest and appeal which we had suggested in March. He was promptly arrested by the Gestapo. Szalasi's thugs then set upon the Jews. Throngs of Jewish children between the ages of four and twelve were driven through Budapest to the Danube embankment and machine-gunned into the river.

During the 1943–1944 period mainly spent in Istanbul, I had to make frequent visits to our Cairo headquarters; had to visit Italy in the summer of 1944; go down to Smyrna to help in the escape from Athens of a Hungarian diplomat whom the Gestapo wanted to arrest, and do other such jobs in addition to the day-to-day work of our Hungarian section.

In my free time I wrote my first book in English, *In Darkest Hungary*, which was published with Michael Karolyi's preface in November, 1944, by Victor Gollancz. It was during this period that for eight months I studied Russian at least an hour a day. My political convictions, the events of the war and the pathetic incompetence of the Horthy-Bethlen-Kallay set had converted me into an enthusiastic advocate of the Tehran and Yalta agreements. I looked forward to a postwar world which the Anglo-American-Russian alliance would make prosperous and progressive. The National Park of Feudalism would be turned into a modern democratic state and the serfs would be liberated.

Chapter Eleven

IN DECEMBER the Istanbul S.O.E. office was closed down. I went to Cairo and then in January, 1945, to London. On the fifth of January I was in the peace and sunshine of Morocco. Next morning our plane left Rabat for London. That day fourteen V-2's fell on the London area. All the deep underground stations were still air-raid shelters. The spectacle of families sleeping on the crowded underground platforms, the ruins all over London, the front-line life of the great city, made a very strong impression on me. I was strangely moved and felt a curious sort of gratitude to these people for becoming more human in a most inhuman world. For compared to prewar Britain, people were kinder, friendlier; they did not try to hide the fine fervour of feeling which drove them on to fight and to work amidst most adverse circumstances.

The challenge of the blitz, the challenge of war existence brought out the best in people. In wartime London one had to be true to oneself. But what to do if there were two or three selves? I had some difficult and anxious nights, going home through the blackout to the small Kensington hotel where I stayed. The war was drawing towards its end. Millions would escape the constant risk of death. The survivors in the concentration camps and annihilation centres would get a chance to live. Peace would come, the long-awaited peace of our dreams. And I was afraid of this peace. I read a poem in some French newspaper or periodical. The first line went something like this: *The bony fingers of victory are tapping icily on the windowpane.* I did not know what fears and foreboding haunted that French poet. I only knew my own anxiety.

I would have to choose. While the war lasted, life was simple. One did one's duty, one was driven on by conviction, enthusiasm, determination. The infamy must be erased; the evil must be defeated. One ceased to be a private person. There were private hours, sometimes even private weeks, but all this was incidental. One was not responsible for one's destiny. There was no choice.

But for me the war had already ended. Here I was in London, presumably to arrange my return to Hungary. And I did not feel like returning. I had fallen in love with London again. I had spoken and read English since I was sixteen. I had spent five years of the war among Britishers. I wrote and thought in English; during those decisive and fateful years, I *lived* in and through the English language. All my friends in the Middle East spoke of going *home* when they spoke of London. And I caught myself several times thinking about going *home* to London. Could it be, must it be, that I should leave all this? That I should get used to not thinking in English? That I should become a foreigner?

Yet next morning when I met friends and acquaintances and they asked me what I was planning to do now in London, I heard myself saying:

'I am hoping to arrange my return to Hungary.'

I said what was expected of me. I said what I expected of myself. A hypocrite says what he is supposed to say and does what he wants to do. I was a sort of counter-hypocrite: I said and did what I was supposed to say and do. Why was I an anti-fascist for so many years? Why did I fight in this war, why did I take the side of the Hungarian people, if I did not want to return now? How could I preserve any self-respect if I suddenly followed my inclinations and decided to forget Hungary? Could I simply say, 'I don't want to be a Hungarian any more?'

Would they believe me if I told them that I was not inspired by the immediate future in Hungary? I hated the fascists, but I did not wish to witness anti-fascist man hunts. My heart had ached since I was fifteen for the Hungarian peasants. But I did not look forward to seeing the feudal serfs turned into kolkhoz robots. I wanted a change of regime, but I did not want to be in the mad scramble for positions which is sure to follow any abrupt change of regime. I had thought of myself as a revolutionary for a great many years. But I did not enjoy the thought of a revolution imposed from above, by foreign bayonets.

Would they believe me? But did it matter what they believed, what people thought? Did I believe all this myself? Wasn't all this just a rationalization, a plausible political smoke screen to hide my desperate longing to remain in England?

During the daytime I was rushing about in London, lecturing, seeing people, having long talks with old Michael Karolyi, taking part in Hungarian political exile debates, meeting many British friends – but at nights, the anxiety was there. At times I felt that I was lying, betraying myself, whatever I did. I betrayed myself if I stayed, and I betrayed myself if I returned to Hungary. The war really produced a sort of split in my personality: a Hungarian self, now very much in the background, and a European self who would like to live in England.

Moments of decision? ... Oh yes, in moments of decision, I am very good. I decide firmly and quickly. But then in January, 1945, in the London of frequent V-2 explosions, in the pre-victory England, I had weeks of decision. And while my private selves went through torments, my public self, the man of action, drifted along a line which was determined, predestined: I went on making arrangements to return to Hungary. And as the days passed, I felt guilty even for wanting to remain.

Freedom? Of course, I was free to choose. But is a person free who feels that he has to atone for the crimes of his ancestors? Who feels a traitor if he does not work for the arrival of the Kingdom of God on earth?

London on the eve of victory did everything to help me. The men and women in uniform, the gigantic city teeming with frank humanity seemed to say: Do what you want to do. You worked and fought; now it will be soon over. Then do as you please. The London sky at dawn – crisscrossed with the chalk lines of V-2 trails – seemed to say: Don't lie to yourself. In this city one does not lie.

And then at the end of January I found myself sitting in an airplane, flying back to Cairo on my way 'home'. The siege of Budapest was still going on at that time and the only way there was through the

Middle East, Turkey and Romania. From Cairo I sent my application to the Allied Control Commission in Bucharest for a transit permit to Hungary through Romania. The application was transmitted by the British Embassy in Istanbul. While I waited for the answer in Cairo, I started to write a novel in *English*.

I spent nearly half a year again in Cairo waiting. I wrote one of those 'let's-get-it-out-of-our-system' novels. It was partly autobiographical, as most such novels are, and rather surrealistic, with a lot of stream-of-consciousness presentation. The entire action of the novel took place on the upper shelf of the brain of a fatally wounded man lying in a caved-in cellar. There the hero lay in complete darkness, in utter hopelessness, with a wound which tormented him with piercing pain and the last remnants of his personality, of his sanity, were retreating from the pain. I called it *The Survivor*. Some years later that imagined situation in the red dome of the skull, that curling up from pain, became reality for me. Is it possible that I tried to get out of my system not only my past, but my future too?

At the end of May I was told that my application for transit to Hungary had been turned down by the Soviet element of the Allied Control Commission in Romania. This was a shock to my public self, and a relief to a part of my private self. I wrote to Count Karolyi in London about this refusal. He thought that after all it would be easier for all of us to return at a later date from London. I gladly took the advice, booked a passage to England and arrived in July, on the day of the Labour victory. When I left London in January, it was decided that I should be demobbed from S.O.E. in Cairo before I started for Hungary. So now I was given back my real identity. I had a small grey Certificate of Identity. The war came to a victorious end and I became an enemy alien. And this was my own doing because after my more than five years' service I could have applied instantly for British citizenship. But in my wisdom, sense of duty and leftish obsession I did not apply, although my fallible self wanted to very much indeed.

True, by this time there had been a great change in the situation, which strengthened the position of what I call my public self. All my

The Undefeated

worries concerning the Hungarian peasantry were dispelled. The first step of the coalition government set up by the Soviets in Hungary was a really sweeping land reform. In a country where less than one per cent of landowners possessed nearly fifty per cent of the arable land, six hundred sixty thousand landless farming families were given land. About four and a half million acres of arable land were distributed. The Minister of Agriculture responsible for the reform was a Communist leader of peasant origin, Imre Nagy.

For me this fact and these figures meant infinitely more than the realization of a reform long overdue. My personal nightmare came to an end. My 'humanity pain' had started that day in Orkeny when I realized in what abject poverty, what inhuman debasement, the estate servants and landworkers lived. And they had lived like that for a thousand years. As far as they were concerned, Hungary resembled 'darkest Africa'. And now they were coming out of the darkness.

But the land reform meant something else too. It gave me the impression that communism wasn't a rigid set of dogmas. Being well-versed in Marxist literature, I knew that according to Lenin the peasantry was constantly bringing forth small capitalists. Stalin was most insistent on forced collectivization before the war. But now – after the victorious war fought in alliance with the great Western democracies – communism seemed to become more flexible. The Communists understood the particular situation in Hungary – I thought. For them life came first and dogma afterwards. I thought that all my worries and doubts caused by Marxist-Leninist-Stalinist writings were unfounded. Needless to say, no one could have convinced me that the land reform was just a tactical step, that Imre Nagy was regarded as a 'within-the-party fellow-traveller' and he was entrusted with the land reform only because his 'Bukharinite' leanings and peasant origin made him a suitable instrument.

The fact that it was the Hungarian Communist party which claimed credit for the land reform proved to me that one of the basic tenets of Russian communism had been revised – with the approval of Stalin and the active assistance of the Red army in Hungary. So Marxism can and will be rejuvenated – I thought. Of course there will be many fights yet on smaller issues between dogmatic cliché-mongers and the progressive, flexible Communists, but the general tendency seemed a most healthy one.

Before and during the Second World War the illegal Communist party in Hungary was very small. Just a tiny and very brave conspiratorial set. The number of party members must have been in the vicinity of two thousand, and many of these were killed during 1943 and 1944. It was only to be expected that in addition to some thousands of sincere sympathizers, the party would be joined by opportunists and careerists. The party would need friendly critics, independent Marxist theoreticians who would honestly help in rejuvenation. In 1945 – while I waited for a chance to return – I hoped to become one of them.

I was not homesick for Budapest. The newspapers I read after Soviet troops occupied Hungary gave the impression of a curious *danse macabre*. The most gigantic inflation in history was raging, there was a coalition rule of the democratic parties; jobs and positions were distributed according to party percentages. Every problem of the country's policy, economy or culture had to be related to the four-party rule.

The tone of the newspapers was harsh and at times very primitive. Thousands of people came forward speaking about their heroic democratic behaviour under fascism. There were suddenly millions of brave anti-fascists in the country. This side of the spectacle was nauseating. But the Budapest coalition intrigues, the primitive textbook jargon of the new careerist Communists, and all the other disturbing symptoms were for me counterbalanced by the wonders of the land reform and by the truly great efforts of the workers in rebuilding a country bled white, plundered thoroughly by the retreating Hitlerites, and destroyed by the last terrible months of the war. All the Danube bridges at Budapest had been blown up. The day the Red army entered Budapest, there was not a single lorry in the capital. People emerging from the cellars after two months of siege started to weep. The city was a rubbish heap, there seemed to be no hope of rebuilding it. But rebuilt it was.

I did not know how thoroughly the Red army robbed and raped the defenceless population. When the first reports about the raping came to my ears, I attributed them to reactionary propaganda. The main thing was that my worries were dispelled, I could again believe in the cause. I read Marxist literature with new fervour, mainly the early writings of Marx and Engels. I saw in the *German Ideology*, the *Origin of Family, Private Property and the State*, the *Critique of Hegel's Philosophy of Law*, the original and true basis of Marxism as a flexible and progressive political philosophy. I felt that the theory of the dictatorship of the party leaders disguised as the dictatorship of the proletariat would be revised under the impact of events and the possibilities of the mid-twentieth century situation.

According to Lenin the working class cannot produce its own theory. It has to be introduced from *outside*, from intellectuals who join their cause. I believed that it was the duty of friendly intellectuals, my duty, to free the theory and practice from all that was despotic and unprogressive. It was the intellectuals' duty to help in the rejuvenation of Marxism.

Although I had reservations concerning discipline, my drift towards the party went on. The immediate postwar period with its revelations about concentration camp horrors, the general pro-Soviet atmosphere and the many disillusions of victory – all contributed to this drift. Meanwhile my second application for permission to return was refused. In April, 1946, the Hungarian government delegation which visited Washington passed through London. It was then that I first met Matyas Rakosi, the general secretary of the Hungarian Communist party, who as Deputy Premier was a member of the delegation.

Rakosi was a legend in Hungary in leftish circles. He was a Deputy Commissar during the first Communist rule after the First World War. After the collapse of their dictatorship he went to Moscow, was for a time 'instructor' of the Italian Communist party and came to Hungary in 1925 to reorganize the illegal Hungarian Communist party. He was soon arrested and sentenced to eight and a half years in prison. In 1933 a new trial was staged in his case with the intention of sentencing him to death. There was a world-wide protest against this, lawyers from all over Europe came to Budapest, and he got a life sentence. In 1940 he was exchanged by the Soviet government for the Hungarian flags which the Russian armies captured in 1849. Rakosi spent sixteen years in jail.

This legendary man was very friendly to all of us who came to greet him but did not encourage us to return at once. 'There is a scramble for positions now in Hungary. It will be time enough for all of you to return when you are wanted for a particular job.'

So I stayed on in London, writing books, critical essays and short stories in English, working at the Hungarian section of the B.B.C. and giving one or two days a week to Hungary and to 'the cause'. There was the 'Hungarian Club in London', a Communist-front organization. I took part in its meetings, brain trusts and lectures, and later became one of the nonparty people on its executive. In 1949 and 1950 most of the Communist leaders of this organization who had returned to Budapest were clubbed to death or hanged by the Security Police.

In February 1947, Martin Horvat, the editor of the Hungarian party daily, came to London, and asked me whether I would like to be the managing editor of a popular front weekly in Budapest, a sort of Hungarian *New Statesman and Nation*. I agreed. In April the official invitation arrived. On a May morning I drove through London for the last time. My train was leaving from Victoria Station.

I arrived early, put my luggage in the compartment, and walked up and down the platform very bravely and resolutely – as someone who does his duty, as someone who makes a great sacrifice for the cause. My heart was aching for London, for the potential English writer I was about to kill, for the quiet of the British Museum Library, for an English girl I loved, for the smell of Hyde Park after rain, for queuing up at the Old Vic, for the taste of kippers and freshly made toast, for the speech-melody of young girls, for privacy and tolerance and good-natured mumbling, for the huge, sprawling city of eighty suburbs I had grown so fond of.

I tried to work up Hungarian patriotic fervour in myself. I thought of my prospective function as one of the bridge builders between East and West. But there was very little consolation in clichés and parting was such a sorrowful sorrow.

Chapter Twelve

FOR A DISENCHANTED LOVER the passion and happiness of his former self is hard to recapture. The whole emotion seems remote and difficult to understand. I encounter the same difficulty in writing about the period between my arrival in Hungary in 1947 and my arrest in 1949. During that period I was ideologically in love with communism and the 'party', and as blind to the short-comings of the loved one as most ardent lovers are. In Proust's *À la Recherche du Temps Perdu* there is an apt remark about M. Swann, who suffers incredible torments because of his love for a woman in every respect his inferior. To criticize him for this is like saying of a man with cholera, 'How strange that he is willing to go through all the agony of this disease for the sake of the cholera bacilli.'

Ardent faith, conversion to a cause, or falling in love all produce their own highly charged mental and emotional states and strong defence mechanisms against any sort of internal or external criticism, or any 'hostile' phenomena. In those who are possessed by an ideology, this defence mechanism is strengthened by an arsenal of intellectual weapons. Communism produces a complicated sort of controlled schizophrenia with concomitant mental blinkers. Hence my difficulty in giving a true picture of that former self.

The party in those days meant everything to me. When I was arrested and realized that the party had had me arrested, I felt like someone who is kicked in the stomach by his mother. Then after two years in prison, at the end of a long and painful process during most of which I still clung to my faith, I suddenly saw the utter bankruptcy and dishonesty of the 'cause'. For a long time afterwards I was a 'former

Communist', like a religious man who turns into a militant atheist. Then as the years passed, I stopped being a 'former Communist'.

I never take it for granted that I am an authority on myself – or anyone else, for that matter. I really don't know what kind of person I was during my two years as a would-be Communist. I know that in party headquarters I was regarded as a 'within-the-party fellow traveler' whom the party exploits for the time being and then liquidates as a possible source of danger. I also know that all my conscious efforts were directed towards becoming a real Communist. I was a sincere adherent and my sincerity was never believed for a minute.

Although I was not allowed to join the party until six months after my return, I considered myself a Communist from the day I arrived in Budapest. During those first few days I was, so to speak, gasping for air like someone who had plunged into ice-cold water; it was exhilarating and frightening at the same time. I was happy that all the drifting and meandering had come to an end. No danger any more of getting into an intellectual and emotional swamp. No danger of disintegration. I had a good, wise and severe father – the party. A father I could trust and respect.

But I have never yet accepted a 'wise and severe father'. I was a rebel in the family, a nonconformist in life. I had always followed the promptings of my conscience, of my whims and inclinations. All my life I had been in opposition. Would I be able to submit to strict party discipline? Would I be able to change over from general opposition to total approval? But was it necessary to approve totally? Was it in fact good for 'the cause'?

Were these doubts the remnants of my 'bourgeois past'? For the most part I tried to mesmerize myself into the mood of a man who abandons himself to discipline and conformism. I felt – or wanted to feel? – like a man who is called up into the army, who leaves behind a complicated private life, a business with many difficulties and grave responsibilities. But in the army he is no more responsible for himself or for anybody or anything else. It's a hard life, it's a dangerous life, but it is wonderfully simple and one has the feeling of doing one's duty.

I explained often to myself and to others that I regarded my position in the party as that of a subaltern in a fighting army who does

not question or analyze the decisions of the higher command, let alone
the orders of the supreme command. The fight is on for the good of
humanity and the subaltern obeys orders.

Most of the time I tried to transform myself, to suppress the ancestors lurking in my bones, to discard my Bohemian tastes, my 'destruc-
tive' sense of humor. But there were moments of dismay; I felt lonely
and fenced in. The returned Ulysses complex frequently got hold of
me. I simply could not face the fact that the time of travels and adventures had come to an end. I longed for England, for France. In my new
spiritual home, in the home of the Communists, cocksureness seemed
to be an endemic disease; and there were fleeting seconds when I
longed for thoughtful uncertainty, for confusion, for irresponsible
escapades.

But these heretical interludes became more infrequent as I plunged
into learning the everyday life of the party. I soon developed an
instinctive respect for people with working class or peasant origin. I
did my best to acquire the party style. I took a masochistic delight in
'disciplining' my style, which was at first the greatest sacrifice. As I
became immersed in this new kind of existence, trying to meet only
'good Communists', trying with my newly acquired earnest zeal to
learn ideology and party history, taking part in all the approved activities, the awareness of my 'former self' diminished almost to extinc-
tion. I may be wrong in thinking that life within the party destroyed
in me all awareness of myself. Looking back now I think this was so.
Some people were brain-washed. I actively helped to redecorate my
brain, repaint it and refurnish it. It is probably true that propaganda
is only effective with those in whom for various emotional and other
reasons there is a readiness to believe it, to be influenced by it. I was in
such a state.

After spending two days in Paris, I arrived in Budapest on the fifteenth
of May, 1947.

The city looked somehow much smaller than I remembered. There
were ruins everywhere, The Buda skyline above the Danube was almost
unrecognizable and the once lovely Castle Hill had a toothless grin.
Grey dust settled on the battered buildings. Only a new emergency

bridge had been built, all the other bridges were still half-sunken in the Danube. The dirty streets and avenues teemed with hectic life. Having gone through the siege and the ravings of a mad inflation, people were in haste to get their fill of all the good things in life.

The secretary of the weekly which I was to edit had reserved a room for me in a pension, and I drove round my poor and now unlovely home town. After dinner I visited a friend. He was an intellectual who had spent most of his life in Paris, had returned a year ago, and was now a Communist. He and his wife were very glad to welcome me home. They embraced me, produced the best wine for me from a nearby wineshop, told me about their adventures and about life at home, but they nevertheless made me feel strangely muscle-bound. To begin with, their conversation was strange. Some of their sentences sounded artificial, like a quotation from a leading article. There was also a forced and artificial simplicity in their manners. They seemed to be acting a part.

I felt lonely. When I got up to leave, they told me rather hesitantly that I should go home to my pension through the main boulevards because there were still some hooligans who attacked people, undressed them and left them there naked.

'Russians?' I asked.

'Oh no,' they said. '*Mostly* hooligans who have somehow got hold of Russian uniforms.'

'I see,' I said.

'Oh no, you don't see,' my friend said. 'At first there really were Russian soldiers who did that sort of thing, but now it's truly local hooligans.'

I was very much alone with the beating of my heart as my steps echoed on the deserted boulevards. I made a serious effort to think only about all I meant to do during the weeks to come, but beneath these unspoken thoughts there was bewilderment and fear, not because of 'hooligans', but because I was frightened by the impossible possibility of being deserted and disappointed by 'the cause'.

In the stuffy pension I thought of my rooms in Holland Park. Then I read a paper-back detective novel which I had bought for the journey. But I managed to think before falling asleep of the thousands of people who had returned from concentration camps and prisons; of the millions who had spent months in cellars and air-raid shelters, near starvation. They – I thought or made myself think – wanted to build a better world. We humans are born in pain and blood. So is the new world.

So is the new world!

Next morning life swept me along. I went to see the editor-in-chief of the weekly *Tovabb*, 'Forward', of which I was to become the managing editor. Their officers were in the same building as the official daily of the Communist party and most of the staff were Communists. The editor-in-chief, Geza Losonczy, was the son of a Calvinist priest and by profession a lecturer on French literature. At that time he was a Communist member of Parliament and one of the leading publicists of the party. Later he spent five years in a Communist jail; he was released in 1956, became Minister of State in Imre Nagy's revolutionary government. He was arrested with Imre Nagy in November, 1956, and in 1958 was tortured to death.

In Losonczy's room the entire staff of the weekly were awaiting me. Losonczy made a welcoming speech which I had to answer. Afterwards I was taken to the offices of the party daily, where Joseph Revai, the ideological party chief, welcomed me in a few closely clipped sentences and immediately went on:

'Please don't feel hurt if I ask you something. Are you not in the power of the British? Do they have a hold on you? After all, you worked for them during the war ...'

I assured him that nobody had asked me in Britain to act as their agent in Hungary.

'All right, all right,' Revai said. 'I hope you don't mind my asking you.'

Then he told me that the weekly I was to edit was to be a popular front periodical. Its aim was to gather the best progressive intellectuals round the Communist party.

Before taking leave of Revai, I told him I would like to join the party. He said that the time for that had not yet come.

I soon found out that *Tovabb* was considered by everyone to be a

Communist weekly. The public didn't even know that it was supposed to be a 'popular front' organ. Although Michael Karolyi and some socialist and Peasant party intellectuals contributed occasional articles, the paper was written and edited by Communists, and it was not known that I was not yet a member of the party.

Losonczy was a very busy man and only discussed the general policy of the weekly with me. I had to become in fact as well as in name managing editor of a weekly in a political country which I barely knew. Most of the political personalities were unknown to me, and the four-party coalition with its numerous mutually hostile groups and sub-groups had come to an end by the time I had learned all its intricacies. My greatest difficulty was that I did not know the Communist party itself, and now I was editing a Communist weekly without the slightest knowledge of the personalities of the party apparatus.

My work at the weekly, the many articles I had to write for other publications, the lectures I had to give, the need to read all the important political documents, speeches and articles of the past two years, all kept me intensely occupied. In addition I had to get to know the new personalities of public life, with the intellectuals of the four parties whom I had not met before. I lunched and dined out a lot, went to many parties, and was soon swept along in the postwar atmosphere of fast living. In former middle-class and intellectual circles, Communists included, everybody seemed to have affairs, everybody flirted a lot, and I too had several affairs in quick succession. Although from time to time I still felt lonely in this turmoil of public and private life, I was never alone. I never had a second to face myself, to meditate on my actions.

My political home was among Communists and their friends. They spoke with disdain of the coalition scramble for jobs, and seemed to be only interested in the rebuilding of the country. They behaved like earnest adults who are tolerant of the adolescent frolics of other people, that is, the non-Communists, and interfere only if these frolics tend to endanger the common good. It was taken for granted among them that a Communist is a hardworking, disciplined and responsible individual.

During my first weeks in Budapest I met friends from the former

Western-democratic camp, many of whom were now Communists. I did not find it surprising that leading writers, artists and scientists had joined the party, which boasted such transitory converts in the past as Gide, Romain Rolland, Barbusse, Ignazio Silone, Brecht, Koestler, Dos Passos, Auden, Spender and many others. Some of the intellectuals had received the revelation of Marxism while they served in the Jewish labour battalions. Others had got their Marxist schooling in the various Gestapo jails and concentration camps where they were taken because of their activities in the resistance. For many young intellectuals communism seemed to be the best insurance against the return of fascist horrors. To them Marxism and communism was the most consistent and most determined effort to build a world without wars and poverty.

And changed they were, these former left-wing intellectuals. They behaved as enthusiastic lay brothers of the militant order of Marxists. They were all in the process of acquiring the intellectual weapons of this philosophical creed. Most of them had already developed a smooth and strong conceptual technique; they appeared to be superior, calm, and secure after having acquired their consistent world-view, this modern magic stone which can explain everything under the sun. In the past they had been in constant danger of personal disintegration with their aimless lives, their various complexes and anxiety and guilt. Now they had achieved inner peace and security, a firm intellectual and emotional stand.

It appeared that in the 1945–1947 period they had far less doubt about the party than had intellectuals abroad. For them Marxism, that is 'historical and dialectical materialism', was mainly a great intellectual revelation. They found in Marxism all the attractions which the great closed systems of philosophy exert, and never having studied philosophy before, assumed that these belonged exclusively to Marxism.

The party bosses very wisely kept a great part of the sacred books from the Hungarian public. The *Short History* of the Bolshevik Party and many of the most militant and ruthless writings of Lenin and Stalin were not only not published in Hungarian, but were not sold in the bookshops in any other language either. The expression 'dictatorship of the proletariat' was severely forbidden. Those people who used it were denounced as reactionary trouble makers or stick-in-the-mud leftish deviationists. The party line from 1945 till 1947 summer elections was roughly this:

'Hungary never went through the stage of the liberal revolutions of the last century. Hence, for a long historical period yet to come the party and all progressive elements in Hungary must fulfill the tasks of the liberal revolution. From a semifeudal state of great estates Hungary has to be transferred into modern parliamentary democracy. The Communist party must be the dynamo which drives the thorough democratic development and economic rebuilding of the country.'

Only the mines, a part of the heavy industry and the big banks were nationalized. The Communist party leaders announced repeatedly that the Communists would be grateful to those capitalists who helped in the rebuilding of their war-devastated country. Large election posters declared all over the country that the Communist party was defending the private property of small merchants, artisans and peasants. In cultural life the party professed one aim only: to transform Hungary into a truly progressive cultured country.

In this atmosphere the intellectuals and the professional classes were constantly wooed by the Communist leaders. Scores of excellent periodicals made the intellectual scene lively, publishing houses flourished. New schools were founded by the thousand and the 'People's Colleges' movement gave educational chances to the children of the poorest.

Many intellectuals, professional people, industrialists, small capitalists and shopkeepers were taken in by all this. And in a way they were taken in by reality, for land reform was a reality after all. It was a fact that some industrialists and the commercial classes received credit from a state in which the Communists had a decisive voice. The living standard of the people was comparatively high and the intellectuals had a surprising amount of freedom. And none of them ever read the *History* of the Bolshevik Party, or the other sacred books which pointed the future.

I had read these books, but I believed the party leaders when they continually emphasized to us outer-party members and fellow travelers that 'Marxism-Leninism' was flexible and that communism in Hungary would be different. I wanted to believe them.

Communist propaganda was crude but effective. With the help of the Soviet Command and their unlimited financial power, the party exploited their successes in rebuilding the war-devastated country. Gerö, the Communist Minister of Transport, was called 'Gerö, the bridge-builder'. In Budapest, cut into two by the Danube, bridges had the highest importance. And whenever one of them was rebuilt, it was given out that the Communists had rebuilt it. All signs of returning normal life were claimed as Communist attainments. In 1945 and 1946 Hungary was the victim of the greatest inflation in history. When on August 1, 1946, inflation was stopped, four hundred thousand quadrillion pengöes, that is, 400,000,000,000,000,000,000,000,000,000 pengöes, were exchanged for one forint, at that time approximately worth six-pence. This too was heralded as a Communist victory and the Communist party boss, Rakosi, was called 'the father of the forint'.

Although the non-Communist majority in the country knew that the bridges were rebuilt by workers, mostly Social-Democrats, and that the quick economic recovery helped on by a good harvest stopped inflation, we who only met Communists believed our own propaganda. At that time there was very little true intercourse between Communists and non-Communists.

My mood at that time was similar to that of a man who wants to fall in love and welcomes every sign and trace in the loved one of traits that he can approve of. One of the things I welcomed was the People's College movement. In Budapest and all over the country scores of such colleges mushroomed up.

Soon after my arrival I visited one of these colleges. It was in a war-battered building in the residential section of Budapest. Some of the windows were still boarded up and most of the floors were of rough wooden planks, but there was a good library for the students – some eighty boys between the ages of seventeen and twenty-two. Their director, a young lecturer at the university, told me their story.

In September, 1945, a deputation of four peasant lads came to him. They had heard about the People's College movement and had come on foot from Southern Hungary with ten of their friends. Their parents, former estate servants, received small allotments of land. But they were still very poor and there were many children at home, so they had nothing against one boy from the family trying his luck in Budapest. The boys had no shoes and no overcoats. They had no place to sleep. After getting them lunch at the university canteen, the lecturer told them to find an abandoned building, pending the necessary permits. That very afternoon the boys moved into an abandoned house. The inlaid wooden flooring had been used up for fuel during the siege. The boys slept on some wooden planks they had got from a nearby building, and next day they began to tour the city and the suburbs. From abandoned buildings, rubbish heaps, scrap-iron yards and other places, they got their first few 'beds' and pieces of 'furniture'. By the time they were given some army blankets, they had already repaired the floors, mended some of the windows, and had a few electric bulbs. Their sumptuous residence attracted other peasant lads roaming the city, and their number soon reached eighty.

During their first winter they had only one stove, and that was in the great hall where they all studied. They had very little to eat. But they studied – Hungarian, German, French or English literature. And now, after two years they were gathered together in their hall to meet the writer who had returned from distant lands. They were very thin, they had on ill-fitting secondhand suits, but they were scrupulously clean and polite.

There they sat with eager faces and shining eyes, asking hundreds of questions. The questions showed that most of them had worked intelligently, that they tried to think for themselves. I asked them about themselves. Their histories were very similar. Their parents were estate servants living in small crowded huts. In winter, when there was deep snow, they could not go to the distant village school because they had no shoes. Not that now they had everything they wanted. A twenty-one-year-old lad told me that he had already collected thirty-seven books of his own. He was studying English and they were all English books. But now he would like something very much: to have his own copy of Samuel Pepys' diary. After that there was a debate between the English students about the pronounciation of Pepys' name. Later we had a long discussion on Thomas Mann.

I had dinner with them. After dinner they sang peasant songs, and late at night some ten of them walked me home. Going through the deserted streets, I told them about my first meeting with estate servants, when I was fifteen. They listened in silence and did not say a word till we arrived at the house where I lived. Then one of them said:

'Uncle George, whenever you have time in the evening, come and see us. You know we are like a family. Join us.'

The rest of them crowded around me. I had to shake hands with everyone.

For the next two years I spent many evenings at this and at other People's Colleges. For me they were the greatest achievements of the Communist regime. I was already in jail when the People's Colleges movement was banned as an 'anti-party', nationalist, right-wing deviation. But for two years those colleges and those boys were for me a constant source of inspiration and determination.

In the summer of 1947 the Hungarian United Nations Association was formed in Budapest and was affiliated to the World Federation of United Nations Associations. These UNA's were formed as part of a popular movement to strengthen the UNO (and make propaganda for the aims of the UNO). There was a four-party discussion about the foundation of the Hungarian UNA. The government hoped that Hungary would become a member of the UNO sooner or later, and this was a necessary preliminary step. It was agreed that Count Michael Karolyi would be nominated for presidency; all four coalition parties would nominate a vice-president each; I should be nominated as secretary-general; and there would be a Social-Democratic deputy secretary-general. The foundation meeting elected the proposed list of officers. The Communist vice-president of the Hungarian UNA was none other than Imre Nagy, the Prime Minister of the 1956 revolution.

Next year the World Federation elected me to the eight-man executive, as the only member from behind the Iron Curtain. And this election had a great deal to do with my 'elimination' in 1949.

In October, 1947, the Political Bureau of the Communist party decided to discontinue the publication of the weekly *Tovabb*. The reason then given to me and Losonczy was that the weekly did not come up to expectations. We could not understand this because *Tovabb* was quite successful, with a constantly growing circulation. Losonczy and I felt that the weekly was too successful for the liking of the editors of the official party daily. There was very little textbook jargon in our weekly and the articles we published were therefore more interesting than most of those of the official party organ. At that time Losonczy and I did not know that popularity earned by hard work and talent is not approved by the party apparatus. It had to be centrally decided whom to popularize for a time, never for long, and never too much. We attributed the banning of our paper – and after all, the Polit-bureau had banned its own weekly – to petty jealousies and inner-party intrigue.

A week later Rakosi, who was away in Moscow at the time of this decision, gave separate audiences to Losonczy and me. This was the first time I had seen Rakosi since my return to Hungary. It was in his interest to be very friendly to me, to dispel all my doubts, to inspire my loyalty. He gave a full half-hour to the task, and quite naturally succeeded. During the sixteen years he had spent in jail, he had amassed, with the help of a prodigious memory, an astonishing intel-lectual arsenal. He charmed bishops by quoting by heart from the Bible, second-rate poets by reciting their poems, engineers by knowing their special problems. Being articulate in six languages and consulting with his research assistants before meeting anyone of importance, he succeeded for a long time in impressing and charming foreigners and his countrymen alike. He behaved on this occasion as a modest man without any affected pose. He talked freely about political problems, creating the impression that he had full confidence in me. He seemed to be well-informed about my work as a writer and told me that he expected important work from me in the field of Marxist theory, espe-cially on the 'cultural front'. As to the banning of the *Tovabb*, which had been decided in his absence, he told me in confidence that it was based on some mistaken information. It was a mistake of the party. 'But we shall soon have you editing a more important paper, if you still want to be an editor.'

Then he asked me where I lived. I told him I had a one-room-bath-room flat.

'They should have given you a proper flat, completely furnished,' he said.

'I was offered one, but I preferred to buy my own furniture,' I answered.

Realizing at once that he had made a slight mistake, he smiled and said, 'Of course I should have known that you have some principles in these matters. An excusable sin, you know.' Then he walked to the door with me and asked me 'to help the party in the cultural revolution'.

I felt proud to have the confidence of the great revolutionary leader. I was flattered by the fact that he openly admitted 'this minor mistake' of the Politbureau and was reassured as to my future.

A day or two after the audience Joseph Revai told me it would be a good idea if I went to join the party. I did. And the party took me in hand. I had to lead seminars, was sent to lecture in factories, was given writing tasks and in January, 1948, I was made head of the Foreign Language Department of the radio and of the Hungarian Broadcasting and News Agency. My department was responsible for broadcasts in French, English, German, Russian, Esperanto and later in some other languages. This was a most responsible position, because for Communists exact wording has a supreme importance. My department was busy from early morning till well past midnight, and I generally rushed out for a quick break of one or two hours between two principal broadcasts. Meanwhile I was working on a Marxist social-anthropological critique of Freudian psychoanalysis and wrote many articles and essays in various left-wing and party periodicals.

In 1948 and early in 1949 – before the party embarked upon the policy of the dictatorship of the proletariat – I lectured in many factories. After the discussion was over, I usually went with some workers to a pub for a glass of wine or beer. The workers were confident. Their living standard was still high. They believed that we were building a new socialist industrial society in which they would be the leading force. I believed with them that by our hard work and sacrifice we were going to build a future world of plenty and peace.

I was even proud to be able to make small personal sacrifices too. I gave up writing in English. I naturally earned far less in Hungary than I had been used to earning in Britain. My personal future was far less assured in Hungary than in the capitalist West. Knowing party history, I knew that sooner or later the stage would arrive when we intellectuals of bourgeois origin would have to give up our places to the sons of workers and peasants whom we had trained and educated. But all these sacrifices seemed a very small price to pay for being able to contribute to the magnificent work for the future happiness of mankind.

Yes, I think it would be true to say that in those days I mostly thought, talked and felt in clichés. I was not a fanatic, only totally invaded by 'dialectics' and by the party atmosphere. The Communist manipulators at the top knew the art of conditioning. Their Pavlovian technique is always successful if those to be conditioned have a favorable emotional bias towards communism. Whenever that emotional bias disappears, conditioning and hypno-pedagogics lose their effectiveness.

I, for one, wanted to be conditioned. This process was only disrupted on occasions when sudden shocks momentarily revealed the true face of the party. Such a shock came to me in March, 1949, when I was called to party headquarters and was simply informed that next week I was to be transferred from my present position to the 'cultural front', and made literary director of one of the nationalized publishing houses. Nobody consulted me about this. But what's more I knew that this abrupt transfer was a demotion, since my work at the Broadcasting and News Agency was politically far more important. My job there was taken by a former Security Police colonel. His transfer was also a demotion. Both of us pretended to be enthusiastic about the transfer. I told everyone I should be happier in the more congenial atmosphere of a publishing house. But I had my doubts, and it was not easy to suppress the fright which this demotion gave me.

It seems to me now that the Communist party was, and is, a House of Suppressed Fears. With the exception perhaps of the few top-rankers, everybody in the party has to get used to latent and manifest fears. One has the feeling that the party is ruthless, that it does not value individuals. One has very little control of one's fate. Talent, hard work, loyalty, success in work – all these count far less than one's standing at party headquarters. And one is never sure about that. There are secret files, secret committees.

And the frightened ones whistle in the darkness of uncertainty. They try to be more loyal; they try to prove their loyalty. They work harder and they believe that if they succeed in suppressing these ever-present fears, there will be less cause to be afraid.

I, for one, was quite successful in brushing aside these fears. But in 1949 this shooing-away had to be more and more frequent. My reaction was to work up more fervour and enthusiasm in myself.

I was transferred at the beginning of March, 1949. Early in June Laszlo Rajk, a member of the Politbureau, Minister of Foreign Affairs, was suddenly arrested. His arrest caused a tremendous shock and bewilderment. We all knew the story of his life. Son of a Transylvanian cobbler, he became a Communist during his university days. After various prison sentences he escaped and went to Spain, where he had a fine fighting record in the Civil War. After the defeat of the Republicans he went to France, where he was interned in Verney. He got back to Hungary in 1941, was interned again, escaped and became the leader of the illegal Communist party. In 1944 he was arrested again and sentenced to death. At the last minute his sentence was commuted to imprisonment for life. By that time the Red army was already fighting in Hungary. The entire prison was evacuated to Austria, from whence he returned later to become one of the leaders of the party. He was the most outstanding non-Muscovite Communist. Tall, handsome and a good speaker, he was very popular among the workers.

It was next to impossible to believe that he was an imperialist agent and a spy. My Communist intellectual friends and myself were worried by the newspaper campaign against the 'Rajk bandits'. The best we could do was to suspend our judgment till the public trial. It shows what kind of Communists we were, that we believed everyone innocent till the contrary was proven! During July and August many of my friends, mostly Communists who had returned from the West, but also many members of the illegal old guard, were also arrested. There were three among them whose lives I knew well. I was convinced – or wanted to be convinced – that the trial would prove their innocence.

At the end of August, 1949, Rakosi gave a reception in the Gellert Hotel in Budapest. Some artists, writers and scientists were also invited. We sat at round tables while the waiters served the usual over-sumptuous cold buffet. Rakosi, who because of some hormone trouble was dangerously fat and had to keep to austere diet, walked about playing the jovial host. He came to our table too, stood next to me and asked:

'How are you unruly characters, you artists and intellectuals?'

While someone made a noncommittal remark, Rakosi placed his hand on my shoulder and gave me a friendly grin. I had the feeling that he was specially interested in me.

After the reception I felt reassured, because the atmosphere of suspicion preceding the Rajk trial had sharply revived my fears. If the Security Police was not as excellent as I had hoped it to be, my international background, American college education and British war service might put me on the suspect list. Of course I was often told that my behaviour during the war had been praiseworthy, but I still had many uneasy days. Soon after the reception, I was told at party headquarters that I could go to the September World Congress of the United Nations Associations in Rome. This assured me somewhat.

During the last weeks of the summer, I had fallen in love with Agi. She was studying English and French literature at Budapest University. We went out a number of times to concerts and dances; we took long walks. It was the first time I had ever felt as I looked at a girl that I would like her to be the mother of my children.

I visited her and thought earnestly of proposing to her. But I distrusted myself. This time it must be the real thing. I decided – fortunately – to give myself another fortnight to make up my mind.

On the fifth of September, 1949, I visited Agi's home after dinner. We listened to some phonograph records. The maid was just making some coffee when the bell rang.

'Someone wants to speak to you,' the maid told me.

'I shan't be a minute,' I said.

I returned for that coffee more than five years later.

Photographs

George, approximately 9 years old

George, approximately 21 years old

George, approximately 27 years old

George, after his flight from Hungary

George with Agi in Richmond, soon after arrival in Britain

George with Agi and Georgie, 1958

Chapter Thirteen

IT WAS NEARLY MIDNIGHT when the black car stopped in front of 60 Andrassy Avenue, the headquarters of Security Police. The three SP men in mufti took me to a guard's room in the basement. A young lieutenant sat at a desk. He looked at me in disgust, got up and tore the party badge from my lapel.

'Empty your pockets!'

I had to undo and hand over my shoelaces and my necktie. Then an SP guard with rifle took me to a circular staircase which led to the cellars. The cellar corridors were brightly lit. At twelve-foot intervals stood guards with their rifles glaring at me with what I learned to know as the compulsory SP expression of loathing and hate. The cellar was cold and damp. The air was musty, everything smelt of disinfectant, sweat and a combination of various stenches as yet unknown to me.

At the end of one of the corridors I was thrown into an icy cold cubicle three yards by four. There was a wooden plank for a bed and a bright naked electric bulb which threw a harsh light on the unclean whitewashed walls. In the iron door there was a small rectangular spy-hole which was opened and banged shut every five minutes. I stood in the middle of the cell and shivered, my heart nearly jumping out of my breast; I gulped down air as if I were suffocating.

I did not understand the reason for the brutal swiftness of my arrest. Whatever suspicions they might have against me, I was evidently under detention for questioning.

Why does everybody behave as if they took my guilt for granted, I thought. And why these cellar cubicles? Our system should not keep people in such inhuman conditions. Why brag that our Security Police uses no sort of physical coercion if they put people into such awful holes? It's good, though, that they do not torture people. It would be terrible for innocent people like myself to be tortured to give away secrets which they don't know.

How long will it last till I clear myself? I wondered. I ought to be in Rome now. The UNA World Congress had already started, there was that delay with my passport. If I can't clear up everything tonight, I shall miss the Congress.

I walked up and down, five short steps to the door, five steps to the wall. Above the three wooden planks there was a tiny window with heavy iron bars. It opened into an air shaft which probably led up to the courtyard. It must be awful in the winter, the cold streaming down on one's head. From time to time I looked absentmindedly at my non-existent wristwatch, or reached into my pocket for a cigarette. Every five minutes the spy-hole was ripped open, a face appeared with the usual expression of loathing and hate, then it was banged shut again. All through my corridor and in the maze of corridors in this cellar empire spyholes were banging. Heavy boots clattered on the stone floor. Five steps to the wall, five steps to the door. Above the door the naked electric light glared mercilessly into my eyes. What can they suspect me of? What nonsense is this? And why did they bring me in post-haste at midnight if they do not start questioning me right away? I hope to God I shall get an intelligent SP investigator. It would be awful if I got a cliché-mongering ignoramus. Bang, steps, steps, steps, bang, door, wall, bang, steps, clatter of boots, bang, glaring light. Growing impatience in my body, impatience and alarm.

No, this can't go on! I must lie down and try to sleep. I am going to need all my strength! I banged on the door. The spy-hole was ripped open at once. A grim face asked, 'What do you want?'

'Can I have some blankets?'

'No!' Bang.

I was dressed for summer in a light linen jacket and flannel trousers. In the cellar it was cold. I stretched out on the hard planks. I closed my eyes but the lamp glared down on my face. With closed eyes one looked through blood-red light. I turned towards the wall, away from the light. Bang! A face in the spy-hole, a harsh voice: 'Lie on your back. We must see your face.'

I turned into the required position, putting my hands under my head. Bang! A face in the spy-hole and the same harsh voice: 'Put your hands palm upwards on the plank. We must see your wrists.'

They took good care that the prisoners should not commit suicide. One of the SP officers told me later, 'In this building only we do the killing, nobody else.' There was wire netting on the windows to prevent prisoners from hurling themselves to death. After each hearing, when they took us back to the cellar, there was a most thorough search. We had to undress completely and everything was examined for fear we might have stolen some sharp instrument with which to commit suicide. The frequent searches during the winter were further sources of torment.

I remember that night well. It was the longest night I ever spent. I soon got up and paced up and down the cubicle until they changed the guards, until the prisoners were driven out one by one to a troughlike contraption where we were supposed to wash ourselves. There was only one towel, soaking wet already and smelling of emaciated bodies. I did not use the towel. I put my shirt on my wet body. Steps, bang, steps. The prisoners were driven out one by one to the w.c., with a guard standing in the door. Then after another eternity there was a very loud clatter, the metallic clinking of pots. Out one by one again – prisoners were not supposed to see each other – to get 'breakfast': half a pint of lukewarm flour soup and a piece of damp bread. I forced myself to eat up everything. Then we had to put out our dixies, and the 'day' started; crouching on the edge of the wooden planks, walking up and down, counting to seven hundred between bangs on the spy-hole, never ceasing to wonder about my 'case', hopeful, desperate, impatient, apathetic by turns.

In the afternoon the cubicle door was opened unexpectedly. I was hopeful that my hearing was to begin. But it was only finger printing and photographing. A wooden number plate was put under my face. Unshaven, with bloated eyes, I must have looked the typical criminal. But aren't they only supposed to do this *after* they have established one's guilt?

Back in the cubicle, I stretched myself out on my bunk and slept a while. I woke up hungry and shivering. I badly wanted a cigarette. I was thirsty. But at least it must be morning. I waited and waited, but nobody was called out for the morning wash. I banged on the door and asked for water. 'Can't you wait till dinner?' Bang!

My God, it's not dinnertime yet. After many eternities dinner came – some soup and a piece of bread. I wolfed it down. Then I stretched myself out in the prescribed position and with the red glow burning in my eyeballs, burning the back of my head, I tried to sleep.

Bang! The cubicle door was open. A guard shouted, 'Out!'

I came out.

'Put your hands behind your back! Move on!'

Staircase, corridors, more civilized surroundings. I was taken into an office room. Behind a desk sat a small dark-haired young man. In front of the desk four or five yards away stood a chair.

'Good evening, Paloczi-Horvath, sit down on that chair.'

While I sat down, he lit a second lamp on his desk, turned it full into my face. The piercing white light made me blink.

'Tell me the story of your life, with all possible details. Let's start with your family.'

I talked. He made notes. While he wrote I could glance at his wrist watch. It was just past eight p.m. when he started questioning me. At half past twelve he leaned back in his armchair:

'Now I ask you, Paloczi, why are you here?'

'I asked you that already. I am anxious to know. There must be some mistake. Or someone denounced me. If you tell me what it is, I am sure we can clear it up in no time.'

'No, there is nothing to clear up. We know what we know. But it's up to you to tell us what you did. This is our method. You must realize the game is up. If you tell us now, at once, on the first hearing what we know anyhow, then we shall see that you are not a hardened criminal, just someone who slipped … In your case a big enough slip. But if you come clean, if you co-operate with the authorities, we shall help you.'

'I have nothing to tell. I did not commit anything, I made no slip, small or big.'

'Well, if that's your attitude, we have means to get you to talk.'

It was just midnight. He rang the bell on his desk. A guard appeared. 'This man will type his autobiography till four in the morning. Then take him to the cellar, but he is not to sleep.'

Turning to me, he said: 'You will be given a typewriter. Write down everything you told me. And think it over. Till tomorrow you will have time to think, because you are not going to sleep.'

He left. I typed. The guard had orders to prod me on with his rifle butt if I stopped typing. So I typed, half asleep, with reeling head, typed and typed, till the time came to go down to the cellar cubicle. A piece of paper had been stuck on my door. Evidently the order that I should not be permitted to lie down.

Bang. Five steps to the wall, five steps to the door, glaring light, bang, hard eyes looking in. I staggered up and down and looked longingly at the wooden plank. I would not mind the red glow in my eyeballs. Only to stretch out, only to get a second of oblivion.

Morning wash, breakfast and staggering again. At nine o'clock in the morning I was taken up to another officer. A young man behind the desk. In front there was a chair at five yards' distance. The curtains were drawn. As I sat down, the desk reflector was turned full into my face.

'Well?' the officer said with a questioning look. 'Do you like this? An intelligent man like you should realize that there is no point in resisting. You are at our mercy. We know everything about you. We have a great organization to fight against your resistance. You might be fit and strong, but nobody is fit here for long ... Don't you realize that we can do anything to you, I say, *anything*.'

'Communist police cannot use methods of torture.'

'That's what you believe, Paloczi. Why do you think I have this in my desk?'

He took out a long rubber truncheon and brandished it into my face.

'However, I don't like to use it, if it can be avoided ... We know all about you.'

Then it started all over again – I wanting to know the accusation, he wanting me to confess. After a long debate he told me to go on with my life story. The hearing lasted four hours. Then a guard was called in and I had to type till nine p.m. till the original interrogator arrived. He questioned me till midnight, gave an order that I should type till four in the morning, then down to the cellar to stagger up and down in the cubicle.

Just before washing, they changed the guards. It must have been five-thirty a.m. Bang! I did not look at the spy-hole. Bang again. A young peasant face. 'Hey, you!' he whispered. 'Come here. I'll let you sleep till they take you to the interrogator. I will put a piece of bread on your bunk ... Don't sign anything!' Bang!

I did not even think. I just staggered to the bunk and slept like a log.

At nine in the morning the routine started again. The two SP officers went on questioning me in turn, twice a day I had to type my life story. From four in the morning till the first hearing I had to spend the rest of the twenty-four hours walking up and down in the cubicle. This went on for three weeks. As far as the SP officers were concerned, I never slept. But every second day the young peasant guard was on duty, and some other guards were slack. And I learned to sleep while staggering up and down. Sometimes a guard let me sleep during typing hours.

During those three weeks I had to write the story of my life over and over. They made me write some eight thousand words a day. Their orders varied. They would tell me to write down my life story from 1937 to 1941. Then from 1932 to 1934. Then they picked a simple incident which I had to describe in great detail. After that 1939 to 1942, and so on, endlessly. They hoped to catch me out. But I always wrote the truth, and at the end of the second week they started to curse my blasted memory.

The young SP man who questioned me for the first time used a mixed language of Marxist textbook jargon and Budapest underworld slang. He frequently interrupted me by shouting: 'boloney, bunk, bull-shit', or 'tommyrot'. At the end I called him Tommyrot. From his style, accent and general behaviour I concluded that he must have been a shop assistant in one of the disreputable districts of Budapest or a barker in a fun fair. The only way of life and the only type of government he knew was the Communist one. He imagined the 'capitalist state' as a monolithic organization run by a sort of Politbureau of monopoly-capitalists.

The capitalist political police in his mind was a Security Police with capitalist policy. Most capitalist organizations were according to him front organizations of the Secret Service or Deuxième Bureau, and so forth. Britain, for instance, was run by the Intelligence Service. Any ministry, organization or institution which had a research department or intelligence section was naturally a secret branch of the I.S. The most sinister branches of the I.S. were, according to Comrade Tommyrot, the British Conservative party, the Liberal party and the Labour party. These parties, under the central direction of the I.S., had each their own way of working toward the same end – that of betraying the working class of Britain. And through their contacts abroad they did a great deal of spying. The other important I.S. front organizations were the International Red Cross, the BBC, and the World Federation of United Nations Associations.

It was very fortunate for me that I had actually worked for a period for the BBC, that I was Secretary-General of the Hungarian UNA, and most of all, that I 'worked for the British during the war'. The only reason they did not start torturing me right at the beginning was that these facts alone gave them a good case against me. It helped too that in describing my escape from Hungary in 1941, I wrote at length about the day on the Yugoslav coast when the British sent us foreigners off by flying boat. Being half drunk with sleeplessness, I typed mechanically what I thought and felt. Next day Tommyrot was quite pleased with it.

'I see at least that you confess your loyalty to the British. Don't you see that after this there is no point in denying that you are and always were a capitalist at heart?'

'I don't remember exactly what I wrote last night,' I replied. 'It is true that those British diplomats behaved in a most humane way. The fact that I recognize their human qualities does not necessarily mean that I share their political views.'

Tommyrot laughed. 'Says you ... Why pretend that you are a Communist? Nobody believes you. We never believed you. We know that you are an agent. We exploited you while you were useful for us, but had you watched all the time.'

'If you had me watched all the time since I came home, you must know that I did nothing against the regime. You must know that I behaved, wrote and lived as a sincerely convinced Communist. And whatever you do to me, I shall stay a Communist.'

'Tommyrot, tommyrot! ... Stop making speeches! You think because you are a writer, you can get away with anything. You think because the I.S. trained you to be a Marxist, you took us in? Not even for a second! When you came back to Hungary on your agent's mission, your fate was sealed. Of course, you've taken in some people. They saved you in July. You were supposed to be in the July 6 batch of arrests, but some ideological bigwigs saved you. But on the fifteenth of August we received permission to pull you in with the next batch. You know of course that Comrade Rakosi signs all such lists?'

He talked on, but I did not hear anything he said. My head reeled. So on that day of the reception Rakosi had already signed the order of my arrest. No, I can't believe it! But I remembered the strange curiosity in Rakosi's eyes. That look ... God, that look made me think that Tommyrot is perhaps telling the truth. No, it can't be true ...

The weeks passed. I was still impatient, but now I waited for the end of the police investigation. After all, sooner or later they would have to hand me over to an investigating judge, then I should learn the accusation, I could enlist legal aid, clear myself within a few days. It would never come to a trial.

During those first sleepless weeks everything was vague and blurred. Even suffering. It was a hideous feeling to be jailed by my own state, to realize that I, a good Communist, was confined in a Communist jail. It was worrying that the Security Police was not the intelligent organization I imagined. The investigators were brutal and ignorant. And the reactionary talk about torture, which I had never believed for a moment, was true! Everywhere in the building one could hear screams, groaning, whimpering, sudden shrill shouts. At all hours of the day these sounds broke into your cubicle and disturbed your attempt to escape in imagination from all the horrors. There was a girl nearby who started to sob loudly whenever they took her out from her cell to be interrogated. Sometimes I heard her sobbing when they brought her back. I heard her faltering steps, the inarticulate sounds she made as each step hurt her bruised body.

Another torment was the revolting sensation of one's unclean body. I had the same shirt, light summer jacket and flannel trousers on all the time, for weeks. Up in the interrogator's room after half an hour I still could smell the prison-cellar stench emanating from my clothes, from my body. They did not shave me and still gave no permission for the weekly hot showers other prisoners had. I felt sticky with dirt all the time.

Then 'coercion' began. The first occasion would have been comical if it had not been the beginning of torture. One morning Tommyrot asked me where I met Professor Szentgyörgyi, the Nobel Prize winning Hungarian scientist during the war. I told him truthfully that I met him in Istanbul.

'You lie, you fascist swine!'

I kept silent. He asked me again, 'Where did you met Professor Szentgyörgyi?'

'In Istanbul.'

'All right. I'll teach you Istanbul.'

He rang the bell, whispered something to a guard and I was taken to a whitewashed room. I was ordered to turn to the wall.

'Stand closer. Still closer ... All right now, stand at attention. Don't move, if you don't want to get kicked.'

There I stood, my nose an inch from the whitewashed wall. They changed the guards every four hours. The guards had only one duty, to kick me or hit my back with their rifle-butt in case I moved. I stood in that position till the evening. About nine p.m. Tommyrot came in.

'Where did you met Professor Szentgyörgyi during the war?'

'In Istanbul.'

'All right, that's O.K. with me. Then you go on standing.'

After the first twenty-four hours I had to take off my shoes because my feet were enormously swollen. Standing there I learned about the famous 'cinema' of prisoners. By the first evening the unevenly white-washed wall had started to vibrate. The little particles, the slight cracks, the dust on the wall took on various shapes. There were mirages on the wall. My dazzled eyes played tricks on me. Soon I saw snarling, squinting and grinning faces, eyes burning with hatred and loathing. There were hallucinations too. I heard quite clearly the banging of the spy-holes. The wall became full of spy-holes and through each a miniature SP thug glared at me. Next dawn I became quite faint. I hoped I should pass out soon. Curiously enough this thought gave me some strength; I was almost relieved. The wall cinema, which till then had been black and white, took on delicate colours. I saw all sorts of pinks, purples and reds. Lovely girls walked away from me with a voluptuous undulating walk. They always disappeared into the infinite and then started to walk away again.

On the second evening Comrade Tommyrot asked his question again. I again answered with Istanbul.

On the third day I fainted twice in the morning. In the afternoon, when the four o'clock guard came in, there was a great commotion outside in the corridors. They had their weekly party meeting in the big auditorium. When the building became quiet again, the guard – a young sandy-haired boy – told me, 'Sit down now and try to sleep. I'll wake you up if someone comes.'

I staggered to the chair and slept. It was already dark when he woke me up. There were steps on the stairway.

'Stand at attention now. And stick to the truth, whatever they do to you!'

It was again nine p.m. They took me to Tommyrot's room. As I staggered in he turned the reflector into my face but did not tell me to sit down. I stood there. Every inch of my body was hurting me, my skin, my bones, my insides. Everything in my body seemed to be terribly heavy. I stood there reeling. Comrade Tommyrot said pompously with a victorious smile:

'This will teach you, you fascist swine, that it is no use to lie to us. We knew all the time – we have it here in writing – that you met Professor Szentgyörgyi not in Istanbul but in Constantinople.'

There was an explosion of anger in my head. I jumped forward, trying to grab him and shouted:

'You stupid idiot, if you don't know that Istanbul and Constantinople are one and the same ...'

I went on shouting. In the next second there were two guards in the room. I was manacled hand and feet to a chair. Tommyrot sat in front and spat repeatedly into my face. The spittle was flowing down my face.

This was the beginning. Later, when my solitary confinement period was over, I never talked to my cellmates about torture. I won't now either. There were many people who had a far worse time than I. There is no point in describing pain. There are so many ways to cause piercing pain to the human body. All of us prison graduates had days when we were tossed about on a stormy ocean of pain. We were alone with our agony, alone like a small abandoned star in the vortex of a hostile universe.

Torture alone did not make us 'confess'. Sleeplessness, hunger, utter degradation, filthy insults to human dignity, the knowledge that we were utterly at the mercy of the SP – all this was not enough. Then they told us that they would arrest our relatives and torture them in front of us. We heard women and children screaming in adjacent rooms. Was this a put-up job for our benefit? I still don't know.

After the period of torture we were sent back to our solitary cubicles to 'rot away for a while'. Now we were tormented by the intense cold, by the glaring bulb and the four walls which threatened to collapse on us.

We had to be awake eighteen hours a day. There were no books, no cigarettes, only thousands of empty minutes. Now our fear was insanity. Our heads were whirling, we imagined sounds and colours. Some of us had a nightmarish feeling of being drowned. Our emaciated bodies and feverish brains produced eerie visions and hallucinations. Is it any wonder that many of us had no sound judgment, no will power to resist our tormentors?

I realized quite soon that I ought to confess something, but I have an impossible temperament. The way Tommyrot had spat into my face, his insults and all the physical indignities made me stupidly stubborn. I still did not know what crimes I was supposed to have committed, but it was fairly obvious that it had something to do with spying. It was obvious too what I should confess: that all my life I had been a fanatical enemy of the workers and peasants. I could not bring myself to do this.

The Undefeated

During my first period of 'rotting' I was officially permitted to sleep six hours each night. But the banging of spy-holes, the frequent screams, the clatter of boots, and most of all, the intense cold, woke me up several times each night. My stubbornness was punished by their continuing to refuse me any blankets. It was a cold October. The guards on the heated corridors wore military fur coats and fur caps. I was still in my linen jacket and trousers, now ragged with wear and rough treatment. And I slept on the wooden bunk right under the window to the air shaft. By now there must have been surface frost in the courtyard. Many a time I awoke, freezing. I had to get up and force my tired body to do violent exercises. Then I got warmed up, stretched out, slept a while ... and so it went on.

Gradually I became an experienced prisoner. I invented mental play for myself to ward off insanity. During the waking hours I never left myself a free moment. I either lectured to myself, relived a part of my life, recited poems, translated lectures into other languages, attempted to recapture the argument of books, or played simple games. Then there was wall-tapping. This was very dangerous because it was punished with severe beatings, but I was never found out. We tapped with the simple ABC numbers system. One knock: A, two knocks: B, and so on. Later we used the ABC group system. You divide the alphabet into five groups. The letter 'A' is then two knocks with an interval between, because 'A' is the first letter of the first group. And so on. This was a quicker method of tapping.

Through the wall telegraph I learned that Rajk and his associates were mostly sentenced to death, that the investigations were directed and supervised by General Bielkin of the Moscow MVD and his staff. Many of my neighbors were tortured in the 'Russian villas'.

These villas had a curious history. An elegant residential section of Buda was called the Swabian Hill – Svabhegy. Two large luxury villas were used during the war by the Gestapo for their 'investigations'. After the war the place was renamed 'Hill of Liberty' and the villas were taken by the Soviet MVD. General Bielkin and his officers conducted their hearings in these villas.

They described General Bielkin to me and I realized that one afternoon I had seen him on the corridor when I was taken to Tommyrot.

Bielkin was a fat man in mufti, bullet-headed and dignified. Some of my neighbours were heard by General Gabor Peter, the head of the Hungarian SP too. I met him in October, 1949.

I had already spent five weeks at Security Police headquarters when one day the iron door of my cellar cubicle opened with a bang and a grim guard shouted, 'Out!' In the dimly lit cellar corridor two other brutes waited, seized my arms and led me through the maze of cellar corridors to a narrow staircase.

We proceeded to the ground floor, mounted three stories, where a Security Police captain took over. He conducted me through another iron door to the adjoining building. Here the wide corridors were covered with thick red carpet, Security Police officers and their elegant secretaries hurried to and fro, barely looking at the pale, unshaven prisoner in rags.

We progressed through two more buildings, to arrive at last at the inner sanctum, and I was ushered into the Presence. In the middle of the room stood an enormous baroque desk. Behind it sat a thickset, short, sunburned man in plain clothes. On either side of the desk, at a respectful distance, sat Security Police officers. Facing the desk, some ten feet away, stood a simple wooden chair, incongruous in the midst of all the opulent baroque splendor.

The man at the desk, Lieutenant-General Gabor Peter, looked up now and said in a dignified declamatory voice:

'Please, do sit down. I want to talk to you.'

I sat down. He switched on a reassuring smile but his small pig's eyes remained unlit. Then he turned to the colonel who brought me in:

'Why isn't he shaved?'

'He is kept in the cellar, Comrade General.'

'Wrong. He is to have decent treatment, normal room, good food, books, cigarettes.' (Through the wall telegraph I was already aware that by demanding the fulfillment of such promises one could earn an extra-special beating.)

'Files, please.' An aide placed on the desk five bulky files, four of which would normally be kept in the 'Cadre' department, the Control Committee of the party and the personnel departments of the Ministry for Public Enlightenment and the State Publishing Directorate. The fifth and thickest was my Security Police file. The boss opened this last one and nodded with godlike serenity when one of the aides told him that an up-to-date summary was on the top.

While he read it, I studied his face with its short-clipped mustache. It was barely recognizable as the thin, ferretlike face of a market-town ladies' tailor which I knew from photographs in party publications. Those pictures taken in 1935 gave the impression of a nervously cunning little man. Now, after long years spent at the top of an empire of torture, Peter's face was fat and calm like that of Bielkin, whom he imitated in every respect.

He raised his head at last and looking at an invisible point above my head, spoke in a fatherly tone:

'You have behaved most unwisely up till now. There's no point in having yourself beaten to pulp. You know very well what we want from you. You are a writer. Your task is simple: write it down! I am going to have a long talk with you soon. Till then – write!'

A gesture and I was ushered out. I spent another year down below in one of the cellar cubicles, in the same rags, unshaven, hungry, shivering. But I was not sorry we never had 'our long talk'.

On the third of December, 1949, after a long period in which I was left to rot, an SP lieutenant came to fetch me. He took me to a carpeted corridor. Here I had to wait a while, turned to the wall, till I was taken to a small well-furnished room. An elderly man sat behind the desk. He just motioned with his hand that I should sit down, and did not turn the reflector into my face.

The room was well heated yet I shivered; my teeth chattered; all the freezing seemed to come out now. The man opposite me took up the telephone receiver: 'Send me up lots of boiling hot tea and sandwiches. At once.'

He did not say a word till I had gulped down the first tumbler full of tea and had eaten two ham sandwiches. By that time I had stopped shivering.

A captain came in with some files. He addressed the man as Comrade Colonel. When we were alone, the colonel started to speak:

'Still innocent?'

I nodded.

'We don't like innocent people here. Anyone we pull in is guilty. We never make mistakes.'

'So Lenin wasn't right after all,' I said. 'According to Lenin, everyone commits mistakes. Everyone, that is, who works at all.'

The colonel smiled:

'A Marxist, eh? ... Now listen, you don't seem to understand the set-up. All this has very little to do with you personally. It is a great case, a vast international case. You are a little piece in it. But each little piece must fit.'

'I don't understand. Do you mean to say that there is another trial going on, something as great as the Rajk case?'

'The Rajk case is not closed yet. The main trial is over, but there will be many supplementary trials. And the Rajk case was not only against Rajk either. It was against the imperialists and against Tito ... You know the Rajk case of course?'

'No, I don't.'

'A slight mistake.' The colonel smiled. 'They should have given you the Blue Book published on the Rajk case to read. I am going to give it to you. You read it, and then we will talk again. You just lie on your bunk all day tomorrow and read.'

'I can't lie on my bunk because it's forbidden. And I have no blankets.'

'You will be allowed to lie down and you will get blankets. Here is the Blue Book.'

I was escorted down to the cellar. I started to read and I forgot all about blankets, which never came anyway. But I read, walking up and down, or crouching on my bunk. I was appalled by it. By the evening I had read it through twice.

I was shivering again when I sat down in the colonel's room. He seemed to be annoyed that they hadn't given me blankets.

'Well, have you read it? What is your opinion?'

'I've read it, Mr. Colonel (we had to address all SP personnel as 'Sir' or Mr.) but I ask your permission not to talk about it.'

'Why?'

'Because I don't like being beaten.'

'You won't be beaten. You can tell me everything. I guarantee that whatever you say, nothing will happen to you.'

After some hesitation I told him how appalled I was by the whole thing. That everybody in the movement knew how the political police had come to arrest the Eotvos College Communists in 1932. One of the Communist students, Janos Bertok, left a bunch of leaflets in one of the lecture rooms, forgetting among them one of his personal documents. Why say now that Rajk denounced his comrades, when everyone knew it was not true?

'What else?'

'I think it ludicrous that in 1939, before the war started, Spanish Civil War veterans interned in France were talking about a Titoist conspiracy. Even an elementary school kid can see the impossibility of this.'

'What else?'

I went on talking. When I had finished, he asked me what I should like to have for dinner and told me to order anything I liked. He waited patiently while I ate a good meal. Afterwards we smoked for a little in silence.

'Now listen, Paloczi. You've told me you think that the whole Rajk case is a pack of lies. But you know nevertheless that Rajk and his accomplices were hanged. What conclusions do you draw from this? No, don't answer at once, think!'

I thought. The room started to squint, the whole universe seemed to be out of focus. What about the Moscow purges? The Trotskyites? Bukharin, Rykov, Yagoda? What about Kirov's murder? What about Gorki's murder? What about the case of Cardinal Mindszenty? What about Stalin? Rakosi? The party? It's impossible for Rakosi to have been misled by the Security Police! It is impossible for this to have happened without Stalin's knowledge! Why do they kill, why did they kill fanatical Communists? Why kill your best and most trusted adherents? How could Rajk have committed physical and moral suicide by confessing to the most ludicrous crimes? How would this hurt the imperialists and Tito? How can Communists lie? How can Communists murder their own innocent people? The party of truth? How can you build a happier and more decent future for humanity if you do such things?

The colonel smoked. His wise and sad eyes seemed to mock me. He seemed to follow my thoughts. He poured out some more black coffee, offered another cigarette.

'Do you understand now why I made you read the book? Do you understand now your position?'

'I understand the details. I understand the machinery of the whole thing. But I do not understand the reason for the whole thing. Why does our cause need such methods?'

'Think, my boy, think. It is of course for a bourgeois idealist like yourself ... no, don't interrupt me, I use the word idealist in the ordinary everyday sense. I know that in philosophy you are a dialectical materialist ... I know that you consider yourself a Marxist ... But let me go on. Bourgeois idealists like yourself join the movement full of enthusiasm, with fine ideals and completely blind to realities. Now I quote to you. 'You can call yourself a Marxist only if you go on from the recognition of class war to the recognition of the dictatorship of the proletariat.' And what is dictatorship? Terrorism! We are at war with the capitalists. We are at war at a time when our working class is still completely immersed in petty-bourgeois ideology. We fight, we make speeches, we stage trials and the whole world listens. The world of simple and primitive people. We must use simple categories – spy, traitor, agent. We must appeal to the imaginations of thousands of millions of primitive people. We have to frighten our own people. We have to forge our party into a precision instrument, a weapon for our fight. We have to make the Soviet Union victorious. First we have to win, no matter how. Then the famous 'future-building' can start ... Yes, the realities are ugly. Communists must be above it all. Communists have different roles. You can sacrifice your life for the party in many different ways. You can be a hero although you die the death of a criminal ... Think ... You are a small fish. We don't want the supreme sacrifice from you. You can serve as an illustration. You are needed for your propaganda value. If you co-operate you won't stay in prison all your life. But if you continue being stubborn, you will just rot here in the cellar forever. Is it so difficult to understand?'

I sat there, dazed.

Back in the cell, I thought of the millions of honest party members who know nothing about this. But was it true at all? Wasn't it possible that they printed the stuff just to trap a few hundreds of us? Did the colonel say everything that I seemed to hear? Was all this some kind of hallucination?

That night I grew frightened. I couldn't go on thinking about this. I would go mad!

Next day I resumed my normal routine of mental play. I was in such a state that during the day I could not sit down; I had to walk up and down eighteen hours a day and force myself to go on with these futile mental distractions. While I paced to and fro in my cubicle, I was clutching at the last remnants of my sanity. I recited a poem all morning, again and again. Or I found myself counting, counting all the time, in breathless hurry. At times I fainted. The guard came in, gave me something to drink. And so it went on ...

Chapter Fourteen

O N THE MORNING OF DECEMBER 16, 1949, a guard came into my cubicle, manacled my hands and took me to a waiting car. After a short run the car stopped. We were in front of the Marko Street jail, the ordinary prison of the central criminal court. My heart was beating like mad. I thought they were taking me to the investigating judge. In a few days' time I would be free.

As we passed in through the side entrance, I saw with pleasure that the guards here were not SP people but ordinary warders in their blue uniform. They put me in a second floor cell, a large cell with the usual prison windows high up. After a hundred days underground I caught a glimpse of the sky. An old man with a big moustache sat at a table with a book in his hands. A book! He got up when the door closed behind me, smiled and shook my hand. 'Welcome to the sanatorium!' he said. 'I know you, Paloczi-Horvath, my name is Dr. Lajos Bokor.'

I shook his hand. There were two iron bedsteads with straw mattresses and blankets. There were chairs and there were books and cigarettes on the table. The cell was well heated. It looked like heaven.

'Isn't it wonderful to live like an ordinary murderer?' Dr. Bokor asked. He offered me a cigarette, telling me that the food was good and plentiful. His other news was less reassuring. We were not here to meet the investigating judge. The SP had taken over one floor of this prison for people who had confessed or for people who had reached the danger point of death because of torture, sleeplessness and solitary confinement. Dr. Bokor did not know how long they would let us recuperate here.

I sat there listening while he told me his story. I was weak and the first cigarette went to my head. His great misfortune was that his sister married one of Laszlo Rajk's brothers way back in 1927. Dr. Bokor was a police captain in the legal department of the Ministry of Interior in Horthy times. In 1932 when Laszlo Rajk was first arrested as a young university student, his brother-in-law asked Bokor to get the young man out. Rajk was arrested as a member of a Communist group at the university. There was nothing against him, just the fact that he had taken part in meetings. Dr. Bokor went to the chief of police and intervened, and got him to agree that if Rajk signed a promise not to take part in politics any more, they would release him. At that time it was the line of the illegal Communist party for everyone to sign such a document in exchange for being released.

Then after two years Rajk was rearrested as a Communist. There was proof that he had taken part in a leaflet campaign. Dr. Bokor was asked to intervene again, but this time the chief of police refused to help. Rajk was sentenced to three months in prison. Afterwards he was deported from Budapest to a small town and placed under police surveillance. He managed nevertheless to take part in illegal Communist activities. The family again appealed to Dr. Bokor to intervene. Dr. Bokor thought that it would be best for the family if the police deported Rajk from Hungary. That way they would at least be rid of him. The deportation took place.

At the end of 1935 Dr. Bokor retired from the police and joined a firm of solicitors. The Hungarian Nazis arrested him in 1944 because of minor anti-Nazi activities. After the Russian occupation Dr. Bokor lived the life of a retired elderly man. He had an orchard of two acres in which he worked with his wife, selling the produce to Budapest fruit stores. He was very proud of his wonderful grapes, peaches and cherries. Being an anti-Communist, he never contacted Laszlo Rajk.

In June, 1949, he was arrested by the SP. They tortured him to make him confess that he had been present in 1932 when Rajk signed a promise to serve as a police spy. He was supposed to say that the three-month sentence was just a put-up job, and lastly that the political police had deported Rajk to Czechoslovakia to spy on the Czech Communists and that during the Spanish Civil War Rajk had spied for the Horthyite political police. Dr. Bokor, a God-fearing man, refused to lie. He was then taken to the 'Soviet villas' on the Hill of Liberty. The Russian General Bielkin himself interrogated him. The Russians tortured him very badly. At last, Dr. Bokor declared that he was willing to say anything against Rajk, provided Rajk said it first in his presence. It was arranged that they should be confronted. So Dr. Bokor recited the well-learned accusations. Rajk recited the whole 'script' in a monotonous voice. When they came to the Spanish Civil War case, Rajk said:

'Do you want this too? Isn't it too stupid for words?'

When General Bielkin heard this remark from the interpreter, he reddened and sent Dr. Bokor out. After a while they called him in again. Rajk was willing to confess and the confrontation was concluded.

After a while Bokor was taken back to the SP cellars where he began to have hallucinations. So every day they took him into a room on the second floor, gave him good food, books to read and cigarettes. Before the Rajk trial in September, 1949, they assured him that he would be released after the trial. He was just a witness, he must understand, in a most important case and it was for this that he was being kept under lock and key. They let him write to his wife and even order his first dinner at home. A few days before the trial they sent for his Sunday suit. The guards called him Mr. Doctor. On the morning of the great Rajk trial, he was waiting in the room for the witnesses. General Bielkin came in, shook hands with him and asked whether he should have him sent home by car after the trial. Dr. Bokor declined. General Bielkin smiled.

'So you prefer to walk? All the best, my regards to your wife, Doctor.'

In the witness room Bokor saw the other witnesses of the Rajk case reading through their typewritten testimonies; going over parts in which they were not letter-perfect. The whole scene was reminiscent of a schoolroom before final exams.

At the trial he recited his well-memorized testimony, and after it was over, they took him back to the cellar, took away his Sunday best. There he rotted from September till November when he was brought here. He had no idea what was going to happen to him.

I did not know either. I sat through all this, dumfounded. Of course, after having read the Blue Book, it was not news to me. But the whole management of the trials, the callousness of the promises, the part played by General Bielkin, Stalin's personal representative – all this was too much.

Then lunch came, a good lunch, and afterwards we lay down for an afternoon nap. The crude straw sack felt like a bed of orchids. The blankets were warm. I slept till dinner and then again till breakfast. Dr. Bokor did his best to nurse me back to life.

Next morning he took me to the window to look at myself. There I saw my mirrored image, a hollow-cheeked death's-head.

I had three wonderful weeks with old Bokor. He was a Transylvanian Szekely. His people were famous in Hungary for their wit, wonderful storytelling abilities and all-round liveliness. He was sixty years old, but with the spirits and eager curiosity of a boy. I had to tell him about my travels and lecture to him on anthropology. He told me hundreds of tales and funny anecdotes. We played chess, read books. Both of us hoped that by the next summer we should be free.

Dr. Bokor was sentenced later to ten years in prison as a Nazi police officer who tormented Jews in 1944. (He was retired in 1935 and was imprisoned by the Nazis in 1944.) He died in the Vacz jail in 1950 of heart failure.

And I was taken back to the cellar cubicle.

The change was like a transfer from the Ritz hotel to an ordinary prison. The cubicle was bitterly cold, the wooden planks seemed to be harder, the stench more nauseating. After some two weeks of being left to rot, I was taken in hand by a new SP investigator. His method was simple. In the cellar the ordinary prisoners – I was one now – were permitted to sleep from ten p.m. to six a.m. This new investigator – I called him 'Ham-hands' because of his enormous hands – began to question me at half past ten at night and usually went on till four or five in the morning. Otherwise he was scrupulously 'correct'. He did not order beatings, he used no reflector in my face. His approach was that of a Marxist intellectual.

'Paloczi-Horvath, you say you are a true Communist. All right. A good Communist has to achieve self-criticism. Now write the story of your life for me in the spirit of bolshevik self-criticism.'

I was transferred to a basement cell with a table and a chair. Each morning they gave me twenty sheets of paper, each evening they took them away, filled with my scribblings.

After I had become a party member, I had had a taste of self-criticism. Once at our Broadcasting House, I had criticized the executive of our party cell for some mistake they had really committed. Two weeks later I had to get up and say that I was mistaken, the executive was right. I saw other similar incidents, but some true self-criticism too.

Now I felt that I had to convince them of my sincerity through the frankness of my autobiography and the severity with which I judged and evaluated my actions and writings. I wrote on in a state of mind which could be best described as a trance of self-criticism. The basic assumption in everything I wrote was that the party was always right, that good Communists must always prove it to be right. In the same way, in the Middle Ages, true believers always confessed at last because the Church must be right. To be accused by the Church is to be guilty. For people who lived all their life within the Church as true believers, their personal innocence was less important than the repentant's glorified death, which meant ultimate salvation in the hereafter, an inner peace during the execution. If it was true, as the wall telegraph informed me, that Laszlo Rajk's last shout was: 'Long live the party!' then he too preferred to die at peace with the party, as a true Communist. Because how can you be a Communist without the party's blessing?

Many of those who were hanged during the 'monster period' between 1949 and 1953, were the most faithful of the faithfuls. As members of the Communist old guard they had nothing else in their lives but the 'cause'. Their entire past would have been futile, a tale told by an idiot, had they abandoned the faith of the true Communists. So, although they knew that they would be killed soon, killed in innocence, they were intent on making their peace with the party. They were the more loyal, more 'pure' in their Communist fervour, simply because there was nothing left over, just the death of a good Communist. By that time very few true believers remained outside the jails. There were many party members, but the great majority were disenchanted, disgusted and had secretly turned against the party. The minority was entirely cynical. The remnants of the ever-shrinking groups of true Communists were in jail, mostly awaiting execution.

In my trance-like state while I wrote, there was a semiconscious ambivalence in me concerning my future. Although I tried to repress it, intellectually I was convinced that I was going to be executed. (And in this I was right, because at that time this was the official decision.) Emotionally, however, I was certain that I should survive.

Anyhow, death was ever-present in those modern catacombs of ours, in the catacombs of doubly blind martyrs. Doubly blind, because in some of us even the internal eye was blinded. Doubly blind, because we were to be sacrificed on the forsaken altars of a creed abandoned and betrayed by its own high priests. Blindly, or double-blindly, I went on writing in a masochistic fervour of self-vituperation.

'*C'est tout?*' asked Ham-hands contemptuously, showing off his culture. 'I read your effort. *C'est tout?* … I see it is. Do you think you can escape confessing your criminal anti-party activities, your spying and sabotaging, by belly-aching about your bourgeois leanings and slight deviations from Comrade Zhdanov's line? We don't care about the purity of your theoretical line. We don't care about dialectics. We want disciplined party members and honest citizens. You are not here because of your deviations. You are here because you are a spy and a saboteur.'

'I am sorry, but I was no spy and no saboteur.'

'I am sorry, I am sorry … You are incorrigible.' He reached for the bell.

'Please, if you send me back to the cellar, tell them to give me new trousers. These are in shreds. And blankets.'

Ham-hands sneered:

'No favours from you, no favours from us.'

There was a further period of 'rotting'. After the rejection of my self-criticism, I was transferred from the basement cell to the watery section of the cellar empire. The cubicle was no bigger than my former one, the only change was the two or three inches of water on the floor, and the weeping walls. Day and night, with maddening regularity, the walls wept fat and dirty tears. This watery section was deep below the surface and there was a constant seepage of subsoil water. Every morning we were given a bucket and some rags to 'wipe it up', and by working on this for hours, we succeeded in keeping the level constant. But the customary five paces to and fro in the cubicle made a different sound; without shoelaces our shoes normally clap-clapped, now it was squelch-squelch. The banging of the spy-hole did not change, nor the routine and all the prohibitions: *Do not turn to the wall while sleeping, your neck and wrists should always be visible. Do not lie down between six* a.m. *and ten* p.m. I still had no blankets, no cigarettes, no books. The ocean of empty minutes seemed vaster and more frightening. The wooden planks became harder as I lost more weight. It was as if I slept on my naked bones. Each morning every bone hurt. Numb, hungry and freezing, I vegetated on.

But I made my resolution: I will not give up. I was worried lest the constant damp cold should make me ill. By that time I would have given up exercise because, with the very little food we got, I was afraid to lose weight with each unnecessary movement. Yet walking up and down, even ankle-deep in water, was most necessary; I could only forget myself while walking. So although walking, or rather staggering up and down made me tired and impaired my physical health, I had to stick to it to keep sane.

My mental diversions went on. Slowly I reconstructed in my brain a fair-sized library; I practiced my languages, having imaginary debates on various subjects; I relived all my travels; I recalled all the girls I had met; I planned and wrote short stories in my head and translated them into other languages. Being ambitious and industrious by nature, I developed a rigorous routine in my fight against insanity. The intentional daydreaming of my childhood was developed and amplified. My ambition was to be victorious over my body, over the cellar cubicle, over my situation. I did not write short stories, I lived them. Space and time were no limitation. The walls could not hold me. In imagination I lived through hundreds of varieties and possibilities of my own life. Then I developed tastes for other existences. I became a Venetian nobleman of the fourteenth century, or one of

Cromwell's Roundheads, or a Japanese shogun. All this entailed a lot of 'research'. For if as a Venetian nobleman I could not improvise realistically enough, I put the 'play' aside and rummaged for days in my memory for information about fourteenth-century Venice.

At times I had a feeling that I owned the world and all human history. As the spy-hole banged – I grew so accustomed to it that I no longer heard it – and an SP man glared at me for a second with compulsory loathing and contempt, I pitied the poor man. Here he was constantly in this damp and evil-smelling cellar corridor, looking at poor wretches in their holes, while I had just had a long conversation with Hypatia in Alexandria, an enchanting talk about the mystery of numbers, on the impossibility and unavoidableness of the infinite. He, the SP guard, would still go through this drudgery while I was sitting with Erasmus of Rotterdam in that small turret room of St. John's College in Cambridge, sampling wines which the good Desiderius had received from friends in France. Or I might walk in the cool Mediterranean dusk with *her* in Portofino, now, in 1950. And I am sure none of the holiday-makers who actually walked that night in Portofino were as raptly happy with the beauty of the scene, as the inhabitant of cubicle No. 37, whose shoes squelch-squelched at each step.

Hallucinations threatened us with the deadliest danger – insanity. But they helped us too. In a self-hypnotized trance one could shut out the stench of the cellar, the brutal noises, the constant hunger, the various pains attacking our bruised, benumbed, shivering bodies. In these good hallucinations one smelled the air of a Greek island in spring, sage and all; one's skin felt the soft warmth of sunshine … hallucinations helped us to defeat our body, defeat our jailers, defeat reality.

There were other moods. It was terrible to live week after week, month after month in a world bereft of colours. How I longed for the green of young April trees, the blue-green variations of the morning sea, the orgy of colours of an afternoon on the Champs-Elysées. It was terrible to spend the two-hundredth day without music. No doubt, we intellectuals were fortunate to have the world in ourselves, but this was also a source of misery. For those whose ears are attuned to music, a world of drab and harsh noise is hell.

The months passed. Summer must have come, because the guards grew sunburned. At the height of the summer there were a few days when even our cubicles became tolerably warm, so that one could sleep all night.

And the 'rotting' was periodically interrupted by weeks of 'interrogation'. The SP officers were of various types. There was the thin schizothyme captain whose eyes glazed over and defocused after hours of watching others squirming in pain. There was the fat, elderly brute who watched with the steely cruel eyes of an old hen. Their approach varied, their aim was the same: Confess. In the spring I still had seemed to be a candidate for execution; a pompous ass of a captain had looked meaningly into my eyes and asked:

'You would have sacrificed your life for the party many a time, wouldn't you?'

I nodded. He expected that. He raised his hand and hit the desk with the back of it.

'Well, sacrifice it now!'

There was silence in the room. He thought he had shaken me to the core. How theatrical and untrue all this was! I thought. I simply answered that I was not prepared to sacrifice my life for the party by lying to the party. Then I made some unwise remarks and was punished for them.

But by the summer it seemed that they had dropped the plan for my execution. Most of the SP interrogators were rather loquacious. From their manner I could guess that they no longer saw in me a candidate for death. (Previously I often heard the usual greeting: 'Good evening, corpse-candidate!') I managed to get books to read and six cigarettes a day but was still refused permission to write or receive letters. (I learned after my release that Agi and my family were told that I had been hanged.)

I read the books of the cellar library. One could not choose: one day it was the second volume of Marx's *Das Kapital,* next day some revoltingly silly Soviet novel, and then as an unexpected treat, *Dr. Faustus* by Thomas Mann. How I read! Once for pleasure, once for double pleasure, the third time to store away all important facts for possible future solitary confinement periods. I did not read the good books, I plundered them, memorized them, expropriated them. What world-shattering good luck it was, after a week of Soviet trash, to get a volume of Proust or Jane Austen or Kafka!

The prison library contained some books confiscated from the prisoners (they confiscated my library the day after my arrest), so from time to time one got good books.

But then came a transfer to another cubicle in another corridor. This meant a new regime. No books, no cigarettes, just empty time. But one sailed victoriously through these short five or six weeks' periods without anything to read, being enriched with recently read or reread books.

There were some worrying symptoms. The defence against insanity used up a lot of energy, which one could ill afford. I grew ridiculously cadaverous. By now I was allowed a weekly shower and shave. The SP guard who shaved us with five or six quick strokes, complained that my face was all bones. The SP guards called to each other in the shower room while I was enjoying the hot water, saying:

'Look, this one will soon *puff out* [their slang for death], his belly has shrunk to his back.'

I had become seriously weak. A toothache which during the first half year was nothing to bear, became now almost intolerable. I had a headache almost constantly. I did not ask to see the SP doctor, for the wall telegraph told me that he kicked prisoners who reported sick without being desperately ill.

By October, 1950, I collapsed once or twice a day. By that time I had spent three hundred and ninety-six days in the cellar. (One always counted the days. Had I foreseen that I should have to count up to one thousand, eight hundred and thirty-two before my release, I might not be here to tell this story.) Each addition to the number of days meant a victory for me. Three hundred and ninety-six days in SP cellars without signing a confession! Some of my neighbours with whom I was in tapping-coversation told me I was an idiot. If one could satisfy them with a non-death-sentence confession, one should do it. The sentence means nothing anyway, they said. If there is a major change in the political line, some of us will be set free; if not, we stay.

On October sixteenth I was taken up to an SP officer. He seemed to be in a hurry. He said:

'Listen, Paloczi, we won't bother you any more with questions. We know all about you. Here is your confession, sign it. If you refuse to sign, we'll make you sorry you were ever born.'

I read the 'confession'. It started with the usual statement about having been an enemy of the working class all my life. Then came the main confession: the World Federation of United Nations Associations was an imperialist spy and sabotage organization. The Hungarian UNA, of which Michael Karolyi was president and myself secretary-general, conspired to overthrow the people's democracy. John F. Ennals, secretary-general of WFUNA, was my spy-chief and I handed him spy reports in Budapest daily from 1947 till the time of my arrest in 1949. Additional criminal acts of mine were that I succeeded in getting Count Karolyi appointed to be Hungarian ambassador in Paris and that through George Heltai I was running the Hungarian Foreign Office in the interests of the imperialists.

I told the officer I refused to state that I was always a fanatical enemy of the working class. As to the other accusations: Ennals spent only three days in Budapest between 1947 and 1949. He was either at the Geneva headquarters of WFUNA or touring the five continents.

The officer interrupted me. 'Never mind that. No word of it will leak out. Your trial will be kept secret.'

'But why tell a lie if it will be kept secret? Whom do you want to mislead?'

'That's none of your business. Are you willing to sign or not?'

'I am but not if you insist on this nonsense about Karolyi and the Foreign Office. Ambassadors are appointed by the President of the Republic on the proposal of the Council of Ministers. And how can an outsider run the Foreign Office?'

'Never mind, will you sign or not? Look – I erase this bit about hating the working class. O.K.?'

He offered his fountain pen. I signed. Immediately he became very friendly. He looked at his wrist watch.

'You should be heard now by the Attorney General, but there is no time for that. We shall waive this formality. I shall send you over to the

Marko prison at once where you will get good food, plenty of books, cigarettes, anything you want.'

'I want to write to my family.'

'Of course, that will be arranged too.'

He rang the bell. A guard took me to a waiting car. My hands were manacled. In a quarter of an hour I was back in a cell opposite to the one I had shared with old Bokor. The cell was splendidly furnished with a table, chairs, a straw mattress and brand new blankets. I had barely looked around before a smiling guard came in and asked how many cigarettes I wanted a day. He was followed by another guard who offered me a choice of books with the friendliest of grins. Like an overeager shop assistant he assured me they had a fine selection of books in 'every language'. When the third SP guard came with an all too sweet smile on his mug, I realized that these good men wore uniforms on their faces. In the cellar they had to fix on their faces an expression of loathing, hatred, disgust. Here the script called for good cheer and friendliness, hence the ever-present silly grin.

There was a clatter of dishes outside. An SP guard, whose goodness of heart must have overflowed all over his face, asked me in a friendly tone:

'Are you a Trotskyite?'

'As far as I know, I am not.'

'Have you signed a confession today?'

'Yes.'

'Then you are a Trotskyite.'

'Thank you for telling me.'

'This is no joke. Trotskyites get extra good food, you'll see.'

I saw it. They served an over-rich three-course lunch with half a pound of steak and lots of sickly sweet cakes. Naturally I wolfed everything and was ill for three days.

But the SP guards fussed over us like old aunts with their favourite nephews. They got me a friendly doctor (smile and all) who prescribed medicine, special biscuits, diet. After this incident was over, I ate my fill. The good SP aunties popped in ever so often, inquiring about our appetites.

'Won't you have a snack of something?' they would ask with beaming, expectant faces. 'Some fruit, or cheese, or cake?'

The smiling faces started to lose some of their attraction when the SP officer who had made me sign my confession showed up one day.

'I came to see you about your confession. You realize of course, that your offence is not at all serious?' (I nodded; why not?) 'You will naturally stay in prison for a bit but not for long. A year at the utmost. Then you will live somewhere in the country for another year or two, quietly but free, and then, *then* you can return to normal life.'

I did not say a word.

'Now, Paloczi, I would like to leave your confession here. You may keep it. As a matter of fact, you should memorize it. It's a new version, not quite the same as you signed, but basically the same. This is really the script of the trial, as far as you are concerned. The questions of the judge, your answers. I will come again soon, then we can start rehearsing. Yours will be the ninth sub-trial of the Rajk case. Your friend George Heltai will be the principal accused, and you will be the third.'

Then he left. A week later he returned. We rehearsed the script of the trial. Before going, he told me that there was some slight change of plans. I was to be the principal accused and Heltai the third.

'But why me?'

'Your name is better known.'

'But the trial will be in camera, will it not?'

'Yes, yes, but still ... Your sentence will be a bit stiffer ... no, no, it won't be death, I assure you. But nonetheless you'll be free soon.'

I nodded somewhat uncertainly, which worried him.

'You won't try any silly tricks on us, will you? ... Listen, there is no point in retracting your confession. The trial is in camera. Only we shall be present. If any one of you speaks out of turn, or deviates from the script in any way, the judge will stop the trial. And in such cases my chiefs are merciless. You are either tortured for months, or simply put into a dark cell for a year or two, where you will surely go mad ... You understand, I hope, that I am not threatening you. I know that you are an intelligent man. But one has impulses. Be careful.'

'Look here, I signed your silly confession, I will play my part in the comedy.'

'That's the spirit, Paloczi ... You are right. The trial is just a comedy. But it has to be played. The real thing is your behavior and the political situation. But as I told you, you won't be in jail for long. To show you that I have confidence in you, I will tell you now that you will be sentenced to fifteen years. But in fact – as I told you – it will last barely a year.'

I nodded, but I was not so sure. As matter of fact, I did not believe a word. It appeared that they would let me write to my family as soon as the trial was over.

November 29, 1950, was the great day. I had been fifteen months in the hands of the Security Police. Justice Jonas of the Supreme Court had come in the previous day to rehearse. We were six in the dock. Behind us were SP guards, behind them a crowd of SP officers. On the right-hand side sat our counsels for defense, who never spoke a word to us. On the left was Attorney General Julius Alapy, he who had prosecuted Cardinal Mindszenty.

The script went through without a hitch. Justice Jonas read out the questions and I recited the answers.

The Attorney General, hands in pockets, recited a *Pravda* editorial about imperialist scum, about despicable spies and anti-party conspirators. Hands in pocket, he asked for the death sentence for all of us.

Then the SP men playing the role of defence attorneys delivered the second prosecution speeches. Mine pointed out that there was an extenuating circumstance for my being the scum of the earth. After all, I came from a feudal family. My mother, father, all my ancestors were feudal swine, so naturally I had turned into a spy and an anti-party criminal.

Then the court withdrew. Justice Jonas committed the slight mistake of forgetting the typed and signed judgment on the desk and sent in one of his assistants for it. After twenty minutes' deliberation they had not only reviewed all six cases, but had had time to dictate the judgment, the reading of which took a good hour and a half.

We stood to hear the verdict. I was sentenced to fifteen years of hard labour and to the confiscation of all my belongings. George Heltai, whose script they forgot to change, had made the confession appropriate for a principal accused. He had been spying – according to the silly script – since 1945 for half a dozen countries, and had sold the documents of the Hungarian Foreign Office to every conceivable imperialist power. But he received only ten years.

As soon as the verdict was read, the SP officers disappeared. There was no question of our writing to our families.

The SP guards arranged their facial muscles into position one, that of loathing.

I asked one of them, 'Shall we have some lunch now?'

'Shut your mouth, you filthy convict!'

Chapter Fifteen

A S FRESHLY SENTENCED CONVICTS we were marched down the staircases to a waiting Black Maria which drove out from Budapest. We soon guessed that we were being taken to the infamous Vac Jail for 'heavy politicals'.

In Vac we were undressed, our heads and whole bodies shaved. The SP guards threw us some filthy convict uniforms and boots. Then they marched us into the special 'MZ' (solitary confinement) section, which had been built in Horthy times as the punitive wing of the huge prison. According to the law at that time, convicts could be given a maximum sentence of a month's solitary confinement for bad behavior. The cells in this wing were accordingly very small, yet the six of us were crowded into a single cell. There were four palliasses, a w.c. bucket with a badly fitting cover, and a large open water pail. During the day two palliasses were piled under the window, the other two along the wall, so we had an L-shaped 'divan'. At night, the four palliasses were lined up in a row, completely filling the cell.

When the heavy iron door was banged to and bolted, we fell on each other's necks, shook hands, laughed, talked excitedly, nudged each other, shook hands again, talked all at once – madly happy, supremely relieved that the torments of solitary confinement were over. Not only were we in company but – supreme luck! – we were in congenial intellectual company and some of us were old friends. Looking at each other we broke into fits of laughter, we looked so desperately funny and pathetic with our freshly shorn heads, our ill-fitting coarse convict uniforms and enormous black boots. We had a lot to tell each other. Every one of us wanted urgently his fill of talking. The bliss of conversation, the warm glow of human company, the end of terrific tension, all this made us forget our situation for a while. After the agonies of solitude, the fight against insanity, after the gigantic efforts to keep our brains occupied from our own resources, we could relax at last, relax and find safety in company.

We were drunk with happiness. The guards came again and again all that afternoon to bang the cell door and to threaten us with lashing if we didn't stop laughing. We did not notice that we were given nothing to eat, though we had not eaten anything since the night before.

After the first frenzies of laughter, we split up into groups of two, as well as we could in that crowded space, and tried to talk more seriously. But time and again someone had a story which everybody had to hear, and the merriment started again.

At the evening inspection it turned out that we had missed dinner as well. Soon a sort of cowbell announced the last post. We hurriedly spread the straw sacks, stretched out next to each other, crowded like sardines, pulled the coarse blankets up to our necks and carried on a whispered conversation. And then a most wonderful thing happened: *they turned off the light.* For fifteen months we had lived under the glare of bright electric lamps. For fifteen months we had slept with a red glow in our eyeballs. Now we bathed our eyes in the good, soft velvety darkness. There we were, close to each other, under warm blankets, in a good, safe, black world. We were going to talk in an undertone to each other for a while, then go safely and peacefully to sleep. Nothing could happen to *us*. Outside people might have their fears and anxieties. They might be frightened of losing their jobs or being suddenly arrested. The ring of their doorbell at night would bring terror to their hearts. But we were not worried. We should sleep. There would be no jail, no convicts. There would be dreams. There would be freedom. And blessed darkness.

Next morning we began to get familiar with prison routine. It was still dark when the cowbell woke us up. The guards and the convict-orderlies started on their rounds to empty the buckets and fill the pails with drinking water. An hour later breakfast came, the usual coffee substitute and about a pound of bread per person. This was the bread ration of the day, but we ate it up at once. The cell was very cold, although our six bodies provided some warmth. We learned that for the time being – actually for three months – we were not supposed to take part in the daily walk round and round one of the courtyards.

Shivering and hungry, we started to talk about our situation. All six of us were members of the Communist party till our arrest. I assumed that my five cellmates remained Communists.

'The fact,' I said, 'that we were stupidly and brutally smitten down, the fact that we are imprisoned without cause, that some innocent people have been hanged, does not mean that the three volumes of Marx's *Das Kapital* suddenly become untrue, that the exploitation of workers is a good thing, that the Left is wrong.'

The others – with one exception – stiffened. B., the oldest Communist among us, a party member since 1932, said with some emphasis:

'Let's not confuse the Left with the bureaucratic despotism of the so-called Communists. As to Marx's *Kapital* ... one should reread it. I am not so sure about it. True, an ideology cannot be proved wrong by the behavior of some of its adherents. But this is not the case. Remember the purge trials before the war. Security Police rule, rigged trials, all these are not just appendixes of the system. They are its bases.'

We started to argue, two against four. The debate went on for a long time. The partners changed, the debate was the same. Some former party members had become disenchanted during the first year spent in the SP cellars. Others, like me, still believed in the cause. We were even proud that no amount of suffering could shake our belief.

In our first cell the six of us decided after a while to stop this debate, because it got to a stage of endless repetition. We started to organize our time. We decided on a lecture course on world history from prehistoric times till the present. Everyone volunteered for the period he knew best. In the afternoon there was an hour of general conversation followed by language lessons. B. taught Spanish; I gave English lessons; G. was the French teacher. After dinner we played various games, including word poker and twenty questions.

The guards left us alone provided we did not make too much noise. It was December and bitterly cold, but we decided to keep the small window open because of the stench of the bucket. We sat around covered by our blankets. We even took turns in walking. If the other five crouched on the strawsacks, the sixth could make four steps to and four back.

After the first month the crowded existence in our very small cell started to affect our nerves. We were constantly together day and night. Eating, sleeping, drinking, excreting – all our functions were performed in common, and we had to consider each other all the time, dividing our scanty water, making every movement with care and being careful not to offend each other in conversation. And though everyone in that first group was considerate and did his best, our frayed nerves produced quarrels. Solitary confinement was of course far worse but one would not have minded a little privacy now and again. One of us spoke loudly when someone else had a headache; X. turned too often in his sleep, disturbing his neighbours. Y. snored too loudly.

Early in January, 1951, our nights were disturbed by the screaming and wailing of a convict who went mad.

He started to scream and sob incoherently and then shouted in a clear voice, 'Long live Stalin! Long live the glorious Soviet Union! Long live Comrade Rakosi! Down with the fascists who keep us in jail! Long live Stalin, long live Stalin, long live Stalin!' This went on for half an hour, till one of the guards entered his cell and he continued to scream till he was dragged to a cellar. Later on we found out that he was the poet Endre Havas, who had lived in exile in England during the Second World War and returned to Hungary as the private secretary of Count Karolyi. When Karolyi became ambassador in Paris, Havas was one of his counselors. He was arrested in 1949 and went mad in January, 1951. In 1952 the SP guards clubbed him to death.

One day in January, 1951, I was taken from Vac to the new Budapest headquarters of Security Police in Fö-utca. After some hours of frightened waiting in a cell, I was taken up for 'interrogation'. It was again Tommyrot, this time in the uniform of a first lieutenant.

'Good evening, Paloczi, we are preparing a new trial ... No, no, no, don't be afraid. It is true that you will play a part in that new trial, but this time you are in a very lucky situation ... Listen, I know that you were sentenced two months ago. That trial was a farce. It had nothing to do with truth, we all know that. Now we are going to stage a new trial in which you will be one of the lesser accused. It will be a public trial, which shows you how much confidence the party has in you.'

'I was sentenced to fifteen years. I don't want a new trial. I want to be left alone. This is horrible. Can't you leave us in peace even in prison?'

'Now, don't misunderstand the situation. You'll see that this is to your advantage. The party wants to stage a sort of sample public trial to throw light on some of the secret trials. As you may know, we have arrested a great many politicians, from the President of the Republic, Arpad Szakasits, down to many MP's, mainly Social-Democrats and Communists. Their names will be mentioned in your trial and your fellow spies and conspirators.'

'No, a thousand times, no! You had me sentenced to fifteen years. I signed the stupid confession. But as you said, it had nothing to do with truth.'

'Yes, of course, not a word of it was true.' (On my retrial in 1954, before my rehabilitation, Tommyrot admitted that he made this statement to me.) 'We don't want to force you now to lie about yourself. You'll tell the truth.'

'The truth is that I was no spy. The truth is that I am totally innocent, yet you had me sentenced to fifteen years. And all my cellmates are innocent too.'

'I am not interested in your cellmates. And don't take that innocent line. We are going to sentence you this time too, but to a far shorter term, and if you behave well you'll be soon free.'

The interrogation, without coercion, lasted two weeks this time. The statement which they made me sign was much milder, spying was left out of it altogether. I simply had to confess to some anti-Communist activities. In my very weak state I did not risk too much resistance. But this second confession was too mild and it never came to a second trial.

After the interrogation period was over, they sent me back to the Vac Jail. This time I was put into another cell. My new cellmates were my friend, Paul Ignotus, the writer, and two other intellectuals. The other three were intended to take part in the same public trial. We shared a cell for a long time, till the time of my 'salvation' in August, 1951.

The Professor was halfway through his lecture on ancient Indian philosophy. The audience – though a bit groggy from his torrents of erudition – listened avidly because he had an uncanny gift of trans-forming abstract theories into vivid and tense dramas. He sprinkled his lectures with a good deal of incidental information concerning the sex life of aboriginal sects, the technology of pre-Aryan Indians, the psychology of language formation, or the conflicting theories about the various submerged continents.

He was just about to explain the influence of phallic cults in Indian dialects when he was interrupted by the clatter of iron pots in the corridor and the noise of the prison guards opening cell doors to hand in dixies half full of a nauseating brew called soup. He rushed to our cell door to be first to receive the stuff and stood there impatiently looking, in his striped convict uniform, shrunk from repeated boiling in disinfectant, like a giant baby in outgrown clothes. He was six feet six and still tremendously fat, although he had lost more than fifteen pounds during his year in prison.

'Incidentally,' he said after he had gulped down his share and had begun to wash up the pot, 'this utensil is called in English *dixie* or *dixy* which is a corrupted form of an old Sanskrit word. In Hindustani it is called *degcı*, in Persian *degscha*, which is a diminutive of *deg*, that is, iron pot.'

Paul, the essayist, said in a weary voice, 'Yes, you've already told us this three or four times.'

'You go to hell,' the Professor said and started to devour the day's ration of bread in large chunks.

'You will be very hungry again tonight,' the composer remarked, but the Professor paid no attention to him.

We ate the second course – fodder beets prepared like mashed potatoes – in silence. I was hoping that the Professor would omit this time the etymology of the word for fodder in various languages and that he wouldn't have a bowel movement before we had finished eating.

The Professor and his audience sat on the piled-up palliasses that they slept on at night. The audience consisted of Paul, the essayist, an emaciated man of about fifty, the young composer and myself.

The Undefeated

Our cell was twelve feet long, six feet wide and contained three straw mattresses, two very small tables, a pail and the w.c. bucket. On a rough wooden shelf there were four tin drinking cups, eight dixies (corrupted Sanskrit word for iron pot!), some books which we had to translate as 'hard labour' and a couple of dictionaries. On one of the tables stood a rickety old Remington portable. On the opposite wall there was a small shelf with our personal belongings – toothbrushes, pictures of wives, children and relatives, toilet paper, a few cigarettes and neat stacks of cigarette stubs.

In the Soviet system (copied to the letter in Hungary) people sentenced to hard labour are supposed to be paid for their work. Our 'hard labour' was translating. Between the four of us we knew some ten languages and we translated for the 'authorities' spy novels, textbooks on electronics, infra-red photography, Egyptology, new secret Russian technological processes (generally outdated by a couple of decades) and 'spy documents', such as Viennese or Stockholm guidebooks of 1927 or 1935, two-year-old British railway timetables and similar spy material. For all this work we were paid in principle quite a good salary, one thousand to fourteen hundred forints a month. From this they deducted fifteen forints a day for our keep and the usual tax, some eight per cent for the national health service. We were permitted in principle to use up from the remaining one hundred to one hundred fifty forints a month to buy extra food, toothpaste, toilet paper and cigarettes.

But all this was only 'in principle'. As a matter of fact our money was constantly stolen by somebody on the prison staff. It was a very exceptional month if we could buy some onions, a pound of lard, a pound of sugar and ten cigarettes a day. So everyone was saving cigarette butts. We smoked only four-fifths of each cigarette, very carefully put it out and stored the butt. When hard times came – that is when the guards stole even our cigarettes – then we carefully unwrapped the butts and rolled cigarettes from the tobacco and toilet paper. An envelope full of butts was a very treasured possession. Pessimists even stored the butts of the butts, and so on.

The Professor and his audience sat on the palliasses and smoked. We had made a pact to keep silent for an hour after lunch every day. During that hour everyone was supposed to sit still and noiseless – a most difficult undertaking for the Professor. The young composer, who had a nervous tic, so that his heavy convict boots tap-tapped from morning till night, sat Mohammedan fashion with crossed legs on the mattress. There was silence. Nervous silence. Paul, and I – the chief silence fads – were the nervous ones. We had no watches, naturally, and it was anyone's guess how long an hour lasted. Although we had a complicated system of telling the time by the progress of sunshine on the opposite prison building, which we just could see through the narrow window very high above our heads, there were many arguments and even heated quarrels about the progress of time. In the absence of sunshine we could tell the time only by various phases of the daily prison routine.

The Professor intensely disliked sitting still and he cut us short so that we never had a full hour of quiet bliss.

He was a roaring extrovert, very bouncy, and he loved to shout. The typewriter clattered twelve hours a day; the composer's boots tap-tapped with a maddening monotony all the time; screaming quarrels flared up; outside the guards shouted at the old privileged convicts on orderly duty; in the locksmith shop just across the yard hammering never ceased for a second during the twelve hour workday – the post-prandial silence was indeed the greatest of blessings.

A convict in our part of the world has many nightmares. One is the eternal silence of solitary confinement, another an overcrowded small cell in a noisy jail, another again a cell shared by two persons for years. Solitary confinement without books, cigarettes and work is frightening; from minute to minute madness grins at you.

The hysteria of the overcrowded cell or the hell-for-two of the double cubicle – both have their own special kind of torment. Yet a convict dreads nothing as much as change.

And on that August day in 1951 change fell on me again. We were in the middle of the silent hour when heavy steps echoed outside, the bolt was thrown back, the iron door opened and a guard said: '1380, out! Bring your things!'

The Undefeated

I got up, searched for my convict cap, pocketed my toothbrush and paste, a few cigarettes, the little parcel of butts.

'Hurry!' The guard said in a bored voice. My three cellmates went pale. On such occasions one never knew if we should see each other again. I looked longingly at them, but the guard grabbed my arm.

He took me through a maze of buildings and corridors to the main courtyard where near the gate stood a brand-new Soviet model Black Maria. This was really a miniature ten-cell prison on wheels. On the two sides of a narrow corridor were the cubicles, each just large enough for a man to stand in it at attention. The guard pushed me into one of the cubicles and locked the door.

Now I had silence.

I was glad that I had met this type of Black Maria before; my first meeting with it had been horrible. At that time I had not yet heard of this grand product of Soviet civilization, and thought that it was a mobile execution van in which I should be gassed. Now I knew I should have to stand in this narrow cubicle for half a day at the most.

One of the van's doors banged. The two Security Policemen probably went off to lunch or to play a game of cards with the prison guards. In an hour or two we should start. It all depended whether they were taking me to Budapest which is only an hour's run or to some country jail. The thing was to be patient.

The convicts called this type of Black Maria a 'coffin'. And there I stood in the coffin, in complete darkness, the two sides of the cubicle against my shoulder, my back touching the coolness of the metal, and got busy. The thing was not to let yourself go. If I had started to think about my situation or pay attention to my actual circumstances, the result would have been despair. It was urgent to start some mental play at once, before silly thoughts about execution get a chance to creep in. The night before, the Professor and I had played an interesting game of chess with figures made out of kneaded bread, the black figures dyed with imitation coffee; and I plunged at once into replaying that game. After it was over I began to plan in detail the lecture I was supposed to give tomorrow on the functional school of social anthropology. Then the van started.

In complete darkness when all the other senses are turned off and all contact with the outside world is through one's ears, it is surprisingly easy to tell what is happening outside. After the jostling came a very smooth, even run, the main concrete highway to Budapest.

I counted the villages, then came the well-known city noises; the suburbs of Budapest. After a while the dub-dub announced the Stalin Bridge. Yes, they were taking me to SP headquarters in Fö-utca.

When the van stopped, the SP man came in, opened the cubicle, put a blanket over my head. 'Jump' he said, holding my arms. I jumped. He manoeuvred me over a courtyard and some downward steps, then along a long corridor, at the end of which he took the blanket off. In semidarkness the SP man turned me toward the wall.

'You stand here,' he said and disappeared through a door. The smell of carbolic and refuse reminded me of the first night after my arrest and for a short while I lost my grip of myself. It was cold. I shivered and thought that nothing unbearable could happen to me. If they decided to hang me, that too would be soon over and it does not hurt anyhow. Maybe it would be better than years of prison. And then I thought I had probably missed dinner here and that it would be good to be back with the Professor and Paul and the composer. After that I pitied myself for longing to be back in prison and thought about the world outside the prison, about thousands of summer resorts full of people, about planes and trains and ships hurrying all over the globe, about the feel of a warm bath, hot food and a bed not smelling of urine.

A door opened nearby and someone said, 'You! Come in!'

Cap in hand I entered a room full of filing cabinets. A sergeant sat at a desk and the SP man stood there smoking a cigarette. The sergeant – a gypsy with pockmarked face – asked of my particulars. I hated this, because I had to answer, 'Date of release, 1964'. I had to 'deposit' everything I had in my pockets.

The questioning over, the SP man took off and pocketed my manacles. The sergeant got up and said in a self-important tone:

'I am putting you into a large cell with many people. But you are not supposed to talk. Am I understood? Not a word to anyone!'

We went through an iron door into a very hot and stuffy corridor.

The Undefeated

The rows of small iron doors on both sides showed that we had arrived at the prison section.

In front of one of the doors we stopped. Pockmark whispered to me: 'I am putting you into this cell. Forget your old number. Here you will be Number Sixteen. You don't tell your name to anyone, nor your old number. Am I understood? You are number sixteen and keep your mouth shut!'

He opened the door and whispered, 'You will find an empty place. There you'll lie down.'

The large cell was divided by iron bars into a small antechamber with a lavatory and the cell proper. Pockmark unbolted the inner door and motioned me inside. A naked electric bulb showed me a very large room. All around the wall a wooden platform was erected leaving a small well in the middle, and on that platform some twenty people slept. Just under the electric bulb a young man in a railway conductor's uniform stood at attention and wept. In one of the corners there was an empty place. I climbed up to the platform and lay down.

Pockmark tiptoed to the young railway man and whispered something into his ear, then looked round, locked the inner door and left. The young man wept quietly, swaying on his feet slightly.

I sat up again and looked around. My cellmates were not convicts but 'new ones', meaning that they had spent anything from two days to a year or more here, but were not sentenced yet. Most of them slept. On the opposite side a red-faced old man was looking at me, but did not move. When my gaze met that of the weeping young man, he looked at his feet. I looked too. His bare feet were red and enormously swollen.

He whispered something I did not understand. Then he risked a louder sentence.

'Two weeks ... I have been standing every night for two weeks, because I would not confess.'

'Sit down,' I said.

'They beat me if I do.'

'Risk it,' I answered and closed my eyes. When I woke up, the red-faced old man was knocking at the iron bars. A guard came in. The old man asked to go to the lavatory. The guard snapped, 'In the morning.'

The old man whispered to me; 'I try to hold it back half the night. Now I can't go on.' He took his boots from under the platform and urinated into them. He placed the boots carefully under the platform and stretched out. I thought of my first trip to Sicily and went to sleep.

When I woke up a new guard was standing in the ante-chamber handing some tin basins to two prisoners. Everyone stripped to the waist, went to the lavatory and washed himself in turn in one of the basins. There was only one towel and no soap.

While waiting for my turn, I counted the men. There were twenty-three of them. The first two to wash were mere kids. Next to me sat a muscular grey-haired man of about fifty. I looked at his hands and thought he must be a steelworker. I was surprised and sad to see that most of them were workers.

There was a lot of noise. The grey-haired man spoke to me without turning towards me. He asked why I was sentenced, for how long, since when, my name, everything. He was the type of man I would have been happy to have been with in a tight spot.

After washing we all had to sit down on the edge of the platform, our feet dangling. Now I looked them over and they eyed me with great interest. I was probably the first convict they had met and they saw in me their own future. From the terror in their eyes I could judge what an awful cadaver I must be.

I wanted to say something but my grey-haired friend whispered: 'Not now.' It turned out that a sergeant nicknamed 'Tiptoe' was on duty; his only ambition was to catch us talking.

Then breakfast came, a chunk of bread and the bitter black brew they called coffee. During the din of dixies my neighbour said, pointing to me, 'With the exception of the kids everyone is to give him a piece of bread.'

Everyone obeyed, and pieces of bread were passed along a chain of hands to me. I hid them behind my back. 'Eat it all up except one piece,' my neighbour ordered.

When the empty dixies were taken away, Grey-Hair told me about our cellmates. His quickly whispered sentences sounded like a report to a superior officer. It turned out that he had great respect for me as a member of the 'Rajk conspiracy'.

The kid next to him was a seventeen-year-old middle-school boy, who because he failed in Latin, tried to escape to Austria. He was caught in July. The red-faced man who urinated in his boots was a Catholic priest. The other kid, a nineteen-year-old university student, had planned to escape from the country and was denounced. The railway conductor, who was now sound asleep behind the backs of the others, was denounced by his wife who had had an affair with an SP man. Next to the priest sat a tubercular Yugoslav Communist who had escaped to Hungary in 1948 when Tito broke with Stalin. He had been promptly arrested and had been questioned ever since.

The rest were workers from various factories whose story was mostly the same. They had protested against the piece rate, or the bullying of the party secretary, or had warned some functionaries that their turning-lathe was beyond repair, that there would be a breakdown. They were arrested either because they protested or because the breakdowns actually occurred.

'It is quite simple,' Grey-Hair said, 'for every stoppage, for every mistake in planning, for every miscalculation some workers are arrested. The party, the leadership, the factory management – all these must be infallible. So they arrest us. But of course you know all this much better than me.'

'Unfortunately not,' I whispered back.

Grey-Hair turned his surprised face towards me for a second. Then he turned away and only the corner of his mouth moved as he whispered. 'Then why in holy hell did you conspire against them?'

I explained that Rajk and associates were not conspirators and that I had nothing to do with Rajk. I told him that I still kept my Communist convictions after my arrest, after the nightmare period in the Security Police cellars and even after having been sentenced.

Grey-Hair smiled. 'I am beginning to guess why people like you have been smitten down,' he whispered. 'The really bad period only started after your arrest. The Rajk trial probably served many purposes, one was the anti-Tito drive. And also it introduced the period of full terrorism. In this Rajk case they eliminated those important Communists who were blind idealists like yourself, who could have been suspected of elementary decency. The dictators got rid of

all the political parties, the Communist party included. To the cliques
of murderous bastards ruling in Moscow and in the various slave
states, convinced Communists are just as dangerous or perhaps more
dangerous than Social-Democrats or liberals.'

'What are you?' I asked, unsure what to answer.

'I was a party member till my arrest. Of course I hate them like
poison, just like everybody else … Funny, we outside, as glorious
Communist workers, hated and despised the party, while you,
enemies, hyenas, spies and Trotskyite cads, you remained loyal to the
party. The only Communists left were some fools like yourself in jail.
But in the greater jail, in the country, we could see that this stupid and
murderous tyranny has nothing to do with socialism. The true
monstrosity of the regime was exposed only after your arrest.'

'You said that it had nothing to do with socialism … Then you still
believe that there can be a decent sort of communism?'

'Indeed I don't,' Grey-Hair said. 'This rottenest of all the conceivable rotten systems is made possible by the great Communist lie. We
are all against communism because the Soviet system was born of it.
And that system stinks. The whole of it. It's not a question of mistakes
committed here or there. The whole thing stinks as it is.'

'And you say that all the Communist workers, that is, workers who
are still in the party, feel like you?'

'Ask the boys here … I don't say that you could not find a few fools
or hypocrites who still are or appear to be Communists. In our factory
we might have a dozen or so, among more than three thousand people,
but the great majority detest them.'

'Who are "them"?' I asked.

'The few thousands on the top. The cynical thugs and their paid
hirelings.'

'What about Marxism-Leninism?'

'Look, my friend,' Grey-Hair said, turning towards me, 'this
damned ideology has been rammed down our throats for five years.
For me one ideological statement is enough for the rest of my life: the
whole thing stinks as it is. This "cause" … it is an evil cause, a bankrupt
cause, a hopeless cause.'

'But look here.' I grew excited. 'What you say is terribly important for me. Do you mean to say that the monster period is a logical and inevitable consequence of Lenin's writings?'

'Why only Lenin? Throw in Marx and Engels too ... Did they or didn't they write about the dictatorship of the proletariat? Well, this is the muck to mislead the well-meaning intellectuals, the stupid workers into heroically fighting for the dictatorship of groups of power-mad bastards in the name of the proletariat.'

He talked on. He sounded convincing. I thought it possible that many workers thought as he did. And what about the peasants? How could one tell about them?

Then I remembered my 'serf'. It had happened some months before when I was arguing with Paul, who said that ninety per cent of the Hungarian population hated the regime. I said that he only met reactionaries. The workers and peasants were solidly behind the regime. For instance our guards were brutal to us because they thought of us as the enemies of the regime and hated us for it. We were in the middle of this argument when the spy-hole was opened and a voice asked, 'Which of you is Paloczi-Horvath?' I went to the door. A new guard stood outside, a corporal. He asked me, 'Is your family from Orkeny?' I told him that my uncle had an estate there. The guard smiled.

'Those were the good old days. We kids used to go up to the tennis courts as ball-boys for the young ladies. They gave us a pengö each time as a tip.'

Behind me the Professor snorted with merriment. The corporal told me he would get us double rations and do everything he could to help us. When he was gone, my three cellmates said in a chorus, 'Those were the good old days!' The corporal was on duty for three weeks in our wing and really did everything to help us. Paul and the others called him my 'serf'.

After lunch 'Tiptoe' went off duty and open conversation began. For a while they talked about interrogations. It turned out that Grey-Hair was no steelworker but an electro-technician whom the party had sent to the Tiszalok project where a huge hydro-electric power station was being built by eighteen thousand convict laborers. Grey-Hair as a free foreman should have co-operated with the Security Police running the project and the concentration camp. He realized that most of the convicts were simply arrested and sentenced to hard labor in order to furnish cheap labor for the project. He spoke up for them and after a very severe beating was sent to this cellar. Now he was supposed to confess that imperialist agents had paid him to worm his way into the camp. Grey-Hair smiled and quoted the party daily: 'The enthusiasm of the Hungarian people creates the great Tiszalok hydroelectrical power station.'

Three young workers who sat in the opposite corner were conspirators. Early in the year the large-scale deportation of bourgeois elements from Budapest had begun. An old engineer from their factory was deported with his family to a small village near the eastern frontier. The deportees were not permitted to take money with them and if they did not find some agricultural work, they simply starved. The workers of the factory collected some money and sent the engineer food parcels. For this conspiracy the three workers who organized the collection were promised ten years hard labour by the SP officers conducting their hearing.

It must have been nearly three o'clock because we were disturbed from then on by guards who took some of the men away for hearings. The first to go was the railway conductor, who started to cry the moment his number was called. The three conspirators and the two boys were taken upstairs too. The last to go was the Catholic priest. I was left with some workers who questioned me for a long time about the way the SP got false confessions, about the personalities involved in the Rajk case, their past history and prison behavior.

At four o'clock we had our dinner – beans and a piece of bread – and their questioning went on. Later the younger boy returned with a swollen face and a defiant look in his eyes. The 'conspirators', the three young workers who had made a collection for deportees, hobbled back; their feet had been clubbed with rubber truncheons. The last to return was the railway conductor with enormously swollen hands, sentenced again to stand at attention till the morning.

And all the while the questioning went on. Grey-Hair and his friends asked me matter-of-fact questions. They were not interested in theories, just facts.

At last we got permission to lie down. Twenty-two men lay on their backs, staring at the ceiling. The railway conductor stood at attention in the middle of the cell. The Catholic priest was still 'upstairs'.

The two boys talked about girls. Someone raved about a cigarette. I shut my eyes. I was scared. This was something new. Up till now I had weathered everything without loosing my grip on myself, or getting frightened. But now there was fear in me.

A guard opened the door with a bang and let the Catholic priest in. He was not a nice sight. He stumbled to his bunk on the platform, turned towards the wall and started to pray.

Next to me lay Grey-Hair. He watched me with an earnest look. I looked back at him and tried to smile. He reached out and touched my hand for a second. Then I closed my eyes again.

During the next three days they treated me with tact and consideration, but each of them told me his story and many stories about their friends. 'You should know how the workers live,' they remarked time and again.

Though conversion to the Communist faith had been prepared by a long process, by many outside influences, mental and emotional factors, the first steps towards conversion were through theory, through ideology. And during the salvation period the same theory, the same ideology fought a desperate rear-guard action, trying to save something from the wreckage.

Looking back, I sometimes feel that this poisonous delusion produced its own antitoxin. While the basis of the ideology is the supreme importance of the working class, middle and upper-class converts are originally motivated by an abstract love and real respect for the workers. Grey-Hair and his companions helped me to liberate my mind from the worker myth. The fact that the workers had turned against the system helped to give the last push to the already tottering edifice of my *Weltanschauung*.

When I had entered their cell a few days previously, I still thought of myself as a Communist; I had grave doubts about Stalin but believed that Marxism-Leninism was on the whole sound, still the only possible way to the future. In the big cell the desperate rear-guard action had started. Retreat from Stalin to Lenin, then from Lenin to Marx, until finally he was abandoned too.

When I entered the cell, I had a clear-cut world view. I felt intellectually safe and strong. Everything, the whole universe, all the phenomena of society, science and art were neatly ordered. I felt I was on the right side, on the side of the future of mankind.

When the click came I felt neither proud nor happy.

I spent six or seven days in the mass cell with its stifling air, its unhappy human stew. The railway conductor still stood every night to attention. Some were taken away, replaced by an arrival bewildered by our nightmarish cellar existence, telling new stories about the monster period outside. We still sat nineteen hours a day perched on the edge of the wooden platform. We still talked a lot.

And then one morning without previous meditation, without any planning or decision I suddenly began to speak as a non-Communist. Up till then I had been pretty reticent. I had asked many questions, discussed facts, but I had never joined their 'ideological platform', that is, '*the whole thing stinks as it is*'.

That morning we had an almost tolerant sergeant on duty and we could talk properly. Suddenly I found myself using the same language that they did and exposing the Soviet system and the Bolshevik party history in great detail. The cell was interested. I told them about Lenin's suppressed testament, about the systematic falsification of history, about the monster Stalin must have been in his youth.

Grey-Hair, who was still with us, interrupted me once to ask how long I had known all this. I automatically told him the truth: a long time.

Then I stopped talking. Great God! What did the word 'know' mean? For clearly I had *known* all this and much more and at the same time had not known it. What was this? Insanity? Idiocy? Yes, of course I knew how history was falsified. Of course I had heard about the mass purges in the Soviet Union. Of course among thousands of other facts my memory stored the facts about elimination of whole peoples and nations by the Kremlin leaders. Of course I knew everything.

What was I? An erudite idiot? What kind of schizophrenia had got hold of me? What monstrosity infected me? With what monstrosity had I helped to infect the world?

That night the hard wooden planks on which we slept seemed to be red hot. I turned and turned and tossed myself, disturbing my neighbours. I had to exercise the utmost self-control to keep myself from shouting and raving. There was a tremendous rush in my body. I wanted to run and run and run. To run out of the world. The greatest enemy of convicts, impatience, got hold of me.

The neatly ordered world became a chaos. I was tossing now on waves of despair, in outer darkness. I craved all sorts of action. I wanted to make order in my brain in a desperate hurry. I must decide at once, but with great care, with all the prudence and sanity I could muster, to do ... what? Where was I? To find my position? To have a new faith instead of the lost one? Instead of the faith I long to destroy? Hurry, hurry, hurry! Clarify everything! Hurry!

Grey-Hair called the guard. I had an attack of fever, and was permitted to lie down during the day, was even given two blankets to lie on. Grey-Hair nursed me.

He told me that during my attack of fever I kept repeating, 'Nothing left to believe.' He smiled tolerantly and just said:

'You intellectuals ...'

Chapter Sixteen

I SPENT A FEW MORE DAYS in the company of my worker friends, recuperating. Then suddenly I was transferred to another part of the building, to a solitary cell. I had barely started to get acquainted with myself as a non-Communist when I was taken for interrogation to the same colonel who had given me the Blue Book about the Rajk case to read, and whose cynically frank talk started me perhaps on the first steps towards disenchantment. He again ordered food for me and began a general conversation about the political history of Hungary since 1935. This conversation went on for days. He had me transferred to a better cell, ordered special food for me, but gave still no indication of why he discussed with me the history of the illegal Communist party in prewar Hungary.

Then he handed me over to one of his assistants, a captain who during the next two weeks tried to persuade me to turn state's witness against some of my friends and acquaintances. He was interested in Geza Losonczy with whom I edited the party weekly *Tovabb*, and other non-Muscovite Communists. As I was not prepared to invent crimes against them, the usual round of sleeplessness, standing at attention, reflector in my face and threats about worse things to come, began again. During this interrogation period the captain hinted that the arch-criminal in the present conspiracy was Janos Kadar, who was Minister of Interior during the Rajk trial.

When I got back from the hearings to my cellmates, I lay ill and crushed for weeks.

By this time we had heard about the equivalents of the Rajk trial in some other satellite states. In Bulgaria Traitso Kostev, the famous

Communist who spent eighteen years altogether in jail for his conviction, was hanged as a spy, although he retracted his police confession at the public trial. We heard about similar trials in Albania, Romania and Poland. By now we were taking part in the daily walks in the courtyard, we went from time to time to the prison hospital for treatment, we talked to the convict-orderlies, and heard a lot of outside news. We knew that former Communists who lived at one time in the Hungarian parts of Czechoslovakia, were being interrogated about some Czechoslovak Communist leaders. So they were preparing a rigged trial in Prague too.

The SP network in the Soviet orbit is really international, with a concomitant convict's international. Although at times, mainly during the first custody period, the SP takes great care to keep prisoners apart, after the court sentence they get mixed up. As a precautionary measure they often transfer convicts from cell to cell, from wing to wing, and even from prison to prison. Convicts having some particular information are frequently exchanged. The various 'national' SP organizations make arrests on each other's behalf. For the preparation of the Rajk case, for instance, Istvan Stolte, one of the principal false witnesses, was kidnapped by the Soviet MVD from Wasserburg near Munich, then taken to Baden in Austria to the MVD headquarters there. The Russian General Bielkin brought him personally by car to Budapest. The American Noel Field was arrested with his wife in Poland and sent to Budapest to be another state's witness of the Rajk trial. Stolte was then sentenced to imprisonment for life (I shared a cell with him for a while), and Noel Field to fifteen years in prison. In a larger rigged trial most of the Soviet orbit will contribute incriminating witnesses. If there are not enough witness candidates, say, in Romania for a Zionist plot, then Zionists from Hungary, Poland and Russia are 'loaned' to the Romanian SP. All SP minutes, files, testimonials, trial reports are prepared with nine copies. (We all had to sign nine copies of our confessions.) One copy of everything is sent to the Moscow MVD headquarters, which is the nerve centre of the SP network. The many millions of files enable the producers of the large and small rigged trials to have a wide choice of actors in the planned trials. When the scripts are written, these actors' names are generally included, even before their first hearing.

This system makes it possible for the convicts to get inside information about the SP international. In a larger cell in one of the SP headquarters one might meet a convict who was loaned for interrogation by, say, the Czechoslovak SP. In a week or two this man could tell one about the collective knowledge of the convict population in Czechoslovakia. As in the rigged trials the Communist old guard has generally a large role, former party secretaries, former members of Central Executive and Politbureau can clear up mysteries of party history which puzzled Communists for a great many years. The 'suicide' of Jan Masaryk, the Foreign Minister of Czechoslovakia, might for instance be a mystery to the outside world. Inside the Czech prisons, convicts even know the names of the two SP thugs who threw him out of the window. They also know that throwing people out of windows is one of the less frequent methods of getting rid of people in the Soviet orbit. The convicts in other countries know that too. The man from Czechoslovakia has information about Russian, Polish, Romanian and Hungarian convicts who were loaned to their SP. In this way, through the underground information service of the prison international, one might learn in Budapest about events which happened half a year before in the Ljubljanka Jail in Moscow or in one of the punitive camps in Vorkuta. The information might be even less up-to-date. One might learn about events that had happened two or three years before. But those events, of course, were still not known in the outside world.

As our batch of heavy politicals were released within the jail from the rigid initial purdah, we had information literally showered on us. I was grateful that by this time I was already known to be disenchanted, because all the convicts talked openly to me. Only those were shunned who were still 'under the banner of idiocy', that is, those who clung to their old faith.

In the autumn of 1951 we began to realize that the Soviet MVD, General Bielkin and his apparatus of experts, traveled from capital to capital in order to direct and supervise the large rigged trials. Be it the Rajk case in Hungary, the confession trial in Albania, or the Traitso

Kostev affair in Bulgaria – the most important hearings were conducted by the Soviet General Bielkin himself. The trials were far too important to leave their management to the colonial Security Police organization. (We started to use the word *colonial* instead of *satellite*. The moon is the satellite of the earth. But the so-called satellites are colonies *within* the Soviet orbit.)

It was in the company of Paul Ignotus that I first started to get to know the real face of Communism. While I was possessed by the obsession, the defence mechanism of the convert, the impatient faith of the true believer, and the mental blinkers of a closed system of thought made it impossible for me to see *the system as a whole from the outside*. And even many of the details were blurred. There were details which I simply failed to see, there were other details again which I did not understand. And even such a very large 'detail' as our own rigged trial prompted me to many explanations, but I never saw its true nature.

Now most of the convicts were whispering about the impending trial of Janos Kadar. Many of our prison mates were interrogated about him or his associates. And in hurried conversations during chance meetings in the hospital corridor, through wall telegraphy and other means, we exchanged our information.

At the beginning of December Paul and I were again taken to SP headquarters and again heard about Kadar and his associates. In trying to piece together for myself the life story of Kadar, I attempted for the first time in my life to analyze the real development of a Communist leader. It was only when I tried to picture Kadar's life and development that I realized how much I knew of real Hungarian party history. All the various details which were suppressed in me by the defence mechanism now came to light and it was easy to fit them into a general picture. By that time I had revised for myself the political history of Hungary since 1945. The convicts of various vintage furnished adequate details to this version.

I knew that sooner or later I should see Kadar in the dock. He was always considered by Communists in Hungary to be the 'real thing' – an industrial worker who joined the party in his teens, was educated by the party and became one of its leaders. In picturing Kadar's story for myself, I tried to analyze the pattern of development of a 'working-class cadre'.

The start is quite ordinary. A very young worker of working-class origin is spurred into activity by moral indignation. He joins the small illegal group of Communists who fight against social injustice and for a world of peace and plenty. The fine fervour of feeling which radiates from the small group infects him, inspires him to learn. He has blind faith in the two or three fully fledged Communists he meets. They have quiet assurance, immense knowledge and the power of fanaticism. They can give him the key to the future: that Marxist theory which will make the working-class invincible. He learns 'Marxist thinking' before he has had time to learn to think. He enters a world of abstractions when totally ignorant of the world. After very little schooling and still less reading, he reads 'theory'. He learns about Feudalism and Capitalism and Surplus Value, about Formal and Real Democracy. Later he meets a long series of sublime word-gods like the elusive Negation of Negation, and the Change from Quantity into Quality. He grapples with Dialectical Logic, that wonderful Aladdin's lamp of the movement, when still unspoiled by the bad bourgeois magic of Formal Logic. He has not yet heard of Plato but his enthusiastic head is filled by the Holy Platonic Ideas of the movement.

He learns party history too. At times there are slight hitches. On his second seminar it turns out that he was under the impression that Opportunist is just a synonym for Social-Democrat. But on the whole his advance is swift and soon he is teaching theory to others.

He leads a puritanical existence. The Hungarian Communists are at that time 'sectarians'; even according to later official party histories. They are on the whole a sombre, muscle-bound lot. Young girls in the movement are encouraged to conceal as far as possible the fact that they have young, bulging breasts. The comrades are very earnest, very dignified and lead a most frugal life. Their life is under very severe party control. The party watches you all the time. Soon you have your own telescreen in your skull. You reprimand yourself severely on those rare occasions when your thinking strays from the straight and narrow path of the present party line and party mood. In Freudian terminology:

you produce your own Superego or Father (or Big Brother). On the uppermost shelf of your brain a tiny security police officer starts watching you.

All this is well known. The fact that Janos Kadar is called a steadfast and promising young comrade by the leaders shows that he has advanced swiftly through this process. He soon becomes a leader in a small way himself. By this time the epoch of Hitler and the Spanish Civil War is on, producing current proofs of the Theory.

Janos Kadar is still comparatively normal. There is no divergence between his private thoughts and public utterances. His thinking is monolithic. He thinks that his party is the Party of Truth. A Communist is honest. A Communist never lies. All inconsistencies are explained away by 'dialectics'.

During the Second World War Kadar is one of the ten-man leadership in Budapest. The leader of the illegal party, Laszlo Rajk, is his friend. Rajk is Kadar's ideal – a man of working-class origin who became a 'university-educated intellectual', a great Communist, hero of the Spanish Civil War. Rajk, whose illegal name is now Kirgiz, is the bravest of the brave. So is his wife. In 1943 she is arrested by the Hungarian Gestapo and tortured for weeks. They do not know that she is the wife of Rajk, they have only a well-founded suspicion that she must know the illegal leaders. They hang her up by her feet and beat her naked body with rubber truncheons. They want to know only two names: that of the leader and his deputy. Mrs. Rajk saves the lives of her husband and Janos Kadar by not talking.

In 1944 Kadar tries to escape over the frontier to go on a mission to Tito. He is arrested but soon released. At the end of 1944, when Budapest is besieged by the Russians, Kadar is sent on another mission by the party. He has to cross over the fighting lines to the Russians to establish contact. He succeeds in that and meets the Muscovite Hungarian party boss, Matyas Rakosi and his deputy, Erno Gerö.

Gerö and Rakosi initiate the non-Muscovite Hungarian Communist party leaders into the antechamber of Stalinist leadership. Here ideology is taken seriously or utterly disregarded – according to need. Here people are prepared for the great Stalinist principle: you are justified in killing a few thousand people in order to build *a happy life for billions of the coming generations of humans*. That wonderful future can be built only on the basis of a strong and ever stronger Soviet Union, so the interests of the Soviet Union coincide with those of the human race. It was obvious in 1945, when the party had not yet attained power, that the great strategical aims of the party must not be disclosed to the masses. The masses must be won over by the proper tactical steps. Tactics: there is the secret of everything. By clever tactical moves you can ensure your piecemeal advance and liquidate your enemies one by one.

The 'realities' of political struggle teach the Communist 'cadres'. There is still a telescreen in the brain of every faithful party member, but his thinking is not monolithic any more. His private truth differs all the time from the public 'truth', that is, from the propaganda line of the day. There is a mental split between the private and public self as far as truth is concerned.

But this is only the first of a long series of splits caused by political 'reality'. While organized public falsehood takes the place of public opinion, the first moral split occurs. In private life one is or tries to be a decent person – loyal to friends, not given to fraud, theft, slander and murder. But your public self approves of all of these if committed for the welfare and happiness of coming generations (that is in the interest of the great Soviet fatherland). If you are a rank and file Communist, this moral split does not cut very deep, you do not see much of what is going on behind the scenes. Your part is to approve of deeds done by others, by the higher ups. Your part is to defend those deeds and feel enthusiastic about them. If you are sincere to yourself, you explain your doubts and anxieties by the fact that you are still under the influence of bourgeois sentimentality, that you are ideologically not strong enough. If you are higher up in the hierarchy, you have less time for moral bellyaches and are more exposed to the hypno-pedagogics of the great leaders.

By this time you hear nothing else but textbook jargon. A man like Kadar, as first secretary of the Budapest party organization, meets life only in the form of reports by subordinates. And they report not reality but the officially obligatory Marxist clichés they are just in the process of learning. Not 'objective' truth but political truth is reported. 'Truth is what helps the party to advance.'

Intellectuals have a bad habit of intellectualizing reality. Of taking 'broad views' of things, of having a sweepingly theoretical approach to everything. But these shortcomings of the intellectuals are generally counterbalanced by culture. In men of Kadar's type there is no such counterbalance. In their generally far-too-long speeches they quite often betray a surprising degree of ignorance. They become experienced cliché-mongers and quite clever political manipulators while remaining essentially uncultured. And anyhow they consider themselves tough fighters in the war for socialism and teach others to be like that. In 1947 there is still an *esprit de corps* among the Communists. In public life there are members of the three other parties not yet liquidated. So Communists are loyal to Communists. Strong friendships are formed. Such a friendship exists between Janos Kadar and Laszlo Rajk.

Kadar is by now one of the popular leaders of the party. He is a member of the Central Committee and the Political Bureau of the party. He is known to be a mild-mannered, very brave and industrious man. In 1947 in Miskolc there are disturbances among the industrial workers. Kadar alone faces an angry mob and quietens them.

But those who knew him before discover a change in his face. His eyes have a colder look. He has a curiously neutral gaze. Once he 'adored humanity'. This has changed into abstract feeling: into adoration of the humanity of the day after tomorrow and into an indifference toward the fate of present-day humans and countrymen.

In 1948 the Communist party gets absolute power. Kadar is Deputy Secretary General of the party. At that time Rakosi sets up the Soviet system in Hungary concerning Politbureau members. They all have luxurious cars, sumptuous houses and villas at their disposal. Each Politbureau member receives a checkbook *without limitations*. They have no bank accounts, they can just draw *any* amount from the *National Bank*.

The leaders of this fight for the cause of the working class lead the existence of hard-working millionaires. They rush about in their huge automobiles, protected by thick curtains from the inquisitive gaze of pedestrians. They take part in conferences, state banquets; they direct the affairs of the state and of the party. They get up early, go to bed late. They all learn Russian to be able to converse with their Soviet opposite numbers – and try to relax according to taste. After the hard and frugal life of early days, Kadar relaxes in a modest way. He has a girl friend of petty-bourgeois descent. The party does not permit him to marry her, but they live as the most faithful of suburban couples, surrounded by the streamlined luxury produced for Politbureau members by the housing department of the party.

The workers do not have much place in Comrade Kadar's life at this time. The old fervour of feeling returns to him only on his visits to Laszlo Rajk and his wife. Rajk – a blind idealist – retains his old enthusiasm and is at this time still nearest to the simple faithful Communists of the West. His friendship with Rajk gives Kadar some sort of moral grip on himself.

In the beginning of 1949, Rakosi cunningly cajoles the chosen few top-rankers into accepting the brutal tactics of the following period. After the party gets power – instead of persuasion, promises and good pay – the workers must be driven by terrorism to work. Rakosi teaches his disciples to despise present-day humanity, workers included. His argument is most simple. In order to ensure global victory of communism, all Communist countries must develop the largest possible heavy industry and must be victorious in the armament race. But the workers want better wages and better living conditions *now*. Hence they have to be forced by terrorism to sacrifice everything now for the bright future of coming generations.

The party is in power. It is 1949. The loyalty between Communists is a thing of the past. The huge purges – as yet only leading to expulsion – have been made. But Rakosi soon announces in a speech that 'hostile elements who have wormed their way into the party will be expelled and locked up.' Rajk has been demoted from the rank of Minister of the Interior to the unimportant position of a Hungarian Minister of Foreign Affairs. His successor in the Ministry of Interior is Janos Kadar.

Personally, they are still good friends. In the spring Mrs. Rajk gives birth to a son. Janos Kadar acts as godfather. A few weeks later Rajk is arrested. The Russian General Bielkin is in town. Scores and later hundreds of old-guard Communists, Spanish Civil War heroes, well-known Marxists and tried comrades of illegal days are arrested. They are called 'the spy band of Rajk'.

Janos Kadar, the mild-mannered Minister of the Interior, declares in speech after speech that Rajk is a despicable spy, imperialist and Titoist agent, who started life as a stool pigeon of the Hungarian political police and later on worked for the Gestapo, for the French Deuxième Bureau and the American OSS. He repeats accusations which he knows to be totally false.

Janos Kadar is Minister of the Interior and Mrs. Rajk has inflammation of the breast in a cellar cubicle of the SP prison because her infant son has been taken away from her on higher orders. (For a long time all of us who were in neighbouring cubicles during these events thought that this was the doing of Kadar. Years later we found out that we were mistaken.)

In 1951 Janos Kadar himself was arrested. His arrest must have been a great shock to him, but by no means a surprise. Kadar – the intimate of Rakosi, who was responsible for planning and directing several rigged trials – knew that the life of the party was an endless series of rigged trials, small ones and big ones. The practice of 'criticism-self-criticism' in everyday party life is nothing but a miniature confession trial when party members furnish the trumped-up charges against themselves. They get up and take the blame for mistakes committed by the organization, by the higher ups, or by the supreme leadership. Self-criticism is satisfying only if one overstates one's crimes and mistakes. Of course everybody present knows perfectly well that the person confessing various mistakes and political deviations has not committed them at all. But without this system the party line cannot be changed all the time. Without this system every party member cannot be constantly at the mercy of the party leadership. And without this, of course, the party leader cannot appear infallible. Every confession of mistakes, every political recantation is a potential confession of guilt in one of the future rigged trials. 'Self-criticism' can also lead to arrest any minute. 'Self-criticism' – that is, the system of voluntary scapegoats for the mistakes of leadership – is forced on all party members by threats and by the general atmosphere of terrorism. To refuse self-criticism can and will get you in jail.

These are the small rigged trials in the everyday life of the party. The big confession trials, which serve the purpose of periodically getting rid of emerging personalities – and are used at the same time to propagate the new political line of the party – keep up the atmosphere of terrorism so necessary for the Stalinist system. Here party members and top-rankers who are constantly being prepared for their roles by the institution of self-criticism are tortured, cajoled, threatened and tricked into committing moral and physical suicide.

Kadar knew this very well. But he did not think that after being a victimizer for a long time he was to be a victim of the same process. He was smitten down with the utmost brutality, and tortured for a long time, because he knew from personal experience that promises made to candidates of rigged trials are never kept, and therefore he did not sign the confessions demanded of him. Top-rankers are generally from the very start tortured with the most vicious intensity. They are degraded and humiliated so as to make them forget what important persons they were. 'We shall beat the Politbureau membership out of you!'

Torture affects different persons differently. This is a truism. One can only guess the effect on Kadar. It must have had the same effect on him as the sixteen years of prison on Rakosi – making him even more inhuman or infra-human. Utter degradation and unbearable pain leave curious traces on the subconscious mind. They lead to almost senseless moral perfectionism in some people, and to a pent-up craving for revenge in others. This latter type feels that by his past suffering he is justified in doing anything. I repeat, one can only guess. But having seen hundred of persons before and after such an ordeal, I feel that my guess is not far from the truth.

On the eleventh of December, 1951, we were taken again to SP headquarters and the trial took place the same day. Only SP officers were present. I was the first witness. On the dock sat Janos Kadar and three others: Gyula Kallay, the former Foreign Secretary, Ferenc Donath and Sandor Haraszti. The others had been tortured just as much as

Kadar. But their faces had gained somehow in dignity. Kadar's was frightening. He looked at me with a terrified stare. He knew that I had every reason to dislike him. He knew the methods of the SP and was prepared for the worst. The others looked at me with encouraging eyes. One smiled. Some people trust human beings. Some do not.

The vile creature who acted as presiding judge, Dr. Jonas, who had sentenced me barely a year before to fifteen years of hard labour, now read out the questions prepared by the SP. He fidgeted in a most uneasy manner when instead of the expected replies I answered only in generalities. I did not utter the names of the accused at all. After me Ignotus was the next witness. He too answered only with erudite lectures about politics, mentioning no names.

When the whole thing was over, Ignotus remarked, 'Funny, everything we said during this trial could appear in the London *Times*, without us having to be ashamed of it.'

We were sent back to jail manacled to each other. We two 'enemies of the people' of 'bourgeois descent' did not help Dictator Rakosi and the SP to kill their accomplice, Kadar. He was sentenced to life imprisonment.

But to get back to Kadar's face. Before giving his testimony, the witness is asked by the presiding judge to look at the accused persons and tell the court whether he knows them or not. I took a long time to look. A new face is a sensation within prison circumstances. And one's eyes become more sensitive, more perceptive. I looked at four faces, all known to me previously: at that of Kadar and those of his three fellow accused. One of the latter had been previously a tough and rather insensitive party official. His face now – after many months of torture and nightmarish existence – was strangely human. The last accused, Sandor Haraszti, a fiery old revolutionary, had become beautiful. Kadar's once handsome face had grown more distorted. He had not been above it at all. His face had a cowardly, and at the same time, ferocious expression.

After I had made my testimony facing the judge, I turned again and went out slowly so as to have a good look at them. The other three looked at me with friendly, approving eyes. In Kadar's gaze there was only misunderstanding and wonder.

I had the impression that torture had not made Kadar a better man. But later on, when I knew that he was being kept in solitary confinement I thought that perhaps he would change. He spent nearly two years in solitary cell, called MZ (*maganzarka*) in Hungarian. We all knew by experience that solitary confinement is a very effective purgatory. There is a chance for expiation, for facing oneself and one's past squarely. Indeed, it is most difficult to pose to oneself, to go on lying to oneself about anything. Favourite ideas about one's 'personality' are rewarded and the general effect of it all is catharsis in the original Greek sense of the word.

But not in everybody!

Janos Kadar still had many surprises in store for the world.

After the trial Paul Ignotus was taken to the prison hospital and I remained alone in the cell. I had some translation work and spent long evenings and nights thinking through my new problems. Just before Christmas a guard brought in a great pile of books for translation. It was a wonderful Christmas present! After the dull nonsense we had translated up till then we received the following books: The first four volumes of Churchill's Second World War Memoirs, Butcher's *My Three Years with Eisenhower*, Basil Davidson's *Partisan Picture*, Ian Colvin's *Chief of Intelligence: The Story of Admiral Canaris*. All during the bleak Christmas holidays I was reading Churchill, enraptured by his tremendous personality, his rich style, his vitality. Later during the next year and a half I was translating Churchill with Paul. I am sure it was the most pleasant hard labour ever done in the world.

It was already 1952. Outside, in the greater jail called Hungary, the monster period reached its peak. The new batches of convicts arrived with stories which made us less sorry for being in jail. The liquidation of the former middle classes and the 'rich' peasants, the *Khulaks*, went on. They were deported by the thousands, week by week. Small-town cobblers who refused to join the shoemakers collective, peasants with twenty acres of land who did not join the kolkhozes, former solicitors' clerks who were denounced as clerico-fascists, the families of former army officers, almost all former landowners, bank employees, noblemen, and so on, were deported at half an hour's notice. They had to leave their homes with the exception of a single suitcase per person. They were evacuated to small villages and hamlets in Eastern Hungary and were placed under police surveillance. They were forbidden to leave the village or hamlet. Most of their money was taken away. If there was need for unskilled labourers in the village, they were lucky; if not they simply starved.

In offices, factories, plants, warehouses, shops, schools, scientific institutions, kolkhozes, governmental and municipal offices – in every place that people worked for a living, and those who did not, were deported – people had a nightmarish existence. The holy trinity of the party secretary of the cell, its cadre-man and the chief of the personnel department (the official representative of the SP) was watching over everybody. They preached vigilance – eternal vigilance for the class enemy and the imperialist spy was ever-present.

As in the Soviet Union and all her other colonies, in Hungary too they had the cadre-file system. There is a 'cadre-file' for every citizen which contains his or her detailed autobiography, school record, work record, party record, all information, secret denunciations, 'character-estimates,' and so forth; every bit of malevolent gossip picked up about him or her by SP officers, agents and 'contacts' in the various governmental, municipal, and other organizations; every report about him or her by the various party secretaries and 'people's instructors'.

Every Communist official must be in contact with the SP. In party headquarters there is a cadre department and there is the Party Central Control Committee, both keeping a watchful eye on every party member. In every government department there is likewise a cadre department which watches over the nonparty people. Everyone has to fill out questionnaires at least once a year, and at each change of job or promotion has to hand in a detailed autobiography in several copies. All these are kept in the different cadre files but the main file is in the SP centre.

Let us say that Mr. X. after finishing his schools is employed in the textile retail shop in the Vth district of Budapest. The cadre department of the Vth district textile retail directorate gets his school files. The cadre official questions him. Being an unimportant employee he has to fill out a questionnaire of only twenty-eight questions, among them all details about possible foreign travels undertaken by him or any of his relatives, and all details of past and present political affiliation of himself and family. This and a detailed autobiography are kept at the directorate, at the trust, at the ministry and at the SP – if he is not a member of the party. If he is, there are files about him in the cell, precinct and district-party organizations, and so on.

If he is not a party member, he must join the trade union. The cell organizer there must report about him twice a year. From among the party members – without his official knowledge – a 'people's educator' is appointed to deal with him. This person has occasional conversations with him, tries to collect information from him, from colleagues and reports about his 'ideological development' to his superiors. These reports are also kept in the various files about him. All gossip, accusations, mistakes in work or in private life are reported.

These cadre files make the work of the SP much easier. During the monster epoch the various city, county and town SP offices were in Stakhanovite contest with each other. Within the offices the various departments and sections were in competition. The aim was to unmask the greatest possible number of criminal class enemies and imperialist spies. Arrests by the SP became daily occurrences. Naturally all 'class enemies' became imperialist spies during the interrogation period. There was a time when the number of confessed and convicted imperialist spies was well above a hundred and fifty thousand. As the Stakhanovite competition was very intensive, the methods became cruder. People arrived with missing eyes, with crippled bodies. In the prison hospitals the number of hopelessly crushed people grew day by day. While the blue police dealing with ordinary criminal cases had seventeen prisons in the country, four prison hospitals and one mental home for convicts, we learned that there were about seven SP mental homes for political convicts.

A cellmate of mine who had spent four years in Soviet prisons said that Hungary was really well on the way to becoming like the great Soviet example.

But daily life in the country was nearly unbearable even for those who thought that they had no reason to fear sudden arrest. If work started in the factory at six in the morning, everyone had to be present twenty minutes earlier, so as not to be late for the *Szabad Nep* quarter of an hour. During these fifteen minutes someone had to read aloud the leading article of the official party daily, *Szabad Nep,* the same article which the central broadcasting station read at least twice a day. Naturally everybody had to subscribe to this paper, or to its local equivalent. At times the workers had to come even earlier because of one of the 'movements', the aim of which was to prepare everything at the place of work before starting time. This 'movement' was, as was the reading of the party daily, naturally strictly voluntary and the workers 'unanimously demanded' permission to do it. There was the Kuznietrov movement, in which the workers 'fought for the care of tools and their repair'; the Korabelnikova movement of doing one day's work with materials saved during the previous month; the Nazarova movement to keep your place of work clean and healthy; the Kovaliov movement, in which engineers and technicians co-operated for the intensification of labour competitions.

All such movements were launched by very long and most enthusiastic meetings after work. The workers who left home at four-thirty in the morning often sat at such meetings till nine or ten o'clock at night. There were long speeches. Whenever Stalin's, Rakosi's or some other demigod's name was mentioned, everybody jumped to attention and then the 'stormy applause' broke out. This was then transformed into a rhythmic clapping for minutes. No one dared to stop clapping and after two or three minutes the party secretary gave the sign to stop. On the platform facing the audience sat the factory and party leadership. From the platform SP eyes watched the audience. If someone did not make an enthusiastic enough face during the rhythmic clapping, he was a marked man. People acquired the compulsory enthusiasm grimace, and after a time it cost no effort at all. But the drudges of offices, factories and kolkhozes were not very happy when after ten hours' work and two hours' voluntary enthusiasm they returned home to find the Marxist-Leninist seminar textbook awaiting them. Next day after work it would be the seminar for hours, then something else.

And for all this people received only ten months' pay a year. The compulsory peace-loan contribution equaled one month's wage or salary. People earning more had to 'loan' six weeks' pay or even two months'. Everybody had to subscribe to at least one party newspaper. There were no excuses. If in a family five people were working, five copies had to be subscribed for. Everybody had to belong to a trade union and pay the dues. There were voluntary collections for North-Korean or Greek children, for Guatemalan intellectuals or for the oppressed peoples of America. Books had to be bought. If the personnel department chief received an adverse report from the cultural department of the factory about the book-buying record of a worker, he got into trouble. So everybody had to buy at least some of the Marxist-Leninist classics.

In 1950 the piece-rate system was introduced in industry, which practice is, according to Marxist analysis, the worst form of capitalist exploitation. This was connected with the norm system. The production norms were raised constantly. Rakosi announced at the same time that 'we cannot eat up our future'. Hence the prices of food and various consumer goods were raised by governmental decree overnight by fifty to one hundred fifty per cent. The price of butter and lard was trebled. 'Socialist society is free of the vagaries of the market. Price policy is one of the tools of building socialism.'

The various movements imported from the great Soviet fatherland followed people into their homes. There was the movement to collect scrap paper, scrap textiles, scrap metal. The blocks of flats and tenements were in 'glorious socialist competition for raising the amount of scrap paper (or textile or metal) collected'. You had to have enormous paper bags to collect the different items. Once a month someone called for them. Nonparticipation might have aroused suspicion, so you did your best to collect and collect.

And there were the 'people's educators'! They were Communist party members who had to visit Communist and non-Communist homes alike to explain the latest victory of the Communist government. Sunday mornings were often taken up by such calls. People took the visitors into their rooms, properly decorated with the pictures of the great ones. (Because of the possibility of such visits, people could enjoy even in their homes the beauties of Stalin, Rakosi and the other beloved leaders.) There you sat, facing the two 'people's educators' who explained 'what a great blow it was for the imperialists that our government had introduced the piece-rate system!' You listened with properly enthusiastic face, repeated some holy sentences from the party daily, and the ceremony was over. Again you had to take part in the 'parents' co-operative' of your children's school. This enthusiastic co-operative had to prepare the various festivities, discuss the proper Marxist-Leninist education of the children. This was a 'discussion meeting'. You had to visit many.

You were most enthusiastic; you always voted unanimously; you took part in many voluntary competitions. You were always fighting for something. In your office you decided in a rapturous mood to fight for the reduction of electricity consumption, or to make a better use of paper, or something similar. And first of all, you fought for peace. Thirty or forty office drudges or worn-out workers had to gather in an 'improvised rally' regularly twice a month to fight for peace, that is to repeat the slogans given out by the party secretary.

People were not safe in the streets either. A worker who was on night shift went to shop during the day. But there were plain clothes SP men and women patrolling the streets, watching shops and department stores. They stopped people and demanded an explanation for not being at work.

If all this got you down and if after receiving your pay you went out to one of the remaining very few restaurants to eat a good meal, you were likely to get into trouble. If you ordered a more expensive meal than usual, perhaps with wine, someone called up the SP and by the time you had forgotten for a short while the wonderful life under your beloved leaders, the SP man was there with the question, 'How could you afford this, comrade?'

There were houses in which someone denounced the neighbours on the basis of kitchen refuse. It contained for instance chicken bones or too many egg shells. How could they afford it?

It was dangerous to keep too much food at home or too many consumer's goods. During 1952 and early 1953 many times ten thousand were arrested for 'capitalistic hoarding'. This was also a welcome method of getting rid of unpleasant people. I met people in prison who had been sentenced to two years for possessing five pounds of flour and six shirts.

The slogan was 'The country is ours, we build it for ourselves.'
'But for whom do we starve?' people asked.

When I had a picture of the monster period unleashed after our arrest,
I could understand why all of us were arrested, from Rajk downward
to such 'inside-the-party fellow travellers' as myself. Everybody who
took the cause seriously had to be eliminated. The aim was to build
up a strong war industry, to make the largest possible contribution to
Stalin's war chest. At that time I still believed that this aim was
achieved. Later I learned that with the hecatombs of innocently
murdered people, with all the misery and terrorism unleashed on the
people, this system became a fetter on industry, agriculture, commerce,
cultural life, and everything. The workers were right. The whole thing
stinks as it is.

Moving more freely about within the prison and visiting the
hospital more and more frequently, I learned many details of the various rigged trials. There was a new SP doctor at the hospital, who was
less sadistic than his predecessors. In 1951 the situation was so bad
that when I was smitten down by pleurisy, the convict doctor in our
wing advised me not to report to the hospital. I lay for weeks in an
unheated cell (for all cells were unheated) and the convict doctor tried
to pull me through with his small chest of medicine and by getting
permission for hot tea at nights.

But now I could go to the prison hospital. I was not ill, only terribly,
ridiculously thin. I am six feet tall and weighed eighty-one kilos when
arrested. Now I was fifty-six kilos. I looked like the inmates of the
Bergen-Belsen camps before their death. My legs were thinner than
my arms had been before, and I had difficulty in sitting on hard chairs
because I almost literally sat on skin and bones. What I really hoped
was that the doctor would order more food for me. But he had no
right to do so. He gave me some vitamin pills from time to time.

The pet of the hospital was Lajcsi (little Louis), a large, fat middle-
aged man who was a mild lunatic. The hospital doctor tried out on
him the morphia sleep cure. He was supposed to sleep for three weeks.
Each noon he got his injection. Each morning he regained consciousness and then had to be persuaded to go to the lavatory, to wash and

to eat something. Lajcsi, who spoke and behaved like a five-year-old boy, had one ambition – to become a hussar. When he was reluctant to go, he had to be told only, 'All right Lajcsi, you'll get a nice horsey and you'll be a hussar.'

We knew his story from another convict who was in the same sub-trial of the Rajk case, because Lajcsi was one of us 'Rajk-conspirators'. He was a builder-contractor in the city of Szeged back in 1942. One day he fell from great height when he went to inspect a building. The fall made him a moron. His family tried everything. They could not cure him, so in 1943 they put him into the Szeged insane asylum. In the spring of 1949 the Szeged Communist party secretary and the local SP chiefs got their instructions about the Rajk case. They had to write the script of the Szeged conspiracy. It seems that they worked with an out-of-date book of addresses. In 1942 Lajcsi lived on the second floor of a luxury villa, the first floor of which was occupied by an army major. 'Capitalist' and 'Horthy-fascist' officer – how wonderful! Lajcsi and the army major were entered in the script as fourth and fifth accused of the Szeged annex of the Rajk trial. The script was sent up to Budapest and promptly translated to Russian. By the time the Szeged SP realized the mistake, General Bielkin up in Budapest had signed the Szeged script. So Lajcsi was arrested in the insane asylum where he had already spent six years and the army major was pulled in from Nyiregyhaza where he had been for the four years before a night watchman of the local timber mill. Lajcsi was arrested and sentenced to fifteen years.

When we asked him, 'Lajcsi, don't you remember a cellar, officers, paper? Don't you remember signing something?'

His face lit up after a while. 'Yes, yes, little Lajcsi wrote his name, officers promised to make him into a hussar.'

Poor Lajcsi had almost a better time in the prison hospital than in the insane asylum. But what about Geza Rubletzky, the former literary director of Budapest Broadcasting House? He was slowly dying in one of the separate cells for hopeless tuberculosis cases. His death was helped on by their putting him with six other patients in a dark and very small cellar with only half a ration of food. He died in 1953. What was his crime? He studied in Paris, hence he had to be a French spy, a

Deuxième Bureau agent. During the torture he confessed that two Deuxième Bureau officers 'organized him in' – Frederic Gay Lussac, and Boyle-Mariotte. He did not remember their address, he only knew the district. It was called Père Lachaise.

He thought that at the trial the prosecuting attorney, the judge and the counsels for defence would immediately interfere. But he did not know the system. General Bielkin countersigned his confession too. How could he know that Gay-Lussac and Boyle and Mariotte were scientists who died a long, long time ago? Now for anyone to come forward and say, 'Look here, we can't go on with this ridiculous nonsense!' would have been deadly dangerous. You must not make the SP lose face. So at a solemn trial, at which the former Lord Mayor of Budapest, Joseph Kovago, was also present as one of the accused (Kovago is now in the United States), Rubletzky was sentenced to life imprisonment. Chief Prosecutor Alapy actually asked for a death sentence.

They copied well the example of the glorious Soviet Union. Actually, of course, they did not copy it. These trials were directed by Stalin's personal representative, MVD General Bielkin. All the scripts were approved and signed by party leader Rakosi.

But we still had only a partial explanation for the mass murder of the most ardent Communists, for transforming the 'socialist countries' into the bleakest and most dangerous total prisons.

Chapter Seventeen

THE VAC JAIL housed a mixed lot of 'heavy' and 'medium-heavy' politicals. There were many small and medium war criminals who according to the Security Police deserved a far better treatment than we – meaning those members of the Small-holder's, Peasant, Social-Democratic and Communist parties who believed that the Soviet Union had changed and therefore took part in the coalition regime after 1945. Many of the small war criminals, former Arrow Cross thugs and similar people had easy jobs as convict-orderlies in the Vac prison. Among the pampered intimates of the SP guards was my childhood accquaintance Labay-Leibner, who had taken me around my uncle's estate to see how the serfs lived. His cynical talk started the 'humanity pain' in me. Now he was a convict-orderly in new and clean convict uniform, with special rations and many privileges which made life in prison easier. He and his mates were loyal to the SP and informed against us heavy politicals.

One night in April, 1952, all the 'heavies', some eight hundred people, were transferred to another prison. There were scores of lorries doing shuttle service. We were beaten and kicked all the way to the lorries. There we were manacled and some guards pointed their tommy guns at us all the time.

Then we arrived at the central jail in Budapest, the 'Gyujtofoghaz', the place where politicals were usually executed. Paul Ignotus and I were kicked into a tiny cell full of vermin. We had no cigarettes. We were worried because we knew if we could not go on translating, there would be no cigarettes. An alarming prospect. In our very weak state, the daily dose of nicotine became a necessity of life and death importance.

The books we were given to translate had been taken away from us in Vac. We could not lie down because the two straw sacks positively crawled with vermin.

But then dawn came. A sunny April dawn. Our cell faced the cemetery. There were trees. *Free* trees. The summer before we had seen three miserable prison trees on the daily walk in the courtyard. They were anaemic-looking, dust covered them; one could not bathe one's eyes in the green of a young tree. And now, from our window I could see free trees, bathing in golden glory, their tender new leaves pleasing my poor eyes with a symphony. No, with a song of colors. Having lived for so long in a world bereft of colors, always in cellars, in deep prison yards, always in shadow, always in a black and dirty-white world, the foliage in the golden dawn made me insanely happy. Being weak, having not slept, I was dizzy. But this was good dizziness. It told me: *Always there'll be tomorrow.*

How fortunate that since my earliest childhood colors had meant so much to me. Now for weeks, or perhaps months I should be able to watch the ever-changing colors of the foliage. It is grand if there is something to wake up for.

We were for three weeks without cigarettes. Our frayed nerves made us quarrel about nonsensical things. We were constantly hungry and nearly raving for nicotine. Then at last our books arrived from Vac. We were taken over to the translators' wing. On the third floor of wing B, there were the translators, seventeen people altogether. We had permission to visit each other's cells to consult. We had dictionaries and books. We were given a double bread ration. After two years of constantly feeling hungry, it was indescribably wonderful to eat one's fill of freshly baked bread.

On another floor were the quarters of the engineers, technicians and engineering draftsmen. They too got a double ration of bread and fifteen cigarettes a day. They too could move in and out of the engineers' cells. This was the advantage of this new prison. The disadvantages were far greater. The heaviest of politicals were concentrated here. High church dignitaries, former Horthy generals and Spanish Civil War generals – of the Communist side, of course – the main war criminals, all the Rajkists, people like Prince Paul Eszterhazy, former president of the republic, Zsedenyi, a galaxy of former Ministers and Undersecretaries of State. On the first morning, when the convict-orderlies came on their rounds, we discovered that our floor was served by a former Cabinet Minister and a former parachutist general. One of the gardeners was a count, the plumber of our wing was an old-guard Communist who had served as Undersecretary of State under Rajk. We met great names of the Hungarian, Romanian, Czech, French and Belgian Communist movements. In another wing Colonel Kalcsics was the orderly. He had fought through the Spanish Civil War and then the Belgian Resistance. There was even a street named after him in one of the Belgian towns. In 1948 the Belgian Communist party wanted him to stay. But Rakosi insisted. He pointed out that the great hero was of Hungarian origin, hence he should help in rebuilding the Hungarian army. The great hero returned early in 1949 and was sentenced to life imprisonment as Rajk's accomplice. One of the leaders of the Hungarian-American Communist party was dying in one of the solitary cells, while a former professor of the Soviet Staff Academy, the Frunze Academy, was now teaching other convicts how to wash prison floors.

High church dignitaries were given the dirtiest and most unpleasant jobs in the prison button factory. On the occasions of the periodic mass beatings, all the aristocrats, priests, former officers and heroes of the Communist old guard were badly clubbed and lashed.

And at nights the most horrid concerto conceivable began. For the least little offence, convicts were sentenced to 'short-iron'. This very cruel and dangerous punishment, a relic of the past, was used at times in the Horthy army before the war. But it was forbidden to punish with it people over thirty, and for longer than two hours. A doctor had to be present all the time. In our socialist fatherland men well over sixty were put into 'short-iron' for four to six hours.

They manacle one's right ankle to one's left wrist and vice versa. Then they fasten one to an iron bar in such a way that one is completely folded up. Elderly people suffer incurable injuries at once. Most people faint instantly. Many get heart attacks. When they are folded like penknives, an SP guard tramples on their back, while another shortens the manacle to make it more painful. After fifteen minutes the whole body, above all the feet and hands, is completely numbed. Even a touch is horribly painful. The SP guards' duty was to massage the hands and feet periodically till the victim screamed with agony, and fainted again.

Each night on the ground floor five or six or more victims were lined up. We only heard the commands. Then one by one a curious scream. A scream full of surprise. 'Can things hurt so unbearably?' Scream, scream, scream, scream, till all the victims were folded up. Then groaning, sobbing – it is difficult to describe what effect the sobbing of a sixty-year-old man has on one's nerves – all sorts of disturbing sounds. Then silence, long silence. After some twenty minutes, the second movement starts. Piercing cries expressing utter terror and agony. Cries and screams becoming shriller and somehow thinner. By the third movement people listening for the first time would think that a series of specially made sirens emit these inarticulate, piercing sounds. They are no more human, they are produced by the quintessence of pain and they express it well. The victims are in the ultra-agony state, no longer conscious, somewhere on the borderland of death.

And why were you given this punishment? Suppose there was the walk round and round the courtyard. It was winter. From far away a twenty-year-old SP guard approached and you did not take off your cap quickly enough. Next day, if there was a next day, you were slowly recovering from a heart attack, that is if you were an elderly man. Younger people could always take it better.

The curious thing in this most inhumanly cruel punishment within the punishment was that the victims were doubly innocent. They had received their prison sentences on trumped-up charges. Being intellectuals, they had travelled abroad. The architects who studied in France confessed that they spied for Le Corbusier, those in Britain had a spy chief of the Intelligence Service, called Sir Patrick Abercrombie. People in Italy spied for Ignazio Silone. Many in France spied for Voltaire, or Arouet … A friend of mine, George Faludy, the poet, spied for two Office of Strategic Services officers – Edgar Allan Poe and Walt Whitman. For such and similar crimes they received long prison sentences. But in prison they had not the rights of an average criminal. They never wrote or received letters, never received food parcels. But they were punished for the least little 'insubordination'. Somebody was not quick enough to dress after shower; someone's cell was not clean enough. You dropped your dixie while queuing up for food. Punishment? Two to six hours of short-iron.

Yes, the Gyujtofoghaz was a horrid place to be in.

But in December, 1952, a great surprise was in store for those doing intellectual hard labour. Scientists, writers, artists, engineers, technicians were all taken over to a freshly rebuilt building next to the garden of the prison hospital. The whole building looked like a third-class tourist hotel. There were normal windows, a separate enclosure for the w.c., normal hospital beds, writing desks, typewriters, desk lamps, everything. Some two hundred of us were transferred to this place. We were told that they were following the Soviet example. The socialist fatherland wanted to give a chance to talented and well-educated people to work their way back to freedom. They cited the case of a Soviet professor who received the Stalin Prize while serving the sixth year of his ten-year sentence.

We were given production norms and promised that by producing over the norm we could work off some of our sentences. For one hundred fifty per cent one quarter and so on.

This intellectual wing showed another aspect of the regime. Once I received a very complicated scientific text to translate. I told the officer in charge that I should either be given a textbook or preferably consult with an expert. The text was on telecommunication. In half an hour I was taken to another floor. In one of the rooms worked the famous professor of telecommunications of Budapest University with two of his ablest assistant professors. Once when having some problems with a book on oil geology, I was taken to Professor Simeon Papp, one of the five greatest oil geologists alive in the world – if he is still alive. He was sentenced in the MAORT case (the Hungarian-American Oil Company). His crime was that he did not want to produce oil quickly enough. The Communist expert who had told him to do so was also in the prison, sentenced to fifteen years for sabotage. By producing as quickly as Dr. Papp objected to, he caused a most serious stoppage. The Number One in Hungarian electronics was there with Numbers Four, Five and Six. The best architects, electrical and machine engineers, professors of ballistics, and of many other sciences were there busy working to atone for crimes they never committed.

One day I too was told not to sabotage!

'You, Paloczi, are not a simple translator. As a historian you can produce original stuff for us. Prepare a programme of work and send it in tomorrow by the guard!'

I thought and thought and thought. What kind of work should I propose which would be of sufficient importance to them, and at the same time make it possible for me to request as 'research material' important Western periodicals? Among other things I suggested a four-hundred-thousand word 'Encyclopedia of Colonial Changes'.

After two weeks a young officer came in:

'You work out this Colonial Encyclopedia. A sergeant will come every week, you give him the list of research material and he will bring it to you. And now hurry!'

Hurry!

It happened in this way that we received the *Encyclopedia Britannica* (1911 Edition), *Larousse*, scientific and political periodicals and any books we wanted. Having spent two years with the *Encyclopedia Britannica*, I think I am one of the very few men who have read all its articles, with the exception of those on Natural Science.

In another cell, the Yugoslav detachment was translating current Yugoslav newspapers and periodicals for the SP. We were far better informed than the people of the 'greater prison' outside.

In March, 1953, we learned at once about Stalin's death. But nothing changed in our jail. Food was very bad and very scanty. True, our surroundings were less awful, and following the Soviet example we 'working intellectuals' were not beaten up any more.

This life was interrupted by horrid interludes when we were taken to the SP headquarters, where they attempted to turn us into state's witnesses against some of our friends, or wanted our testimonials against some of the top-rankers in the Hungarian or foreign Communist parties.

We found out that the SP everywhere in the entire Soviet orbit liked to have on file testimonials against most of the important Communists, with the exception of the party bosses and their two-, three- or four-men supreme clique. In Hungary at that time, for instance, only Rakosi, Farkas and Gerö were exempted; in France Thorez and Duclos; in England Pollitt and Palme Dutt. But everybody else – in the literal sense of the word: everybody – was a possible candidate for a purge or a smear campaign. People who lived in France were interrogated about such spy suspects as André Marty, Aragon, Frédéric Joliot-Curie. I and many others who lived in England were expected to give testimony against such people as Gallacher, Bernal, Professor Haldane, Jack Lindsay and others. About Gallacher Tommyrot had already questioned me once. He explained to me that they knew Gallacher was an Intelligence Service agent, because his sons were officers in the British army. I told him that as far as I knew Gallacher's sons died while fighting, and many British Communists were commissioned. He had a long argument with me and told me that they had enough material against Gallacher without my help.

I was often interrogated about Professors Bernal and Haldane. Once in 1951 one of the SP officers told me that a young Hungarian scientist was sentenced to eleven years in prison for spying for Professor Bernal. 'How could he spy for Bernal?' I asked.

The SP officer told me, 'Easily. Bernal visited Hungary in 1950.'

I imagined Professor Bernal being fêted by the Hungarian Communist intellectuals, while SP agents were gathering material against him.

I asked these SP officers often, 'Do you think that almost everybody in the French and British Communist party is an enemy agent, and a spy?'

'No, of course not. The heroic French and British working class are all right. But the party leadership is full of intellectuals who are in the pay of the intelligence services. When the party gets power there, they will have to be liquidated, the way all of you have been liquidated here.'

Fortunately they did not torture people for such testimonials against leading foreign Communists. There were plenty among the convicts who were willing to say anything about them. The important thing was for the SP – in Hungary and everywhere else in the Soviet orbit – to have such testimonials ready against everybody.

It was very bad on the other hand when they wanted one to turn witness against one's friends.

My last such interlude came in April, 1953. At SP headquarters the regulations in the cellar were stricter than before. One was officially allowed to sleep seven hours and twice half an hour to walk up and down in the cell; otherwise one had to sit at the edge of the wooden planks and stare constantly at the spy-hole. The interrogations went on at night, so one rarely had more sleep than two hours. It was very hard to keep awake and sit with numbed body in the same position all day long. There were no books or cigarettes. As one sat staring at the spy-hole, one dropped off to sleep. There was one guard for four solitary cells. When one dozed off, the guard kicked the iron door of the cell with his heavy boot. This terrific bang woke one up scores of times a day. It was as if something exploded in one's head. One awoke with a pounding heart.

Six weeks of this kind of life produced a headachy, hungry state in which one had constant hallucinations. The SP officer who interrogated me wanted me to confess that one of my friends, a well-known young Marxist professor of economics, was an imperialist spy. Although I was worried that I might not survive the ordeal I could not bring myself to turn state's witness. By doing that I would have robbed myself of my last hold – my self-respect.

At the end of May I was in such a bad state that the officer told me:

'All right, Paloczi, you don't want to help us. I shall send you back to the Gyujtofoghaz, but not to the translators' section. You will live in solitary confinement, without books or cigarettes, on half rations for six months. In six months' time, I shall ask you again. We shall see. If you resist, back you go for another year ... We have time ...'

I was taken back to the Gyujtofoghaz, to the punitive section. Passing through the courtyard, I looked longingly at 'our' special building.

Would I be able to stand it? In the punitive wing daily life was full of beatings. Once a week when we were taken one by one to the shower room, all the way through the guards hit or kicked us. They had instructions to make our life hell. They fulfilled their instructions to the letter.

On the first of June I collapsed for the first time. I was very weak. I neared the stage when one simply gives up. I decided to think over all the good things in my life, and then give up.

We knew by experience that giving up in our state is not an empty word. It happened that one of my cellmates had told me, 'I give up now.' And he was soon dead. But although my intellect approved of giving up, my emotional-irrational self – should one call it the 'real self'? – knew that I wouldn't give up. There must be a way out, something would happen, I was going to be saved.

I was lying on the palliasse the afternoon of the fourth of June, 1953, when the miracle happened: I heard the wireless! Down below, on the ground floor was the guards' duty room in our wing. The wireless grew louder, so loud that all the convicts could hear it. The guards had never done such a thing before.

We all heard the speech of the new Prime Minister, Imre Nagy, announcing his 'new course'. He spoke against all the evil aspects of the regime. He attacked the grave miscarriages of justice. He promised a new, democratic way of life.

I listened with feverish attention. This was salvation! Next morning when I woke up I thought that the whole thing must have been one of my hallucinations. Surely, surely it could not have happened?

At noon the punitive section was disbanded. A very courteous young SP officer took me back to the intellectual section. I stumbled into my old cell. My cellmates took a look at me and started to offer me their saved-up bread, an onion, some substitute coffee from the morning. I looked ill and starved.

Our 'small hotel' of intellectual convicts was in turmoil. Everybody was talking about the Imre Nagy speech and its consequences.

A fortnight later we learned that General Peter, the head of the SP, was under arrest. Now there were long discussions about his life and career. Our convict barber at that time was a former SP major. He was pulled in in 1951. There were other former SP officers with us from colonels downward. We learned a lot about the Hungarian SP. One colonel served during the war years in the Russian MVD as a captain. He had a pretty tale to tell too.

So I pieced together my 'sinister profile' of General Gabriel Peter, the SP chief.

The occupational psychosis of a Communist Security Police chief differs greatly from that of an ordinary hangman, who is generally a very simple person. The SP chief must be an astute politician, a trained Marxist theorist, a good psychologist and a callous cynic. He has to keep his head while directing a modernized and greatly enlarged version of a Hieronymus Bosch *Inferno*, and must be past master in the art of murderous intrigue and counter-intrigue in the Kremlin. In order to keep alive he should have constant last-minute information on all trends and symptoms in the Moscow-directed gigantic Security Police network from the Odera to the Pacific Ocean. A broker of death, a director of a thousand torture chambers, an engineer of rigged trials, he must undoubtedly be used to hazards, knowing full well that his profession has the highest mortality rate among all human callings.

During Stalin's lifetime all the SP chiefs of the Soviet orbit were constantly at the mercy of the supreme tyrant's whims, fits of insane suspicions or sudden ideas to sacrifice another batch of accomplices. At the same time they were at the mercy of the local tyrants about whom they had to send spy reports to Stalin. By definition they were the most important tools and at the same time the most dangerous enemies of the local party bosses. General Peter, the Hungarian member of this curious fraternity, managed to keep his position for eight years. After Stalin's death when most heads of the international network were chopped off, his enemies managed to save his life hoping to make him chief witness against dictator Rakosi. He was sentenced to fifteen years of prison and is at present in solitary confinement in one of the SP jails in Hungary.

The role of the SP chief in Communist countries is generally as misunderstood in the West as the function of the organization he directs. He is looked upon as a horrid bloodhound kept for special purposes by the party bosses and used on the whole only on exceptional occasions. Nothing could be farther from the truth. The Security Police – officially the State Security Authority – although formally only an organ of the government, having the rank of a ministry, is in reality the political and administrative backbone of the party. It is controlled by a committee of three Politbureau members – the dictator and his two lieutenants, the so-called 'troika' – and controls in turn the *entire party and state apparatus*. The SP has representatives in every party and governmental department down to the party cells, down to shops, factories, collective farms, high schools, village councils. It keeps secret files on all adult members of the party and all citizens of the state. It receives duplicate copies of all reports, minutes, memoranda, documents of the party and the state from deliberations of the Council of Ministers to the village councils, from Foreign Office notes to minutes of factory committees.

In building space and number of staff the State Security Authority surpasses that of all the other ministries taken together and its budget is the second largest after the Ministry of Defence. It has a special army, special air division and in maritime countries, even a fleet.

In actual fact the SP chief is one of the most powerful men in the country and plays the most effective part in the running of the everyday life of the country.

He has, on the other hand, a less important part to play on those special occasions when outwardly he seems to reign supreme – at the times of the bloody purges. The rigged trials were and are directed from Moscow.

General Bielkin and his officers supervised all the tortures, hearings and the actual trials of all the outstanding personalities. Even many of us lesser 'suspects' were often heard by the enormously fat General Bielkin in the secret villas of the Soviet MVD.

All that a local SP chief like General Peter could do on such occasions was to kill some dozens of people who stood in his way personally or who knew something unpleasant about him. The main outlines of the show trials were planned in Moscow. To Hungary, for instance, General Bielkin came with the outlines of the 'script' – the confessions of persons who were not even selected yet for their respective roles as conspirators, spies and saboteurs. There was a conference in which Bielkin, Rakosi and Peter decided on the scope of the fictitious conspiracy. In Budapest they would arrest eight hundred persons, in Szeged one hundred twenty, and so on down to smaller towns and 'sample villages' on the frontier. They selected the main culprits-to-be and prepared the main points of the final 'script', naturally knowing perfectly well that they were going to sentence innocent people to death or long prison terms.

The fact that a local SP chief is only a minor director of the show trials does not mean that he is not a mass-murderer on his own accord. In the everyday life of the country he has to keep up the atmosphere of terrorism. His enormous organization is constantly producing spies. During the Hungarian revolution of October 1956, the attorney-general's files were examined. General Peter's organization had produced in a period of four years more than ninety-eight thousand spies and saboteurs, more than five per cent of whom have been executed. It is the SP network's task in Communist-ruled countries to distribute evenly the necessary arrest among all categories, groups and classes of the population, and naturally among all districts of the country. The atmosphere of constant suspicion and fear can be kept up only in this way.

General Peter was a callous cynic. To corpse candidates, if he talked to them without witnesses, he freely admitted that he does not believe in the cause. My friend, George Faludy, had such an intimate tête-à-tête with him. Faludy, a poet, was an anti-Hitler exile during the Second World War and served in the American army. He is the one who spied for Poe and Walt Whitman. He lives now in London. Faludy told me when we first met what happened during that interview ...'

Faludy: 'You know that I am innocent ...'

Peter: 'Yes, of course.'

Faludy: 'Then why am I here?'

Peter: 'Because you fit into the category. Now that you are here, you'll die here.'

Faludy: 'What about Hungarian literature?'

Peter: 'It does not need such idiots as you ... You silly fool, returning from America to this filth! ...'

The Undefeated

I have mentioned already our convict barber, a former SP major. I happened to know him in 1938 when he was the most fashionable 'hair stylist' in Budapest. He became a member of the SP after the war, and was 'purged' in 1951.

The convicts were shaved one at a time, once a week. During the two years he shaved me regularly, he talked to me a lot. I asked him to explain why most of the Hungarian SP higher-ups and even the MVD officers use the very same gestures and the very same turns of speech.

'That is simple,' he said. 'They all learned it directly or indirectly from Stalin. When Stalin made preparations during the times of Yagoda [chief of Soviet SP], he personally instructed him how to deal with members of the Communist old guard if they were reluctant to confess. One has to look them significantly in the eyes and say, 'You would have sacrificed your life for the party, wouldn't you?' When the person nods, you raise your hand and hit your desk with the back of it and say, 'Well, sacrifice it now!' This gesture was taught by Yagoda to Yezhov; it was used by Menzhinsky, by Beria, by Kruglov and Abakumov, by all the SP chiefs (all of whom incidentally were executed). Their subordinates learned it and now all over the place from Poland to China SP officers demand the supreme sacrifice with the same gesture.'

The former hair stylist and SP tormentor told me about the special SP schools where most of the 'investigating officers' of the Soviet orbit are taught the system. The pink-cheeked, fat hairdresser talked a lot about instructions in methods of torture. He was a most erudite scholar of comparative torture. But he also told me how he nearly went mad when kept for four days in solitary confinement. I did not mention to him that some of us had had more of it.

How are SP personnel recruited? What kind of people are the five thousand-odd officers and men who do the actual tormenting? How did a market-town couturier like Gabor Peter become SP chief?

People who knew him in Bekescsaba in 1935 say that he was a nervous little man, very servile to his employer and sickeningly charming to the customers. At that time he was already a member of the illegal Communist party and shortly before World War II he was in charge of the most secret department of the illegal party, that of 'party security'. He spied on the private life, public actions and jail behaviour of his comrades. In 1945 General Voroshilov and party boss Rakosi made him head of the newly formed political department of the Hungarian Police. In 1948 it was transformed into State Security Authority, and terrorism was unleashed in the country.

The SP was constantly being purged by General Peter. Many former SP officers were with us in jail. They were arrested for the slightest sign of elementary decency. With this method General Peter succeeded in finding in a few years that criminal and potentially sadistic five per cent which is there in any given population.

We had in jail with us one of the former personal chauffeurs of General Peter. He was a peasant lad who became a driver during his army training and was then simply transferred to the SP, and drove General Peter. One day they were going to Southern Hungary. On the highway a convoy of factory lorries did not pull to the side quickly enough when the special SP horn was sounded. General Peter ordered him to stop in front of the first lorry and make the convoy halt. Then he jumped out with his aides, brandishing revolvers and rubber truncheons and clubbed the drivers. When they started on their way again, the chauffeur, half-turning, asked:

'Why did you do that, Comrade General? After all they were simple workers.'

'You are a fool,' the general answered. 'The SP must be respected and feared. People must tremble when they see an SP uniform.'

The chauffeur was arrested at the end of the journey and sentenced to five years in jail. Now he understood how the SP is purposely isolated from the rest of the population.

General Peter was married. His wife, née Jolanda Simon, was for many years dictator Rakosi's private secretary. I do not know who arranged this convenient position for her, her husband or Beria himself. It is a fact though that this most functional marriage did not prove quite satisfactory to the general. He had several villas in Budapest and the country where he used to have much-needed rests after his trying existence in the company of various blondes and redheads. After he got tired of them, they generally went to jail or concentration camp. At this time he had a true love too. In her company he indulged in the dangerous luxury of opening up and talking about his worries. But something must have happened, because one day in the most secret part of Budapest Central Jail a new prisoner arrived. They pulled a white hood over her head, down to her shoulders. Not even the guards were allowed to see her head or talk to her. She was taken to a cell without spy-hole. She was taken for her daily walks by an SP major, who held her by the arm. We once caught a glimpse of her. She was a tall woman who would have been described in American glossy magazines as 'curvaceous'. She was hanged by Lieutenant Colonel Bogar personally and the convicts who took her to the limepit saw only a hooded figure.

Later, during our revolution, SP Major Bankuti, who was at that time governor of the prison, told some officer friends of mine that the hooded prisoner was the lady love of General Peter.

Gabor Peter was no doubt once a believing Communist. That must have been at the very start, when he made tailored suits for small-town ladies. Later he could not have kept his pure convictions – if they ever were that – because as security man he was already in touch with the international SP network. He learned in illegal days that scoundrels have a greater chance to survive among party functionaries than honest men. When the party was in power and he made his frequent trips to Moscow, the entire stupid and murderous nightmare became known to him. We know that in 1950, when he talked to Faludy, he already despised such idiots who returned from America to this 'filth'. But he still carried on because in the Stalinist system there is no retired SP chief.

In 1953 he was arrested. He must have learned about the execution of Beria, Abakumov and Bielkin. When he was sentenced to fifteen years only, he must have immediately known that he was meant to take part in a later trial in which Rakosi would be the chief accused.

Chapter Eighteen

THE FUNERAL CEREMONY OF COMMUNISM had begun. Among the two hundred intellectuals in our prison building there were forty Communists with very long party records. Most of them had spent long years in jail as Communists in various parts of the world. Nearly twenty of them had fought through the Spanish Civil War and had been in the Verney concentration camp in France from the spring of 1939 till the summer of 1941. Then the Pétain government had them transferred to concentration camps in Algiers. There they were together with hundreds of survivors of the Spanish war, Communists from all parts of the world. Some months after the Allied landing in Northern Africa, a Soviet commission came and they were permitted to volunteer to go to the Soviet Union. With one exception all volunteered.

The British sent them in special first-class railway wagons through British-occupied territory to the Persian side of the Caspian Sea. There a Soviet steamer took them on board. They were headed for Mineralnye Vody, a port in Soviet Kazakhstan. They were moved and elated when the steamer neared the port. They saw that a special army guard of honour was awaiting them. The minute they landed, this guard of honour, in fact SP troops, surrounded them and took them promptly to the cellars of the local SP jail. Here they waited for more than a month. Then the Minister of Interior of Soviet Kazakhstan, Comrade Taitlbaum, interrogated them personally. They had to write detailed autobiographies. Some of them were shot, the rest were permitted to proceed to Moscow. There they joined the Soviet army or were transferred to the political department of the army, that is to the army wing of the SP. They fought through the last two years of the Second World War in the Soviet army. And in 1949 they were all arrested. Marshall, Szebeni and some other former Spanish fighters were executed. The rest received sentences ranging from ten years to imprisonment for life.

The others, who had not been to Spain, were mostly in prisons and Nazi concentration camps from 1936 till 1945.

Here was a group, most members of which had given all their life to the party. And now the whole edifice of their ideology, the grand cathedral of their faith, collapsed. They moved about punch-drunk and lost among the wreckage. Through the information service of the convict international they learned about the fate of their friends; about the great heroes of the Spanish fight who were being executed all over the Soviet orbit; about people who were their first teachers; about others who had spent long years with them in capitalist jails. Was everything in vain?

They, and former Communist members of Belgian, French, Italian and Yugoslav resistance, were seeking the company of former Communist theoreticians and economists, historians, top-ranking party and state functionaries to clear up their problems. Our jail was well-provided with such top people. There was a former Politbureau member, a former chairman of the State Planning Authority and several leading Marxist theoreticians in various branches of science.

In the summer of 1953 almost all of them got disenchanted. [I am not mentioning names, because many of them are still within the Soviet orbit.] Not all of them stayed disenchanted though. After our release, when the fight between the Stalinists and the anti-Stalinists was on, some of them joined the Stalinist side. But then, in 1953, they were disenchanted, and even those who were not, behaved in a very 'revisionist', 'right-deviationist' way.

As they were gradually losing their mental strait jackets, they started to talk about secret party history. They spoke freely about events which they had never dreamed of mentioning before. For weeks the discussion went on about events and personalities of the Spanish Civil War. There were debates about Moscow's role. Some maintained that from 1937 onwards, Stalin and the Kremlin clique did not want really the victory of the Republican side. They talked about the purges the Soviet SP people carried out among the Communists in Spain. They told the story of one of the great heroes of the war, the story of General Lukacs.

General Lukacs was born in the Hungarian village of Mateszalka and when, after the First World War, as a former prisoner of war, he became a partisan leader in Soviet Russia, he took the movement name of Mate Zalka. He is well known as such in the Soviet Union. Right after the First World War when Kemal's Turkish army fought against the Greeks and the Allies, some Soviet military experts were sent to help them. The leaders were General Frunze and General Janos Kemeny, in reality the former Mate Zalka and the later General Lukacs. In the Soviet system people often have to assume false identities for some secret missions abroad. When passports are needed, they are given passports confiscated from SP prisoners. Then the technical department exchanges the photos, but the names generally remain. Zalka-Lukacs became one of the heroes of the Turkish war as General Kemeny. In 1936 he was sent to Spain and soon became one of the military leaders of the Republican side. But he was too popular and had too many friends among the Hungarian Communists who were just then being liquidated in Moscow.

In the midst of war, when his presence was very much needed he received instructions from Moscow to give over his command and fly at once to Russia. His aide-de-camp and some others had similar instructions. General Lukacs, having information from Moscow, knew what was in store for him. By this time Tuchachevski and the other Soviet generals were already liquidated. He had three choices: to desert from the war and take refuge somewhere in the West, to go to Moscow and be hanged as a spy and a traitor, or to commit suicide. He chose the latter. On the Andalusian front there was a section of the highway which the Francoists had completely under their fire and for this reason, the people of the Republican side did not use it. General Lukacs one day, after he said farewell to his best friends, got into his car and with his aide drove into the Francoist artillery fire. He received a hero's funeral.

This suicide was a grave failure for Commissar Singer, one of the Comintern instructors of the Spanish Communist party, who was disguised as the secretary of La Pasionaria. According to some cell-mates of mine, Commissar Singer was really the inventor and the Svengali of this famous Spanish peasant woman. La Pasionaria was his marionette. Commissar Singer became well-known later as one of the leaders of the Hungarian Communist party, under the name of Erno Gerö. His stubbornness, sadism and stupidity contributed to the outbreak of the 1956 revolution.

Coming from a petty-bourgeois commercial family, Erno Gerö was one of the most active young men in the 1919 Bolshevik revolution in Hungary. Soon he became a political exile, obsessed by the peculiar *dementia emigrantis* of Communists driven from their country. Living in Vienna, Prague and other continental cities, he worked hard to master political and economic theory.

In the early 1930s he was called to Moscow and made a Comintern functionary. At that period the Comintern had a very close grip on the Communist parties of the world. Each party had one or several Comintern 'instructors', that is, controllers representing Moscow. Some of them were openly acknowledged, some worked without the official knowledge of the party which they controlled. They reported to the Comintern and to the international section of the Cheka, GPU or NKVD – as the Soviet Security Police, now the MVD, was called at different times. Erno Gerö, under the name of Ernest Singer, was 'attached' for a long period to the French Communist party.

When the Spanish Civil War started, he was sent to Spain. There he had a complex role. He was one of the representatives of the Special Commission for 'party purges', manipulating rigged trials against overpopular political and military leaders of the fight in Spain, against 'deviationists' and 'waverers'.

Commissar Singer was severely reprimanded for letting General Lukacs escape the hangman's noose.

But why kill General Lukacs? Why kill thousands of fanatical Communists? Why the purges?

We tried to find the answer. We felt – we were not convinced yet – that the rigged trials and the purges, that the SP system and the general atmosphere of terrorism is in causal relation with Marxist-Leninist theory and with Communist convictions. This relation is not a simple cause and effect connection, but complex and involved. The causation is at times direct and positive, at times indirect and negative.

There was a wise old 'Spaniard' with us, whom we called Uncle Pedro. I asked him once, 'Why can't we arrive at a simple answer?'

Old Pedro smiled. 'Don't talk nonsense, son. A wireless is a very simple thing compared with all the problems of communism and of the Soviet Union. Yet you cannot give a simple answer, explaining in a few sentences to a nonexpert, how wireless works … We party fighters have to tell our stories to you, the theoreticians. You have to study a lot, think a lot, and then maybe, maybe, you'll arrive at an answer.'

The prison library naturally contained a complete collection of Marxist literature. All the works of Marx, Engels, Lenin and Stalin and the lesser ones were there. The Russian and Hungarian Communist periodicals, theoretical monthlies and scientific magazines were ours for the taking. And after the arrest of General Peter, when we all anticipated a trial against Rakosi, most of us former Communists started to reread the holy books, trying to make up our minds about communism, the Soviet system, the secret of rigged trials and about all other connected problems.

We furiously studied the Marxist classics again to find out what could be saved for the left from the wreckage, and to get answers to our problems.

There were some points accepted by almost everybody in our group of old guard Communists:

1. Communism has grown to be identified with the Soviet system.

2. That system has nothing or very little to do with socialism.

3. The very few top-rankers on the summit, the members of the various 'troikas' and foursomes who are the real party dictators, pay lip service to Marxism-Leninism, but in fact care only for power.

4. The Soviet Communist system was and is a bureaucratic despotism. The principle of the dictatorship of the prolotariat is a smoke screen to hide the dictatorship of the party bosses.

5. The Communist party is neither Communist nor a party. It is an

apparatus in the hands of the dictators. The party is really based on the various branches of the Security Police. The Central Control Committee and the Cadre Department of the party are branches of the SP.

6. The Soviet Communist system by its double, treble and even tenfold controls by the party and within the party over the government apparatus and within the government apparatus, over industry, commerce, agriculture and cultural activities and within these, is most inefficient.

7. This enormous party and governmental bureaucracy is built up into an almost feudal hierarchy. The members of this hierarchy from Number One to the party secretary of a small town, from the ministers down to the directors of single factories and state farms, form a new class of bureaucrats. Within this class there are feudal ties. Everyone owes allegiance to someone higher up. If someone on the top is purged, his entire line of feudal subjects is purged too.

8. Bureaucratic despotism by its very nature is reactionary.

9. We knew many Communist parties before they attained power. They were then different. The membership was convinced that the Communist party was the party of truth, of scientific socialism, the party of common sense and decency. With the exception of the Soviet Communist party, the membership of all other Communist parties believed this until 1945. A change came when in Eastern Europe and Asia other Communist parties came to power. We have enough material there to generalize. One significant feature is that most of the Communist old guard is liquidated after the party comes to power. They are liquidated because they take the ideology seriously.

10. Can we call Communists people who are branded as traitors, deviationists and bourgeois revisionists by all party leaderships? Shouldn't we reserve the name Communist for those who approve of the Soviet system of bureaucratic despotism? If so, there are very few Communists in the world.

We mostly agreed as to the relevance of such questions and the truth of these points. There were of course many debates about the details and about the main question: Is the evil and inefficient Soviet system an inevitable consequence of Marxism-Leninism or not?

There was a large group which maintained that a decent, real communism is possible; that Marxism-Leninism was corrupted by Stalin and his associates. We of the opposing group maintained that the principle of class war, the principle of class enemies, the theory of the proletarian dictatorship, the principle of one-party rule by a monolithic party – all these inevitably lead to bureaucratic despotism. The working class in any country is not the absolute majority. The peasantry, petty bourgeoisie, the middle, professional and upper classes and the intellectuals form the majority. But even the industrial workers are not supposed in Marxist-Leninist theory to be enthusiastic adherents of Communist dictatorship at the beginning. They have to be forced to accept this dictatorship. Then they and the rest of the population have to be forced into submission. It can be demonstrated from Marxist-Leninist theory that for a very long historical period, for several generations, the majority of the population has to be forced by terrorism to submit and to go on working. There cannot be a dictatorship of the proletariat because the proletariat cannot have a say in the affairs of the country. The dictatorship is practiced in the name of the proletariat without its ever having a chance to interfere.

Marxist-Leninist theory and the Soviet system inevitably produce dictators and dictatorial cliques. Even the Communist parties of the West are ruled by such dictators or cliques.

I tried to report faithfully what questions our 'conferences' discussed and what conclusions these liberated minds arrived at.

I took part in all the debates. But I was more interested in the psychological and social-anthropological aspects of the question. I asked all my prison mates to tell me the story of their conversion. I questioned them about their later mental states, about doubts and anxieties. I tried to get a clear picture of the great leaders, of the people just below the top, of rank and file fighters of the party. I felt, as most everybody did, that there is something which one could call Communist neurosis. I also felt, as did many others, that there is something schizophrenic about the whole thing.

But first, the thing was to get the real life story of some of the leaders. Here was Matyas Rakosi the butcher of Hungary, clearly the most monstrous figure of the international Communist movement after Stalin. I tried first to understand his personality.

Most people in Hungary and the international Communist movement know only his mask: an ugly, bald and fat old man with the expression of a jolly country grocer who might even sell on credit to people in difficulties. His cheerful eyes, the ever-present smile around his thick lips, his comfortable paunch and his sense of humour led thousands to mistake him for a genial human being.

This is the mask. Once I saw his face. During an intermission in the Budapest parliament when everyone rushed off to lunch and his entourage scattered in haste to carry out his orders, a few of us lingered long enough in the back of one of the press boxes to see the mask drop off. Believing himself alone, Rakosi's shoulders dropped, the jolly smile disappeared, his jaw protruded in vicious defiance. We saw the muzzle of a monster and horrid eyes burning in impatient hatred. We quickly retreated, haunted by dismal forebodings.

His life, like his face, has a well-known mask – that of the great Communist leader, hero of the 1919 Bolshevik revolution who spent sixteen years in jail, was exchanged in 1940, returned to Hungary in 1945 and was Communist dictator of his country till 1956. Some people saw his life as the tragedy of a man who went through terrible ordeals for a cause which he later helped to befoul. So Rakosi would also be one of those 'captive minds', victim and victimizer at the same time. But this is obviously not true. The Rakosi riddle is similar to that of Stalin: How can one become an imprisoner of peoples' minds, how can one become a despiser of humanity and a demented falsifier of human history?

Rakosi was born in 1892, the son of a country shopkeeper. In 1910 he won a scholarship to the Oriental Academy, financed by the Hungarian Bankers' Association (TEBE), where gifted young men were taught Western and Oriental languages to become ultimately Oriental representatives of Budapest banks. After graduation he worked for a year in a London bank. He served in the First World War, was a prisoner of war in Russia, returned as a Communist and became deputy commissar of commerce during the 1919 Bolshevik revolution in Hungary. According to official party history he took a heroic part in the fighting around Salgotarjan, but the only proofs of this are some fifth-rate paintings 'eternalizing' this supposed fact. None of the

Salgotarjan fighters ever saw him. But – as every child knows in our unfortunate part of the world – Communist history is free from 'bourgeois objectivity' and has to be 'one of the weapons in the fight for the dictatorship of the proletariat'.

After the defeat of the 1919 Bolshevik revolution in Hungary, Rakosi returned to Russia, became a Comintern official, served for a short time as secret 'instructor' of the Italian Communist party, then was sent back to Hungary in 1925 to organize the illegal Communist party. He was arrested and sentenced to ten years. In 1933 a new trial was held in his case and the prosecution demanded a sentence of death. To be twice tried for the same offence and to be executed after a long period in jail would have been monstrously unjust, but international public opinion hurried to his rescue. Protest meetings were held in more than fifty countries, well-known legal experts from all over the world hurried to Budapest to help him – and Rakosi was saved from the hangman's noose. In 1940 during the Hitler-Stalin alliance he was exchanged for the historic flags which the Russians captured when crushing the 1848–1849 Hungarian war for liberty.

On his trials Rakosi behaved with a great deal of courage. During his first period in prison he organized hunger strikes and was respected by his prison mates. Then he was transferred to another prison, the 'Csillag' jail in Szeged. Of his cellmates during his second eight-year period very few are alive today. He murdered most of them when he came to power. But two of them gave me a few hints about the ugly truth before they died. For the time being I will not mention their names, as their families are in Hungary.

In the Csillag jail Rakosi had an exceptional position. He was given special food and permitted to receive regularly the Hungarian and foreign press. *He was the clerk of the warden.* All prison graduates of the world know perfectly well that only traitors among political prisoners receive such positions. My friends told me how Rakosi turned stool-pigeon, denounced his prison mates, how sternly he reprimanded Communist convicts if they were slack with their spinning wheels. The murder of his former cellmates and the long list of his nauseating crimes when in power validate these accusations.

In 1945 he returned to Hungary with the Soviet armies and through a long series of tricks, blackmail and fraudulent practices, he cheated, bribed and murdered his way to power.

He established full terrorist dictatorship in 1949. The period from then on till 1953 was called in Hungary the 'monster epoch'. At the height of this, on February 29, 1952, in one of the most cynical speeches of political history, Rakosi told the students of the Supreme Party Academy how his small clique supported by Soviet tanks subjugated the Hungarian people. He admitted that even the majority of the workers was against the Communist party. But by capturing for his party the Home Office, the Security Police and the Supreme Economic Council and using 'clever' tactical moves, they misled the workers and crushed the majority parties.

'In those days,' Rakosi said, 'this was called "salami tactics", whereby we sliced reaction off bit by bit ... in the Smallholders party. In these unceasing struggles we whittled away the strength of the enemy ... In the land reform we applied the tactics of trying to divide the enemy or, if possible, of neutralizing him ... When we made demands we carefully began little by little, in order to make it more difficult for the enemy to mobilize and concentrate all forces against us. Later we increased the demands and whenever possible used transitory forms.'

He admitted that they raised the problems of dictatorship only in the inner party circle. 'We did not bring them before the party publicly because even the theoretical discussion of the dictatorship of the proletariat as an objective ... would have made our endeavors to win over not only the petty bourgeoisie but the *majority of the mass of the workers, more difficult.*' (Published in the February-March 1952 issue of the official *Tarsadalmi Szemle.*)

With the famous 'salami tactics' he first went into a coalition with the Smallholders, Peasant and Social-Democratic parties to crush the Conservatives, then annihilated the Smallholders party with the help of the remaining two parties. Then he suborned the Peasant party and absorbed the Social-Democrats, killing off or imprisoning their party leadership. Politicians were bribed, blackmailed, driven to exile, imprisoned or sentenced to death.

At first in 1945 he appeared as a tolerant man, always ready to compromise. The first intimation of his real personality was given to

Dr. Stephen Riesz, the then Minister of Justice in the winter of 1947. Dr. Riesz learned that one of his Communist judges upon higher orders intended to sentence to death a small merchant for a price offence, perhaps deserving a month in jail. Dr. Riesz went at once to Rakosi protesting against such a monstrous act of injustice. Rakosi explained to him most patiently that there was price racketeering going on and someone had to be hanged to direct the attention of the workers to this fact. Dr. Riesz, a Social-Democrat, asked Rakosi, 'Do you want me to murder an innocent man?' Rakosi laughed. 'Murder … innocence, what big words. It is obvious that in the present political situation a price racketeer has to be hanged. It's immaterial to me whom you choose for that role, only do choose someone quickly. You fellows in the Social-Democratic party are sentimentalists. You have to learn realities.'

Dr. Riesz did not learn realities. He soon went for a week's vacation during which an unfortunate merchant was duly hanged. In 1950 when Rakosi started his campaign against the Social-Democrats, Dr. Riesz was clubbed to death in the SP jail.

Rakosi enjoyed the role of the framer-up, of the tormentor, of the jailer and of the hangman. In the rigged trials he personally gave instructions to the Security Police officers as for how long and with what methods his former friends should be tortured. One of his last cellmates in the Csillag prison had been Colonel Erno Szucs of the Security Police. One day this colonel – himself a vile creature – was taken to the 'liquefying room' at SP headquarters, where people were clubbed to death and then were 'liquefied' in a mixture of acids and let down the drain. The colonel's aide, a naïve old-guard Communist, learning of this, rushed by car to party headquarters and informed Rakosi of the 'terrible miscarriage of justice' about to happen. Rakosi showed himself properly shocked, said that he was going to phone at once and instructed the aide to return to SP and report to him instantly that Colonel Szucs was safe. When the unfortunate man arrived at SP headquarters, he was immediately arrested and beaten up. By some mistake he was sent then to a prison hospital. In a year he could walk and spent only some five years in prison with us. But this was an oversight. Colonel Szucs, with his brother Nicolas, a one-time secretary of the Hungarian Club in London, were duly let down the drain.

Rakosi liked to watch men's faces as they were being smitten down. In 1948 there was the 'fusion' of the Social-Democratic and Communist parties. At the Budapest mass meeting celebrating this fusion, Rakosi publicly kissed the renegade Social-Democratic leader, Arpad Szakasits, and said that 'Szakasits's name will be written with golden letters in the history of the Hungarian working class.' Two years later, when the same Szakasits was president of the republic, Rakosi invited him for a friendly dinner party with Erno Gerö and General Farkas. Szakasits told us in jail what happened at that dinner party. Rakosi was his usual jocular self. Still smiling, at the end of the dinner he took from his pocket some typewritten sheets and gave them to Szakasits to read. The latter realized in utter astonishment and horror that it was a detailed police confession in which he admitted a long series of crimes from having been a Horthy agent to having spied for the Gestapo, the British Secret Service and the British Labour party.

When Szakasits had read it through, Rakosi told him, 'If you sign it, your fate will be that of Zoltan Tildy [house arrest for years], if you refuse, it will be that of Rajk [execution].'

Szakasits said, 'But, Matyas, you know my life as well as your own. You know that not a syllable is true in this vile document.'

Rakosi, instead of answering, pressed a bell on the table. In came General Gabor of the SP, with two of his officers. Rakosi told him, pointing to Szakasits, 'Comrade General, take this filth away.' The chief inquisitor of Hunagry put his hand on Szakasits's shoulder. Rakosi leaned forward in his chair and watched Szakasits's face with a greedy look. Next minute the scene was over. Next day – while Szakasits was being tortured to sign it – Rakosi read this 'confession' to the Central Committee of the party and said, 'This is the filthiest document in the history of the Hungarian working class.' He was in a position to know. It had been written by him.

I too saw that look on Rakosi's face at that reception in 1949, just before my arrest.

With Stalin's death dangerous times started for Rakosi. It was well known that, acting on a hint of Stalin, it was Rakosi who furnished most of the material for the murderous anti-Tito campaign to Beria and the two MVD generals, Abakumov and Bielkin. Sharing Stalin's belief that a historical lie will be accepted as truth if thousands are murdered as an illustration, Rakosi planned the Rajk trial in Hungary and helped to plan similar trials in the other satellite countries. He boasted publicly that he personally discovered the first clues of the 'Titoist imperialist conspiracy' and had 'spent many a sleepless night' planning the swift annihilation of the 'Titoist monsters'.

What kind of people are these Stalins and Rakosis? What do they have in common with their simple followers, with the uninitiated Communists?

Is it possible that people who enter the Communist party are schizophrenic from the time the party gets power? In the West, and in the East European parties before the war, the rank and file members were simple adherents of the ideology. There was nothing schizophrenic about them. But in the Soviet Union and, later, everywhere the party attained power, the splitting of personality in Communists began. Obviously the lower anyone is in party hierarchy, the less he suffers from this. But as the proletarian dictatorship gets into full swing, everybody with the exception of the simplest members and the opportunists, has either to become disenchanted or develop a kind of controlled schizophrenia. This is a conscious mixture of delusion and cynicism, of obsession and opportunism. The mental and moral split between the public and private self widens. The defence mechanism is at work and private personality atrophies. But then a new series of splits occurs within the public self. There are so many contradictions between professed beliefs, aims and programmes and actual practice, that people have to harden themselves and develop a contempt for ideology, for all political talk. Every speech, article, book – every intellectual argument is just a means to further the real aims. The higher one is in the party, the more dangerous life becomes. Marxism-Leninism is very important, because every action, every move, every change of the party line, has to be justified with the holy texts. And at the same time it is completely unimportant, even dangerous. The rank and file should be disciplined party members and nothing else. Only the dictator and his clique have the right to interpret the holy text.

The series of mental and moral splits occur in people who do not *think* in a normal way. Ordinary thought processes are disturbed in them by the daily life of party existence. Stalinist hypno-pedagogics have the greatest effect on people who are within the party apparatus. There are many doubts as to the effectiveness of Marxist-Leninist hypno-pedagogics on the people on the whole, but those who exercise hypno-pedagogics certainly become infected by it. In conversation and in public speeches, in discussion meetings and conferences, in any kind of writing, they always repeat the 'theses' and the slogans of the day. They are conditioned in such a way that any event, problem or aspect of private or public life, of science or literature is automatically associated in their brains with one of the slogans, theses or Marxist-Leninist-Stalinist quotations. The void between two slogans or quotations is filled out by the officially approved platitudes of the day.

I heard a Muscovite saying that 'on the whole, everything is forbidden, but anything permitted is obligatory.' So when you are permitted to say something, you always *know* what you *must* say to the exact wording. Deviation from *Pravda* language entails very real dangers not only for those who utter such a sentence but also for those who listen to it without protest. After years of such conditioning functionaries become similar to automatic phonographs which play in any given situation the officially obligatory records.

The atrophy of thinking could be observed among my cellmates. Although they became disenchanted, and were 'liberated minds', it very often happened that the whole conditioning had got hold of them. In discussions sometimes a sentence or an expression produced a necessary association and they came out with a series of quotations and theses.

Controlled schizophrenia then occurs not in normal and sane people, but in persons whose thinking and memory, whose intellectual and emotional reactions were spoiled and crippled by years of hypnopedagogics, cliché-mongering, and conditioning to the ceremonial repetitions of quotations.

Before people arrive at the very top, controlled schizophrenia is necessary to keep some self-respect. To be entirely cynical and to want power for power's sake is not given to everybody. In order to go on, people nearing the summit often have to hypnotize themselves into that fine fervour of feeling, of fanatical faith, which started them on their way. They often fall back on their former public selves, and even on former private selves. While they exercise double-think and double-speech, their emotional life is ruled not by double but by treble and quadruple feeling. The varieties of this constitute the Communist neurosis. This is built up and caused by the contradiction between ideals and reality, by a series of personality splits in the individual's development and an elaborate machinery of conscious and unconscious self-delusion. Some people on the very summit get cured even of this when they become entirely cynical, when they stop lying to themselves and have no need for 'conscience cosmetics'. Stalin was cured this way. He became a tyrant, with the psychology of tyrants. That was Rakosi's cure and that of some other leaders.

But even after they had been 'cured', they have to talk ideology all the time. Their murderous dictatorship is justified by the ideology of the builders of the future. Through long years of ideological manipulations, they lose their intellectual convictions, even their ability to be convinced of anything. For them ideology is the raw material of propaganda, of the ceremonial justification of their decisions. Their thinking is determined by this sort of scholasticism.

The party life makes people lose the continuity of their personality. And without continuity, one can barely speak of personality. The ever-changing party line forces all true believers to argue enthusiastically against something of which not so long ago they were enthusiastic supporters. In the new 'concrete' situation black is already not black, and white not white. But in order to go on with such antics for years, memory is a most unwelcome ballast. You develop a new side of your defence mechanism, that of forgetting anything whenever it becomes unpleasant.

'Controlled schizophrenia; Communist neurosis; conditioned reflexes and hypno-pedagogics; disintegration of personality' ... Am I overcomplicating matters?

I decided to put these problems aside for the time when I should be free, if that time ever came.

In November, 1953, the new prison commandant came from cell to cell, and handed out ordinary postcards. After four or five years of complete isolation, we were permitted to write to our families, ask for replies and for food parcels. And the greatest thing – early in December we could receive a visitor. And from then on we could have two visits a year.

When the door closed after him, we sat there dumfounded. I, the incurable optimist, immediately said that we were going to be released soon. There must have been a complete change of line in the offing. It was not possible that we – the most dangerous witnesses of mass murders committed by the Soviet and Hungarian leadership – that we should have contact with the outside world. What would happen if people learn something about our experiences?

It was almost treason in the prison to suppose that *they* would ever release us. But I hoped that *they* would be soon demoted.

The SP guards started to behave in a confused manner. It was well-known that SP officers were arrested with General Peter. Our former prison commandant, Major Bankuti, was in the solitary confinement wing of the Vac jail. The most sadistic SP guards started to behave in a friendly way and they talked of leaving the SP if a chance arose. The architectural section in our building, which was planning many new prisons, agricultural stations where convicts work, and other SP building projects, was told to stop. The ever-expanding SP seemed to be uncertain about the future.

And then the first letters begun to arrive in reply to our postcards. New aspects of our tragedy came to light: the fate of our families. Most of the families had been told in 1949 and 1950 that we had been executed. Some of the wives mourned their husbands for two and three years, then got married. Now they were trying to divorce their present husbands, or were confessing in pathetic letters that they loved their new husband. Those wives who knew that their husbands were still alive in jail were forced to sue for divorce. This was the condition for keeping their jobs. They were forced to denounce their husbands as despicable spies. Those who resisted were thrown out of their jobs and had to work as unskilled labourers. In cases where both man and wife were arrested, their children were forcibly taken away from the grandmothers or other relatives. It was fairly well known that they were being brought up in Communist orphanages, under different names.

The Gyujtofoghaz was a huge complex of jail buildings. One of them was for female convicts. Many of our prison mates learned now that their wives were being kept in that neighbouring building. These wrote their postcards to their wives. They were frantic with anxiety about the fate of their children. The widow of Laszlo Rajk was also there. Her son, born a few weeks before their arrest, was taken away from her mother.

I could not write to Agi because she was not my nearest relative. I could not even mention her name in my letters to my relatives, because that might have been dangerous for her.

During the long years in prison, I often thought how fortunate it was that I had not proposed to her before my arrest. As my official fiancée she might have even been arrested with me. But from her standpoint, this was much better too. We were in love for a short time. We had known each other for a short time. She was very young. I hoped that she would soon forget me, get married, have children, be happy. Yes, I told myself that I hoped all that. At times I even earnestly believed that I felt like this. But all the while there were timid little hopes in me that some day we might meet again, that she would be free and …

In prison one has to be very careful with hopes and desires. By having too many hopes one can get oneself into a special hell-for-one, an inner circle of torments within all the torments.

For years I tried not to think of Agi. But one does not think only of persons. Our language is poor in this respect. No, I hadn't thought often of her, but I *felt* of her. There was a nameless aching, a timid craving, a disturbing magnetic field of unanalyzed feelings.

I had fortunately an excuse to think of Agi from time to time. My first novel which I wrote in English, *The Survivor*, was in manuscript form. For various reasons, in 1949 I had had only one copy. I had lent that a few days before my arrest to Agi. Now the normal thing to do in that situation would have been to burn the manuscript. If the SP had reached her house and found the manuscript, they would have arrested her promptly. I 'hoped' that she had burned it. And I hoped desperately that she had not.

Now that there was a possibility that we were going to be released I dared to think of her again. I was very realistic and manly about it. It would be good to see her, spend an evening or two in her company, and that of her husband. An old acquaintance turns up. Of course I wouldn't even mention the manuscript.

What would I do if they released me? I wouldn't get married. That was out of the question. One has to face realities. Wife and children, no, that was not in store for me. I might write. And live, cautiously. Live the life of a reprieved corpse. Live on borrowed time. Enjoy music, walks in the hills, a proper bath, privacy. Anything I still could get from life would be an unexpected gift.

I could not imagine ever being free again. And I could not imagine spending all my life in prison. To be able to go anywhere I wanted to was something unbelievable and even somewhat frightening. Streets, with many people, loud noises, colours – life after years of vegetation. No, I said to myself, stop all this nonsense, get back to intellectual hard labour, to the safe prison routine. There'll be always tomorrow, but don't be too eager for the tomorrows.

Then the time of visits came. One of the main corridors was divided down the middle by a wire netting.

Visits were on Sundays. The visiting relatives were permitted to the corridor in batches of forty. Their names were taken, and forty convicts were lined up on the opposite side of the wire netting. On both sides scores of SP officers and guards were listening in to the conversation. Before the visit we were told that we could only talk about personal matters. We were forbidden to speak about our trials, or anything we had learned in prison. The relatives were forbidden to tell us political news.

In the half-dark corridor eighty desperate people were trying to talk to each other. The convicts were self-conscious in their coarse, ill-fitting uniforms. They knew that they looked terribly thin and ill. They tried to behave cheerfully. But the wives and mothers burst out crying the second they caught their first glimpse of their beloved one. Some convicts and some relatives were running up and down, hysterically searching for each other. The long years of misery and fear, torment and starvation had wrought such changes on their faces, that they did not recognize each other. Near me a former cellmate of mine was standing. He expected his wife. I saw her photograph, she was a healthy and pretty young woman. Now two SP guards supported her, an emaciated, elderly woman. 'This is your husband,' they said. 'This is your wife.' The two clutched the wire netting and wept silently. The visit lasted ten minutes. They spoke to each other only with their eyes.

Eighty people trying to speak, eighty people weeping, sobbing, eighty people trying to outsmart the listening SP guards, eighty people trying to get the most out of this precious meeting. Eighty people swaying in a near faint, craving for a touch, craving for escape, being terribly afraid that the visit would be soon over, wanting desperately that it should be over.

In the general turmoil some people with steady nerves and strong will power managed to have a real talk. Some of the relatives had been told that we were all innocent. They succeeded in telling us about the political situation outside.

The opening of our crypt was a painful shock to us. But it was a painful shock to the mass murderers in the party leadership too. Imre Nagy, as Prime Minister, had started his fight to release all the innocently sentenced people. Rakosi was still the party dictator and fought a desperate rear-guard action. He still had his entire party apparatus and the Security Police. In the ministries he had his own men everywhere and they did everything to thwart Imre Nagy's efforts. But in the second part of 1953 most of the concentration camps, the Recsk horror camp included, were disbanded. Forty thousand innocent people came out. They told their story. The whole country was shaken with moral indignation. People knew of course about the mass murders committed in their midst, but they did not realize the full scope of the murderous regime.

And then the 'rehabilitation' hearings were started early in 1954.

The Undefeated

New SP officers visited the jails and told everyone to tell his *true* story. One by one we had our preliminary hearings and told the SP officers about our innocence. They pretended to be surprised and shocked, but noted everything we said.

We became feverishly impatient. For long years we had vegetated shut up in damp, evil-smelling, ugly cells. For years we were treated by the SP guards as dirt under their feet. For years we had nothing decent to eat. Now we started to dream about food. For four years, for instance, we never had potatoes. Our menu consisted of musty beans, lentils, dried peas, dried vegetables, fodder beets and similar things. During the springs, summers and autumns we were thinking of people who eat fruit; who simply go to a shop, take out some money, and buy themselves fruit. They drink chocolate and coffee; they eat meat. They are free to go everywhere. They can take a walk in the country. They meet women. They laugh, and make love, and hurry, and plan, and travel.

At four-thirty in the afternoon our cells were bolted. There was nothing to look forward to but to go on feeling hungry, doing some work, walking up and down endlessly and trying to escape into some daydream. On the first warm spring evenings, when the victorious spring managed to invade even our prison courtyards and send some disturbing scents through our windows, it was very hard to be cooped up in our small cells. Young men suffered torments. They wanted girls. Some hurled themselves at the cruel walls. Some escaped into conscious self-delusions. During one summer I, for instance, played at being invisible. It started with a dream. I dreamed that I was invisible and my body in its invisible state could penetrate through the thickest of walls. And from then on, often with a feeling of guilt, I rushed up and down the cell for hours, imagining my invisible self going through the prison walls, going out into the free world, invisibly visiting my friends. Making Agi invisible too and escaping with her to the West. And then we were walking in Portofino or Florence or Paris, eating mashed potatoes and listening to good music.

We all went a bit insane during that last period. There was a rush in our bodies; we slept badly and dreamed about being free. The Hungarian expression for release from prison is literally 'to put someone on free feet'. The expression dates from the time when convicts' feet were shackled to a long chain, and through that to the wall. Releasing someone was taking off the shackles. We knew that our release wouldn't make us free, but at least on 'free feet'. And we longed desperately for this sort of freedom.

But Rakosi was putting up resistance. The rehabilitation process took a long time. The first batches were released in May, 1954. Most of the Rajkists were taken in for rehabilitation interrogations to SP headquarters in June. My turn came in August. I spent again six weeks at SP headquarters. But now we had mattresses on our bunks and special food. They wanted to fatten us up before release. With an SP officer I went through my case. All the accusations were proved wrong. The SP officer had in his room all the volumes of *Pesti Naplo* and other Hungarian newspapers I had written for, all the books I had written. Before I was taken in for interrogation, he read through everything, trying to find an article, a statement, or part of a book, which could prove that I was 'an enemy of the people'. But I never had written against the people. So he grew friendly. He shook my hands, called me comrade. The Chief Attorney's office sent a representative to conclude the hearings. This man also said that I was innocent and would be set free at once.

Then nothing happened for weeks. The SP officer told me that my file was sent up to party headquarters and no permission yet was given for my release. The others in my case were set free on the sixth of September. I too was awakened early, I was given a civilian shirt, clothes, shoes, was meticulously shaved and my hair cut. At noon, the civilian clothes were taken away. The guard told me that the others were set free.

There I was, again in convict uniform. The iron door was bolted. What now? I started to knock on the door. The guard came and I requested to see the SP officer who conducted my 'rehabilitation' hearings. Then I tried to read and could not. It was the first time in my long prison experience that I completely lost control of myself. I could not go on with mental games. They grew stale and hideous. I could not bear to think about my situation and it was impossible not to think about it.

In the evening they gave me a tranquilizer. The guards probably reported that I was rushing to and fro in my cell like a lunatic. I was at times conscious of my facial expression – bewilderment and horror. Then I tried to accept 'facts'. I was foolish to hope and believe. They would take me back to prison. I would go on vegetating.

On the third day the SP officer gave me an audience. He repeated that as far as they and the Chief Attorney were concerned, my case was closed. But party headquarters had not yet given permission for my release. He hoped it would soon come.

Four more days of near madness. Then, on the thirteenth of September, 1954, I was again shaved, I got another haircut and civilian clothes. They were ill-fitting, smelling of disinfectant. They probably belonged to someone executed by the SP. I was taken to the prison commandant's office to settle my account. According to my calculations I should have received twenty-nine thousand forints for my work after *the deduction of fifteen forints a day for my upkeep* during the one thousand, eight hundred and thirty-two days I had spent in prison. After all the socialist state cannot be expected to pay for the upkeep of criminals, even if they are declared innocent. But they paid me only two hundred forints, with which I couldn't have bought even a pair of shoes.

Then a bored-looking sergeant took me to the side entrance of SP headquarters. He opened the gate without a word and motioned me to leave. I was on 'free feet'.

Chapter Nineteen

FOR A SECOND I thought I was going to faint. I stumbled quickly into the main street, afraid to be too near the prison building. I was frightened of people, of noises, of bright colours, of harsh sunlight. I felt exposed as if I had no skin to protect me. I wanted desperately to look my fill of the normal world; at the same time something made me afraid of looking at people.

It was an everyday morning, still summerlike, with bright sunshine. My heart wanted to burst out of my breast. There I stood in ill-fitting clothes, thin and haggard and deathly pale, carrying a rough canvas sack containing the thousand typewritten pages of my *Encyclopedia of Colonial Change*, a few chapters of my autobiography and some other manuscripts. I had been told that they could not trace my confiscated library, my manuscripts, photographs, personal papers, furniture – a man without souvenirs.

I longed to get rid of the hanged man's clothes on my body. I longed to rush to the safety of a room where I could be alone.

I took a taxi to my relatives' flat. They were away on holiday but their co-tenants knew about me, and frightened me with their out-burst of joy. They gave me food that I had dreamed of for years. But by then I was too excited to enjoy it. Then they left me alone in a room with a telephone. I did not call up Agi. I spoke to friends who had been released a week earlier. Then I asked for a bath. That first week I soaked in warm water at least three times a day, trying to wash off the prison smell.

My former prison mates, who had already had a week's experience of the 'free feet' world, told me not to be worried if I wasn't able to sleep at all for the first three or four nights. There was no point in trying. I should go to a physician friend at once and do what he said. He helped scores of ex-convicts back to 'normal' life. I had to take large doses of tranquilizers three times a day and was given vitamin injections daily. And I ate. The physician weighed me every day. The first week I put on more than ten pounds, although for the first four days I could not sleep at all.

For that first week I did not want to show myself to anyone: I was too thin and miserable-looking. Then I borrowed money, bought myself clothes and set out on foot to see the city.

I met many people whom I knew. They tried to hide their shock at my cadaverlike appearance. Had they known that the SP had tried to fatten me up for six weeks, and that now for a week I had eaten ravenously ... well, what then? Some of them did know.

The time came when I thought I looked normal enough to visit Agi. It was very early in the morning when I rang the bell. She opened the door and went white.

'Hello. I've come for that cup of coffee I missed last time,' I said, and knew I sounded artificial.

She simply motioned me to come in. She gave me coffee. She said I hadn't changed. I dared not ask questions. She was shy. I told her I had just dropped in for a minute.

'Don't you want to get the manuscript of your novel? I'll get it out. No? ... all right. I hope you'll come to see me tonight ... No? ... Tomorrow?'

I said yes, I'll come tomorrow evening. Yes, I'll stay for dinner. Then I got up. She said she'd come down too. On the staircase she opened her identity card which everybody has to carry and tucked in there was my photograph ...

I stopped. I couldn't say a word, just squeezed her arm ...

Since that time we have never been separated.

Normal life after many years in prison is a very great shock and it is most difficult to get back to it. I was lucky: in a country where long years of tyranny had destroyed the fabric of human ties, where people got used to not confiding in anyone, where they had mostly given up having 'dangerous thoughts', I had Agi and the large group of prison graduates who trusted each other. Although we, the freshly released ones, carried in our minds and bodies many half-healed wounds and scars, although we were shy and muscle-bound, yet we were perhaps the only normal group of human beings in the entire country. We did not go through the monster period. In our cells there was freedom of speech and thought. We formed lasting friendships.

After the first shock of my release was over, a series of lesser shocks revealed to me what had happened to people outside during the long years of misery and terror. There were my two elderly women friends, unmarried sisters who were both scientists, who had worked together and shared a flat for the last twenty years. They had both joined the Communist party at the same time in 1938. Let's call them Anna and Eve. A few days after my release I met Eve. She had aged terribly since I had last seen her. As we walked on the Danube embankment, she asked me about the prison years. Then she said:

'We have been fools. The party is a monster, and ought to be destroyed like a monster. No sane and decent person can think otherwise ... It's awful at the weekly party meeting to have to pretend enthusiasm for the stale slogans, for the murderous lie. But there is no point in giving back our party cards – it would mean prison. So one goes on with this nausea.'

Before parting she remembered something. 'Oh George, I almost forgot. If you happen to meet Anna, please forget what I said. She does not know how I have changed. She still wears blinkers; she is still a believer. How she does it is beyond me. But there it is.'

Some weeks later I ran into Anna. In the corner of an empty café she hurriedly whispered to me, looking around all the time. She was very glad to see me alive. She thought these criminal gangsters had destroyed me, as they destroyed many thousands. They had destroyed the country. 'I'll never forgive what they did to us decent people, who believed in the purity of the cause. I feel as if I were in Dante's *Inferno*, immersed in boiling excrement.' She had to rush off for a party seminar she was leading. But before going she told me to be careful with Eve. She – poor soul – was still a believer. Why make her unhappy?

It was autumn of 1954. The Annas and Eves in Hungary, and maybe all over the Soviet world, shared flats, talked for hours every day without once risking even a sincere look, much less a frank sentence. The great lie had transformed their life into an Inferno-for-one; yet sisters, and even man and wife pretended to each other that they adored pestilence and worshiped the monster.

The people of Hungary in 1954 were a terrorized, atomized, timid, sulking, mollusc-like lot. I witnessed later how the developments of the next two years transformed them into fissionable human material. Only a detonator was wanting to produce an explosion which shook the world of communism.

But in those first few months after my release I thought that everything was utterly hopeless. Imre Nagy was Prime Minister. I knew that it was mainly he who fought for our release. I knew that he wanted a decent 'new course' – communism without terrorism. I was firmly convinced, as I still am, that this is the most impossible of all impossible propositions. The party is dictatorship. The party is security police. The party is terrorism.

There were of course many Communist party members who wanted 'socialist legality', who dreamed of the disbanding of the SP. But the party apparatus, the governing body of the country, was solidly against Nagy. Knowing party history, I did not trust the pronouncement of Malenkov, Khrushchev and Company about 'collective leadership'. After Lenin's death Stalin promised precisely the same thing. There is no such thing as collective dictatorship.

The hopelessness of the situation did not make me bitter or resigned or cynical. I enjoyed the wonders of the 'free feet' life. The first time I went to the Opera House with Agi, I got into a feverish, euphoric state. I enjoyed the music so intensely that I ran a temperature. There were concerts, exhibitions, books, walks in the woods, outings. There were islands of private existence where one could ignore the Nausea.

As far as I thought of the future my ambition was to be a nonentity. I wanted to carve out for myself an inconspicuous existence, a modest life without dishonour. At first my greatest worry was party membership. Of the several thousand prisoners released in the autumn of 1954, the majority were former party members. It was understood that our civic rehabilitation would be followed by party rehabilitation. We were called in one by one to party headquarters, where the SP people, disguised as Central Control Committee functionaries, investigated our behavior in prison. They asked us whether we had given up our Communist faith or not during our prison years. I told the commissar who heard me that I *had* changed. I was not only a tactical adherent of legality, but an absolute one. I didn't believe moral values were relative. Although I could not give a philosophical definition for it, I believed that there was such a thing as common decency; and as far as party discipline was concerned, in the future I must be guided entirely by my conscience.

During the ceremonial party rehabilitation the thirty-two party judges of the Central Control Committee decided I was '*a sincere and honest citizen but not fit to be a party member*'.

I was relieved that without endangering myself too greatly I had avoided rejoining the party. I did not know at that time that party headquarters wanted to bring me, and some others like me, to a point where we were forced to apply for party membership. It was not good propaganda for the party that newly released prisoners did not want to rejoin. They used economic methods to put pressure on us. According to law I should at once have received 'rehabilitation money', five years of my last salary and the value of my library and possessions which they had confiscated. Those who rejoined the party received a large sum; I got nothing for two months, then a very little, and only in the summer of 1956, in the atomosphere of revolution did I get enough money to buy furniture for one room. I was supposed to get a flat to replace my confiscated one, and that they only gave me the following February; so Agi and I could not get married until then. And they made it impossible for me to get anything published. I got an advance on my *Colonial Encyclopedia*, but party headquarters forbade its publication. I wrote another book, but publication was again stopped and the publishers were forbidden to give me translation work.

According to law I was supposed to get a job after release. In December, 1954, I got a small job at the Historical Institute of the Academy of Sciences as a research historian. I received and managed to keep this job because of the six languages I work in. With my salary one could barely exist. But we managed. I did secondhand translating and writing jobs and managed to get an advance from well-meaning officials of one of the state publishing houses. I enjoyed living as a second-class citizen, as the other nine million nonparty Hungarians did.

We, the resurrected unpersons, could gauge political trends by the attitude of some of our friends and acquaintances. In September, 1954, party members thought that the rehabilitation process would go on. They believed that we newly released former Communists were the men of the future. So they were sickeningly friendly to us. I was warmly embraced by several people who had denounced me in 1948 or 1949 as a bourgeois enemy, as a Western-cosmopolitan-intellectual saboteur. They did not know that during the rehabilitation investigation we were shown our files, so we had read all the denouncing letters and documents sent to the party or to the SP. Some of us prison graduates were too tired and too disillusioned to care. If these informers rushed up to us in the street with beaming looks and tremulous voice, we stood there quietly and let them give vent to their warm feelings. Other released convicts behaved differently. SP officers and informers were beaten up, spat in the face at, brushed aside.

There were various types among our betrayers! I received a letter from a friend, an elderly writer:

> *Dear George,*
>   *It is probable that sooner or later we shall meet. Before you shake my hand, I want you to know that in 1949 I betrayed you. I was called to party headquarters and questioned about you. They knew that I was your friend. At that time the Rajk case was on. People with a Western background were arrested. You know that Ily [his wife] is a cripple and would starve without me. So I told them all the slanders they wanted to hear about you. I had to make statements like this about most of you.*
> *Your ——*

We shook hands.

At the beginning of 1955 it was obvious that Rakosi would soon oust Imre Nagy. Some of my ardent new friends tried to avoid meeting me. Others became cold and reserved when we met.

It was a curious experience for Agi. At the opera or concerts or in one of the cafés we would meet my former friends. When we were alone again, she would look at me with a questioning glance, and I would tell her to what category the person whom we had just met belonged.

Before our release the SP made us sign a document in which we pledged total silence about everything we saw and heard in prison. Most of us ignored this pledge. We believed that we made it more difficult for the Stalinists by telling our experiences. So apart from party functionaries and SP agents – one knew about *them* – we told everybody everything we knew, believing that they would not put us back into prison – yet. And if the Stalinists won completely, we would go back to prison anyhow. At that time the Stalinists in Hungary, with Rakosi in the lead, still clung to the myth that Rajk and those executed with him were guilty. We told everyone that there was not a grain of truth in any of the great show trials.

Our rehabilitation, the inside story of the rigged trials, and the release of some eighty thousand innocent people when Imre Nagy opened up the concentration camps shook the country. In ever-growing numbers people realized that mass murders had been committed in their midst. They realized that the murderers and tormentors were still in their respective positions and that everyone in the country was in danger of sudden arrest, inhuman torture and execution.

The anti-Communist majority in the country – some nine hundred and fifty thousand of the one million members of the Communist party included – was better prepared for this shock than the party apparatus. The majority knew about the murderous rule, even if the utter cynicism and monstrous sadism of it was news to many. But the still-believing Communists, many of them medium and lower party functionaries and the so-called Communist cadres, received an enormous shock. Years of hypno-pedagogics, of completely destroyed personality, of badly atrophied memory, the whole technique of controlled schizophrenia, would not save them from this shock. For there were literally hundreds of old-guard

Communists, with the finest fighting records, who told them how callously they had been smitten down. They heard about the monstrous stupidity of it all, and began to realize that thousands of ardent Communists had been slaughtered for a pointless propaganda slogan which misled no one.

I was not surprised by their reactions; I could understand their shock. It took me two years of prison to liberate myself from the 'obsession'. Those who stayed out of jail and went on with their tremendously busy party existence mostly told the truth when they said that they had never dreamed of such insanely evil things. The party saw to it that eighteen or twenty of their waking hours should be taken up by work. The party took great care to keep the blinkers in place. Only the initiated few were permitted to see the real face of the regime.

Some of the Communist writers went through a moral crisis. Three of them had nervous breakdowns. They asked awkward questions at party meetings. They began to write in a guarded tone about the necessity for party rejuvenation. The prevailing wind from Moscow was helping them; Khrushchev and company were preparing the mental climate for the Twentieth Party Congress and the anti-Stalin drive.

The majority of the people paid little attention to 'the moral belly-aching' within the party apparatus and in the 'inner party'. At that time I too failed to see its importance.

But the impact of the 'rehabilitations' went on. Some resurrected persons who rejoined the party and managed to get into higher positions demanded the arrest of some SP officers. In 1953 General Peter, the head of the SP, his Minister of Justice and some twenty high-ranking SP officers were arrested. Then, in 1955, there were more arrests which shook the SP monolith. The SP officers realized that they could not defend themselves by saying that they simply obeyed orders. They knew perfectly well that General Peter and his entourage obeyed the orders of Rakosi and Stalin. But this had not saved them from arrest. They began to have doubts. Some of the less guilty ones tried to leave the SP. Others who remained were afraid of torturing people. The 'iron fist of the working class', that is, the gangster organization of the party dictators, was in danger of disintegration.

The tug-of-war between the Stalinists and anti-Stalinists went on. As far as the majority of the people were concerned, all this went on high above our heads, in the stratosphere of Communist politics. The general atmosphere was changing, though we did not notice it at first, because the changes were imperceptibly small. But people were getting less mollusc-like. Nobody spoke up in public, but there were already shrugs and looks which no one would have dared to risk before.

In 1955 I met a friend who asked why I didn't try to write again. I told him I was on the prohibited list. 'Ah, but this will soon change. You will be a writer again.' I said something polite but it never even entered my head that this could be true.

For a writer who is somewhat graphomanic, such an existence is not easy. Writing is a biological necessity for me, and I felt completely crippled. The writer in me itched like an amputated arm. But I did not write. Not even for my desk. There might be a house search and what then?

I don't know what effect this compulsory barrenness would have had on me if it had gone on for years. At that time I still immensely enjoyed the 'free feet' world. Each season brought its wonders in colours, smells and food. There was music, a full private life and an irrational optimism that some miracle would happen and I would again become a writer.

And we were also optimistic for a personal reason: Agi was expecting a child. We lived in our shabby little flat and were busy getting together the necessary baby stuff. On the twenty-eighth of November, 1955, young George was born. While Agi was still in bed at home, I learned how to change nappies. Our life was taken up by the necessity for sterilizing bottles, heating milk, watching the scales. We talked about the baby all day and thought of him at night. We hoped he would be a great composer. We hoped that by the time he went to school, the Nausea would be over. We lived in our little cosmos and did not notice the gathering storm outside.

And then it broke. The start was the Twentieth Congress of the Soviet Communist party. Although the Hungarian Communist press was forbidden by Rakosi to print the most daring speeches in full, even the little that we could read at once showed that a new period had started. Then a few days later Polish, East German, Italian and other Communist papers arrived in Budapest, and their articles and speeches were translated and clandestinely circulated. Several thousand copies of Khrushchev's secret speech on Stalin's crimes was printed in Russian for inner-party members; a few copies somehow got to Hungary. There was a Polish text and an East German one. Translators worked furiously and soon thousands of Hungarian versions were circulating in Budapest. The party apparatus received a shock the magnitude of which is difficult for outsiders to imagine. The supergod, the fountain of all Marxist-Leninist wisdom, the omnipotent father of all peoples, the greatest military genius of all ages, the leader of progressive humanity, was denounced in no uncertain terms as a sadist mass murderer, a cynical manipulator and a military bungler. The falsifications of three decades of Soviet history became apparent. The Stalin myth was destroyed.

Rakosi, our local dictator, was obviously playing for time. He believed that the de-Stalinization period would soon be over. He tried to isolate Hungary from the Soviet Union. The Soviet Embassy in Budapest had to protest several times because *Pravda* and other Soviet newspapers were confiscated in Hungary. The top-ranking Communists in the party apparatus helped Rakosi in his desperate rear-guard campaign against de-Stalinization, but the great majority of medium and lower party functionaries were either sincerely shaken by Khrushchev's revelations about Stalin, or simply thought that it was safer to climb on the anti-Stalinist band wagon. Dogmatic Communists were shaken because the Hungarian Communist leaders were obviously not following the Kremlin line.

The 'thaw' in Hungary was at first a fight of personalities. By now the non-Communist majority in the country was watching with growing excitement the drama enacted in the 'Communist stratosphere'. The dramatis personae were the late Laszlo Rajk, Mrs. Rajk, Imre Nagy and his adherents on one side and the chief Stalinists on the other. The Stalinists were the criminals of the monster epoch: Rakosi, the dictator-in-chief, and General Farkas, dictator of Army and Security Police; Gerö, the economic dictator; Miss Elisabeth Andics, the cultural dictator. They all had their fanatical supporters in the persons of a few thousand top-party bureaucrats who had everything to lose in case of an anti-Stalinist victory.

One of the principal actors of the drama was Janos Kadar, the former Minister of Interior, in whose trial Ignotus and I had refused to help the Security Police. Although he did not help in the fight against Rakosi, after his release early in 1954, he gave the impression that he was against terrorism.

After his release he made a speech in the Central Committee of the party against torture. He described his own experiences:

His tormentor was a well-known 'public figure' in Hungary, Lieutenant Colonel of Security Police Vladimir Farkas, son of Mihaly Farkas, Minister of War and Deputy Under-Secretary of the Communist party. This man beat Kadar till he collapsed in a faint. When he came to, Vladimir Farkas was standing above him and urinating in his face.

Kadar then added:

'Comrades, we cannot rest while such Security Police methods are endangering everybody!'

Later we learned something else about him. In 1954, after being released from jail, he visited Mrs. Rajk, who had also just been freed after five years in prison. She had once saved Kadar's life, and her husband was once Kadar's best friend. Yet he was the Minister of Interior during the rigged trial ending with the execution of Rajk and imprisonment of Mrs. Rajk, not to speak about others.

Kadar gave her a shock. He told her that he was the one who on Rakosi's instructions persuaded and tricked Laszlo Rajk into making a false confession against himself. He, Kadar, was the one who promised Rajk that only his name would die, but under a different name he would be able to live with his family somewhere in the East.

'Can you forgive me?' Kadar asked at the end.

Mrs. Rajk was silent for a while, then said, 'I forgive you. My husband would have been murdered anyway. It was decided by Stalin, by General Bielkin and by Rakosi. If you had refused, the Bald Murderer [Rakosi's nickname in Hungary] would have used other willing tools instead of you.'

There was silence in the room, then Mrs. Rajk added, 'But can you forgive yourself? … Don't answer me … There is another thing too. If you want to live on as a decent person, you should inform all Hungary, the whole world about the secret of the Rajk trial and about your part in it.'*

Kadar did not answer. After a few minutes he left. And did nothing. He had every means to make a public announcement which would have finished the political career of Rakosi and would have helped to success the anti-Stalinist fight of Imre Nagy, who wanted to go 'the Gomulka way' even then.

In the summer of 1956 the anti-Stalinist wave in Hungary grew enormously in strength. The movement demanding that Rakosi should be called to account for the rigged trials and mass murder grew stronger day by day. It was obvious to the Central Committee and Politbureau members that they would have to sacrifice Rakosi and some of his entourage if they wanted to save their own skins. They thought that Kadar would make an acceptable successor to Rakosi. Kadar probably encouraged them.

But Rakosi heard about this and acted swiftly. At the next session of the Central Committee of the Communist party, he made a few remarks about the 'unwise behavior of Comrade Kadar in joining some people who demand the punishment of those responsible for the Rajk trial'. Then Rakosi looked around with a significantly smug expression and gave a sign to one of his henchmen. This person brought in a tape recorder and started it.

Members of the Central Committee – with a few exceptions – listened in astonishment and horror. *Two voices were recognized by them: that of Laszlo Rajk, murdered in 1949, and that of Janos Kadar.* It was a long conversation, obviously held at 60 Andrassy Street, the former headquarters of the SP. It was a curious conversation. Janos Kadar was persuading his best friend, Laszlo Rajk, not to be obstinate and confess everything the SP and the men of General Bielkin wanted him to confess.

---

* Mrs. Julia Rajak did not tell many people about this conversation. But in 1956, when the taped prison conversation between Rajk and Kadar was produced for the members of the Hungarian Communist party Central Committee, she told all her friends and acquaintances. She told me too.

Kadar did not pretend at all that Rajk had done something punishable. He mentioned several times Rajk's obvious innocence. He argued only that the Communist movement of the world needed these confessions. 'This is the only way to expose Tito.' He reminded Rajk that the latter would have gladly sacrificed his life many a time for the party. The party asked from him now a lesser sacrifice, a sort of moral suicide. Only his past would be slandered, only his name would die. It would be published that he was executed, but instead he would be taken with his wife and baby son to the Crimea after the trial. There they would recuperate and after a while Rajk would get under a different name a very important party function somewhere very far. The party would be grateful to him.

The conversation showed that Rajk – even after many weeks of sleeplessness, hunger and torture – did not accept easily the nightmarish logic of this argument. Kadar cajoled, flattered, promised. Rajk resisted. He said that people would not believe that a lifelong Communist with such a fighting record as his – that such a man was a police stool pigeon, an agent of some five secret services, including the Gestapo.

'Why do you want to make a heel out of me from the very start?' Rajk asked. 'If you want conspiracy, why not say that lately I conspired against Rakosi? That would not be true either, but some people might believe it.'

Kadar explained that the simple masses must be turned against Tito, consequently they had to be turned against Rajk himself. He must be made out to have been a vile character all his life. At last Rajk promised to think it over. Kadar again gave his word of honour that together with his wife and baby son Rajk would be taken right after the trial to some wonderful Soviet sanatorium. At that time Mrs. Rajk was in jail, her son – on Kadar's orders – was already taken away from her. His birth certificate was destroyed and the baby, under a false name, was placed in one of the nursery schools for orphans.

The Central Committee members and some high party functionaries present – about fifty people, all counted – remembered, while they listened, the fate of Rajk and family. Rajk was not permitted to see his wife before his execution. He had believed to the last that he would not be executed. It was common knowledge in Budapest that a high-ranking SP officer committed suicide after Rajk's execution because he knew that the leadership promised Rajk freedom and life under a different name. This officer made some unwise remarks about this and was forced to commit suicide. It was also known in Budapest that some of the fellow victims of Rajk shouted under the gallows, 'You have betrayed us!'

While the tape recorder was played, Janos Kadar sat there with lowered head. He was crushed. In the SP jail, some years previously, he had been humiliated by his tormentors. Now his own past came up and humiliated him before the fifty people present – and soon before entire Hungary. He thought his career was finished. Never again would he have power in his hands. But chance – or fate? – intervened. One of Rakosi's stooges, Erik Molnar, the Minister of Justice, asked the functionary to play the tape again from the beginning. The audience heard now the beginning of the taped conversation, which they were not meant to hear. They heard the voice of Janos Kadar, saying:

Dear Laci, I come to you in behalf of Comrade Rakosi. He asked me to explain to you the position. Of course we all know that you are innocent and perhaps the whole thing could have been arranged in a less brutal way. But Comrade Rakosi believes you will understand. Only really great comrades are chosen for such a role as the one we ask you to play. Comrade Rakosi asked me to tell you, by doing what is asked from you, you will do a historic service to the Communist movement ... and so on.

This had a curious effect. On any group of normal people these revelations – during which Rakosi's face was crimson with anger – could have had only one effect: a decision to expel both Rakosi and Kadar at once from the party and have them arrested instantly. But the Central Committee of the Communist party was not a normal group of people. They looked upon the whole thing as an impasse. They took no actions. Probably many of those present had similar revelations to fear. After all it was clear that Kadar had had no idea that his conversation with Rajk was taped.

But the revelations soon spread in political circles. The Central Committee members talked to their best friends; so did these, and soon the entire country knew about it.

Although international events played into his hands, Rakosi could not save his own position in Hungary. There was such a unanimous clamour for the punishment of the 'Bald Murderer' that with the help of Mikoyan, the party leadership had to evict him. This happened on the eighteenth of July, 1956, session of the Central Committee of the Communist party. Rakosi was just about to propose the arrest of Imre Nagy and four hundred others, when Mikoyan intervened.

A few days later Rakosi flew to Moscow. His belongings went by rail, filling three freight cars. In the airport before departure he gave twenty thousand forints each to his four last bodyguards, to the two cooks and four maids of his establishment. These last bodyguards were indeed lucky. Their predecessors, five groups of them, were hanged in turns. The simple Security Police men were promised that after serving for a term as the great man's bodyguard, they would be sent to special SP officer's school in Moscow. Instead they were taken to Gyujtofoghaz, where they were promptly hanged. With my cellmates I saw the bodies of one group as they were taken to the lime pit.

And what is the explanation for Rakosi? It is quite obvious that he emerged after sixteen years of jail as a perfect Stalinist maniac. He went to jail when thirty-three and emerged at forty-eight. He lost his best years. He lost his health. He lost most of his human qualities, if he had them at all. Gravely ill, on a most austere diet, married to an ugly Yakut commissar for political reasons, the only enjoyment left to him was that derived from power. He knew perfectly well that he was the most hated man in his country. He taught his disciples and accomplices to despise the masses and went on murdering thousands in the name of the masses.

Normal human beings do not understand him. They would have every reason to distrust themselves if they did.

The tape recorder incident, the attempts of Rakosi to force General Peter to make false confessions, his plan to have four hundred people arrested, intensified the indignation in the country. More and more people in the party apparatus turned into anti-Stalinists, and fanatical batches of opportunities thought that it was time to climb on the anti-Stalin band wagon. The fact that Mikoyan arrived by jet plane to remove Rakosi from the leadership shook the Stalinist camp and made the SP organization waver.

The Stalinists saw only one advantageous sign, one ray of hope: Mikoyan and the Central Committee, after ousting Rakosi, made his principal accomplice, Erno Gerö, first secretary of the party and dictator of the country.

Gerö's appointment caused a wave of indignation in the country. I have already written about this Gray Eminence of the international Communist movement in connection with the Spanish Civil War. He was a general handyman and economic expert of the Comintern. He played many roles under many names. His last and longest role was that of economic wizard in Hungary, architect of gigantic Five-Year Plans which totally failed.

Since 1949 Gerö had been Minister of State controlling the Ministries of Heavy and Light Industry, of Transport, of Internal and External Trade. He was also Chairman of the Supreme Economic Council and President of the Economic Committee of the party.

With a stroke of his pen he ordered the one hundred per cent socialization of commerce and industry, and subordinated the entire economy of the country to the interests of Stalin's war chest. He wanted to transform Hungary, with two Five-Year Plans, into a country of heavy industry. Gigantic projects were started and failed. The strategic needs of the Soviet Union required an elaborate deep-tube railway system under Budapest so that the vital east-west railway lines would not have to cross the all too vulnerable Danube bridges. Gerö, tired of the dilatory experts, ordered the huge subway works to be started without proper preliminary investigations. Twenty billion forints had already been spent when the Danube flooded the tunnels, some houses collapsed, and the project had to be abandoned.

His other pet project was the new steel city of Hungary. At the village of Dunapentele south of Budapest, huge steel and coking plants were built. Gerö was again impatient with his experts. Some 'saboteurs' were sent to jail because they did not think that the Hungarian brown coal was suitable for the Soviet type of coking process. When the plant had been built, another group of experts went to jail, because the first group was right, it did not work.

The intensified industrialization produced a shortage of workers. Hence Gerö insisted on the intensification of the kolkhoz policy. Thousands of peasants were forced by Security Police torture into these collective farms. Many of them preferred to become industrial workers. If any of Gerö's projects was still short of workers, the Security Police discovered some rural conspiracy, and ten thousand peasant lads were driven into a new concentration camp for forced labour. Under Gerö some one hundred and twenty thousand people became slave-laborers in the various 'Hungarian Siberias'.

Hungary had been well-known as an exporter of locomotives, diesel engines, radio sets, electric bulbs, Danube-going vessels and many other products. Under the economic wizardry of Gerö, the quality of these products deteriorated. Contracts were canceled. Heavy penalties had to be paid for overdue shipments. By 1952, his economic policy, the unhealthy pace of industrialization, Soviet looting and the terrorist atmosphere had caused a hidden bankruptcy.

The economic dictator then began to stave off complete failure by the fraudulent methods he had learned with his masters. Despite the unanimous opposition of the experts, he signed contracts for machines, machine tools, hydroelectric works, locomotives, and so forth knowing full well that his industry could not produce these items during the all-too-short contract time. On some orders, two-thousand-dollar penalty had to be paid for every day after the time limit. The reason? He needed hard currency badly. On the contract he could borrow money abroad. In order to get two hundred thousand dollars at once he was willing to risk a loss of five times that amount. Under his regime the country paid out millions of dollars in penalties.

Gerö was originally a well-trained economist and a cold-headed realist. At the outset he knew full well the dangers entailed in a centralized bureaucracy and in 'desk-planning'. At the beginning he made ironical remarks about those 'who seem to think that economic laws cease to operate in socialist countries'.

Yet under this eminently sane and experienced economist Hungarian economy turned into something like a surrealistic joke, into a hopeless bureaucratic muddle. The congested railways were carrying goods from central depots hundreds of miles to factories which could get the same goods from neighbouring plants. Seven separate ministries overlapped in all the economic fields; the muddle and red tape grew enormously, and the proportion of the administrating staff of commerce and industry soon grew to thirty-five per cent of the workers engaged in production, processing, transport and retail sale.

Gerö's appointment not only angered the people, it brought back vividly into their minds the all-round economic failure of the regime. The manifestations of this anger should have been suppressed by the dictator of culture, Miss Andics.

The late Dr. Freud would have enjoyed analyzing Elisabeth Andics, whose personality embodies all the worst traits of the female Bolshevik functionary and those of a Stalinist cultural dictator.

Imagine a shrew who has to revenge on all the males of the species an ocean of neglect suddenly given the unlimited opportunity of nagging thousands of interesting and talented men. Imagine a Kremlin-style Mrs. Grundy having at her mercy the entire cultural life of an unruly nation famous for its unconquerable sense of humour. Imagine a narrow-minded virago, a bigoted Marxist cliché-monger, in charge of the 'Stalinist re-education' of dadaist poets, cubist sculptors, post-expressionist painters and surrealist novelists.

She tried to condition with Stalinist hypno-pedagogics everybody from kindergarten infants to academicians. She sought to have a firm grip on people's minds from womb to tomb. And hers was the greatest failure ever experienced by any petty tyrant of the Soviet orbit.

During the short-lived Bolshevik dictatorship in Hungary in 1919, a number of young university students left their middle-class families to become professional revolutionaries. One of them was Elisabeth Andics. After the fall of the Bolsheviks Andics was arrested and was exchanged in 1923 for a Hungarian prisoner of war in Russia.

In the Soviet fatherland, instead of finishing her university course, she went to the Party Academy and studied 'historical and dialectical materialism'.

A young Comintern functionary of Hungarian descent, Andrew Berei, married her but soon volunteered for a dangerous foreign mission. While Comrade Berei roamed Europe or acted as Comintern 'instructor' of the Belgian Communist party, his wife lived with their daughter in various cities of the Soviet Union. She held administrative and teaching posts of medium importance and led the austere life of a female functionary whose charms do not tempt comrades to break the party's morality rules.

Her chance came in 1945. She returned to Hungary at its 'liberation' as the number one Communist woman in the country. Her first function in Hungary was twofold. She was given charge of party education and the 'historians' front. She started at once on her campaign against 'bourgeois objectivity', 'cosmopolitan erudition' and 'the treasonous toleration of imperialistic trends in cultural life'.

In 1945 Elisabeth Andics set out to mold Hungarians to the authorized pattern. Her power was based not only on her Muscovite past but also on her family connections. Her husband, Andrew Berei, the former Belgian party invigilator, also became Hungarian in 1945 and alternated between key positions in the Foreign Office and the Supreme Planning Authority. Their daughter was married to Vladimir Farkas, Lieutenant Colonel of the Security Police, and son of the Minister of Defence, General Mihaly Farkas. Andics's son-in-law was the Security Police officer who tortured Janos Kadar in prison and who urinated in Kadar's face.

When in 1956 there was a clamour in Hungary for the legal punishment of General Farkas and his son, Andics ordered her daughter to divorce Vladimir Farkas. They said in Budapest 'rats desert their sinking sons-in-law'.

These valiant fighters for the working-class cause lived in the Mayfair of Budapest, called 'Meadow of the Pashas', re-named by the people of Budapest 'Meadow of the Commissars'. They had only six servants in their modest fourteen-room villa. They had only two summer residences, one in the mountains and one in the special enclosure at Lake Balaton, which contained the villas of the party top-rankers and was protected by barbed wire and the special pillboxes of the Security Police.

Elisabeth Andics became undisputed dictator of Hungarian cultural life in 1953. From primary school education to nuclear physics, from university curricula to fine arts and literature – everything was under her shrewish sceptre. A few examples will suffice to give an idea of the system she forced on Hungary in order to follow exactly the Soviet pattern.

Children entering school were classified into six categories according to 'class descent':

1. Worker
2. Peasant
3. Intellectual

4. Petty employee
5. 'Other'
6. 'Class enemy' 'X'

Categories one and two had no trouble in ascending through middle schools to university. Category three had very little chance of entering a university; categories four and five received a university education in exceptional cases. Those in category X were forbidden to go beyond primary school.

Category X, children of 'class-enemy' descent, were judged on a stricter basis than the Jews in Nazi Germany. A factory-owner grandfather, or a landowner great-grandfather, was enough to get the child into category X. While a category five child was only a fifth-rate person, an X child was below humanity.

In 1953, when she decided to launch an all-out campaign for the victory of 'socialist realism' in the fine arts, all commissions for paintings and statues were placed under the control of a central authority set up by her. Painters and sculptors did what they were told or starved.

When the painters went to the central authority on fine arts, they were given slips of papers on which Andics's subordinates typed the commissions. There were such titles as 'The heroic Csepel workers in the last week of the fight for the overfulfillment of the revised Five-Year Plan' or 'Our heroic frontier guards fire on escaping class enemies' or a historical subject, 'Heroic members of the builders' trade union hold an illegal meeting in 1933'. Still lifes were branded as 'bourgeois escapism', nudes as 'ivory-tower formalism', landscapes as 'avoiding the issues of the day'.

Hardest to bear was party dictatorship over literature – as exercised by Miss Andics. She expected all novels to be in conformity with the party line of the day. By that time there were five main types of writers in Hungary – and throughout the Soviet orbit: these who were forbidden to write, like myself; those who dared to write; who dared not to write; who did not dare to write; and finally those who did not dare not to write.

Those who dared to write, like Tibor Dery, were constantly under barrage from party headquarters. The well-known writers who dared not to write were attacked for their 'strike of silence', just as those who did not dare to write. Life was not easy for those who did not dare not to write. It takes six to twelve months to write a novel. During that time the party line was likely to change. They had to replan the structure of their novel several times. Entire chapters had to be discarded as certain events of the past became 'unfacts'. Before sending it to the publishers, a quick last-minute revision brought the manuscript in accordance with the party line of the day. If the publisher's reader took a longer time to decide, a new change of line necessitated more changes. If while the novel was at the printers there was a new basic change in the party line, the novel was never published. But the most dangerous time came after publication. If the party line soon changed, the novel was put on a forbidden list and the author got into serious trouble.

Writers tried to escape into the past. They wrote historical novels about epochs in past centuries, the histories of which were not likely to change.

To write short stories was much safer, but you could not make a living by short stories. In the literary periodicals textbook jargon prevailed. There was no state censorship. Each periodical had its own resident censor in the person of a representative of Miss Andics's organization. Controversial articles were sent to party headquarters.

Zhdanovian aesthetics and 'socialist realism' turned into a constant and very boring nightmare for the writers. Nobody ever defined 'socialist realism' for them. None of the Kremlin leaders and theoreticians – no writer or artist among them – had a clear idea what it is. They never saw the impossibility of turning art and literature into a propaganda instrument of the daily, immediate aims of the party.

Novels, plays and short stories were expected to have a positive hero, a good Communist of working class origins who leads a heroic and finally successful fight for the building of a factory, for the over-fulfillment of the Five-Year Plan or the organization of a kolkhoz. He had to be dignified, without human shortcomings. Sense of humour was strictly forbidden as far as the 'positive heroes' were concerned, while writers were expected to depict the 'negative heroes' with vitriolic satire. This primitive snow-white and obnoxiously black world of super-heroes and vile villains had to be described in simple, straightforward language.

The party bosses wanted to determine not only the contents but also the form of the writing. Nothing angers writers more than interference with their style. And dogmatic phrase-mongers like Miss Andics did precisely that. The scientists were constantly nagged by her too. It's no wonder that the artists and intellectuals revolted first. The revolt started among those believing Communist writers who at the start of the epoch tried sincerely to evolve a new kind of Communist literature. They were turned later into the category of those who did not dare not to write. They went on writing, sacrificing more and more their artistic integrity. Through a long series of smaller and larger compromises they debased themselves till they became primitive propagandists. No doubt they thought that in this transition period they served 'the cause' best if they forgot about their 'bourgeois superiority complex', about their 'self-isolating style' and 'decadent visions'. They sacrificed for the cause the artists in themselves. When it turned out that a large part of 'the cause' was a murderous lie, they got into a rage. They were deeply hurt. They were in a moral panic. They had given up what was for them the most sacred thing in their life: their literary personalities. And it turned out that instead of serving the future good of humanity by this tremendous sacrifice, they helped monsters like Rakosi to commit their vile and pointless mass murders.

So they revolted.

Chapter Twenty

THE WHOLE THING started with the rebellion of sentences. Communist writers of the party functionary type found themselves writing imprudent sentences. In a long article which was written throughout in the approved party manner here and there a sentence which was almost human popped up – sentences of which the writer could be proud. And those party functionary writers who in the past had committed grave crimes against their conscience were now in such a mood that they were risking their positions or even jail for the sake of one or two unimportant but human sentences. In 1955 *Irodalmi Ujsag* (Literary Gazette), the official weekly of the Communist-run Writers' Association, started to publish articles and short stories containing such sentences. The general public – the by now disenchanted majority of party members included – did not notice these sentences. The weekly was published in fifteen thousand copies, mainly for party functionaries and the schools, institutions and clubs of the Communist 'cultural front'. I occasionally bought the weekly at that time but found it stupidly dogmatic and boring. Such an issue of the weekly was nevertheless confiscated on Miss Andics's order. But not even this confiscation succeeded in making the weekly popular. I took it, as most of the non-Communists did, for a symptom of the fight in the offices of party headquarters.

After the Soviet Communist party's Twentieth Congress in February, 1956, after Stalin's second death, the Communist writers became more and more daring. One heard rumours about turbulent meetings in the party organization of Communist writers. Some of them openly attacked Rakosi and Miss Andics. These writers had a growing number of adherents among the Communist university students and the younger members of the party apparatus.

The Communist party apparatus was in a turmoil. Communist writers, students and young functionaries pressed for the 'moral rejuvenation of the party'. They thought that they were in line with the Kremlin policy in demanding the punishment of the murderers, in demanding 'socialist legality' and a flexible, cultured Marxism-Leninism. The next period taught many of them that these were impossible demands. But at that time most of them were firmly convinced that they were the real Communists and the murderers on the top were pathological deviations from party theory and practice.

While the country as a whole, the disgusted industrial workers very much included, were still most sceptical about this rebellion, the Communist writers pressed on with their new line. Party headquarters had six delegated functionaries in the executive branch of the Writers' Association. With their help Miss Andics succeeded in firing editor after editor of the *Irodalmi Ujsag*. But it was increasingly difficult to find a new editor. At last both Miss Andics and the rebellious Communist writers agreed on the person of Endre Enczi, a quiet novelist who for years had been very much in the background. But Enczi, though a Communist, was also in a rebellious mood. His first act was to inform Miss Andics and the party headquarters that he would not submit manuscripts for censorship to the party commissars, not even to party headquarters. By this time the rebellion in the party apparatus and the uncertainty in the Security Police had reached such a stage that Miss Andics's request for the banning of the paper was refused by the Politbureau.

Enczi than transformed *Irodalmi Ujsag* from the dull and dogmatic organ of literary functionaries into something unique in the Soviet orbit: a platform of free writing.

In the spring of 1956 we met the Enczi's at a party. And there I heard a sentence from him which I had never expected to hear in my life again:

'Why don't you write for us? You can write as you please!'

I did. And so did some other hitherto silenced writers. We, the freshly resurrected former unpersons of literature, and the rebellious

Communist writers were in a most imprudent mood. Signor Togliatti, the Italian Communist leader, accused us later in an essay of 'having destroyed the Communist party in demented frenzy'. I must state though that this possibility never entered our heads. We believed that there was some ferment going on which might succeed in easing the stranglehold on our lives. All we dreamed of was a little less Soviet and SP oppression, a little less exploitation, a little brighter and more secure life, and – last but not least – some artistic and literary freedom. Were we foolish to hope that bureaucratic despotism could be liberalized and changed into democratic socialism? We certainly were. But in the given circumstance that was the only hope, and we had lived for such a long time without hope.

We had our moods of doubts and dismal forebodings. I remember a day when I told some of my friends, 'We are fools. We hope that plague bacilli will change into Vitamin C.'

But there was the possibility to write as we pleased. And one could not refrain from writing.

When I started to write for *Irodalmi Ujsag*, Rakosi was still in power. Through this many agents he circulated rumours about struggles in the Kremlin which would result in a change of line. Stalinism would return and all anti-Stalinists would be liquidated. We had our child. If I were to be imprisoned again, Agi and the child would be deported. Or even worse they might arrest Agi too, take away the child and bring him up in one of the Security Police orphanages. I was conscious of the possibility. Before I sent my articles off to *Irodalmi Ujsag*, I pondered a lot. But in each case I decided to publish. It was their heads or ours.

Reading these articles now is a curious experience for me. They were literary articles and short short stories. One was about Dostoievski's Alyosha Karamazov posing the famous question: 'If by the torture of a single innocent child you could ensure the future happiness of entire humanity, would you do it?' In my short story – the description of a dream-vision – Alyosha Karamazov puts his question to misguided Communists, to ten million eyewitnesses. He reveals to them their schizophrenia and says that there is no forgiveness for the cynical murderers who did not even believe in the future happiness of humanity.

The Undefeated

For such writing – clearly attacking the party dictators – the answer a year earlier would have been at least prison, if it ever got in print, a most unlikely thing. Now there was only a leading article against me in the party daily, called with Orwellian irony *Szabad Nep* (Free People).

In the spring and summer of 1956 the short stories, poems, essays and articles in *Irodalmi Ujsag* exposed and attacked many aspects of the Great Lie and of party dictatorship. The revolt was not only in the contents but even more so in the form. After many years of textbook jargon, of nauseating *Pravda* platitudes, there was again a human, cultured style. There was again sense of humour, experiments in style; there were unexpected turns in the sentences. The heavy wine of this precarious freedom went to the heads of the writers of *Irodalmi Ujsag*. We revelled in this new-found freedom and were inspired by it.

After years of conformity *Irodalmi Ujsag* was *different*. And it turned out that the general public longed for these rebellious sentences. People found a delight in reading the truth which is difficult to explain to outsiders. Everyone knew perfectly well that Rakosi was a murderer. But to read careful hints stating this fact seemed to them wonderful. The circulation of *Irodalmi Ujsag* grew enormously. Every Friday people fought for it on street corners when the distributing vans arrived at the kiosks and news-stands. Soon the circulation was doubled, trebled; and it would have grown tenfold if party headquarters had not limited our newsprint supplies. The result of this was that our weekly had issues with a black market value of ten, twenty and even fifty times the original price. Some articles were reprinted and distributed by private groups. In a few weeks the weekly became the mouthpiece of the strange ferment going on in the country.

The revolt of writers soon infected the journalists, who were under far stricter party control and in a more difficult position. Yet in a country in which every newspaper and periodical is published either directly by the Communist party or by one of its subsidiaries, like the Communist youth movement, the trade union council, the army, and so on, the 'sentence rebellion' began everywhere. There were isolated attacks against the Security Police, against the murderous collectivization drive in agriculture, against the cruel bureaucratic methods in education.

The 'thaw' in Hungary was much more like a forest fire. By now the university students and even the Budapest industrial workers believed that there was some hope of our success. Although there were no conspiratorial meetings, no agreed tactical plan, the limited aims were obvious. To get rid of Rakosi and his entourage, to expose the criminal record of the Security Police, to build up safeguards against uncontrolled secret police rule in the future.

In July, 1956, Mikoyan fired Rakosi. This made everyone optimistic, although his successor, Gerö, was not much better. But the Stalinists were clearly in retreat. Next General Mihaly Farkas was sacrificed as a scapegoat. The party openly admitted that the Security Police under General Farkas murdered thousands and imprisoned tens of thousands of innocent people; therefore he was expelled from the party and cashiered as an officer. This again made people confident and indignant at the same time.

During the same period the Petöfi Club became active. The time has not arrived yet to tell the full story of this club. It was organized as the club of the university branch of the Communist youth movement. Its name was taken from Alexander Petöfi, the poet-hero of the 1848 Hungarian revolution, which was suppressed in 1849 with the help of Russian troops. The purpose of the club was to bring the problems of Hungary into the open by a series of lectures and public debates. And in a country where people had to be forced to attend lectures by very grave threats, these lectures and debates were immensely popular. People knew that in the Petöfi Club there was freedom of speech. More than two thousand people attended the first debate. The last one was held in the Central Club of Army Officers, which had a big theatre and several large halls. The meeting was timed for six o'clock, but by three p.m. six thousand people had taken their places in the theater, the halls, the large courtyard, hoping to hear the speeches at least through loudspeakers. The meeting lasted till three o'clock in the morning and there was violent demonstration, against the terrorist regime. The fact that it was held in the Army Officers Club demonstrated to everyone that the young officers were also with us.

Two days later the party's Central Committee condemned and banned the Petöfi Club by resolution. The leader of the writers, Tibor Dery, along with a young writer called Tardos, was expelled from the party.

During these months of ferment I had very little private life. After seven years of silence, I was writing again. I started to write a novel – an 'I-write-as-I-please-novel' – and I was asked to lecture a great deal. There were meetings and discussions. Towards the end of the summer a young film producer, an official of the State Film Company who died later in the revolution, came to see me. He said that we should exploit this crazy period while it lasted.

'Do you realize,' he said, 'that nowhere in the world can you write as freely now as in Hungary? There are not even libel laws. The party machinery has stopped functioning. We are gloriously, foolishly free. The Film Company has its huge allocations. We can make wonderful, crazy, daring films. Write a film like that for us. I don't mind anything. The only condition is that it should be good art. I don't care whether your hero is an elderly kangaroo or a naughty idea in the head of an old maid. But write it. We shall give you our best director, best actors, everything!' When he left, I talked for hours with Agi about the impossibly wonderful and wonderfully impossible situation. There was still party dictatorship. Security Police was still formally in control. There were six Soviet divisions in the country. The Soviet Embassy no doubt was sending detailed reports about this revolutionary ferment. How was it possible that nothing was happening? Could it be that the Kremlin leaders wanted the people of Russia, of Hungary and of all their colonies, to revolt and do away with Stalinism? Or what was the explanation? Could this go on indefinitely?

We did not know. But our movement had its momentum. Now we demanded the punishment of General Farkas and his associates. We demanded that Laszlo Rajk get a proper funeral. We demanded that Gerö and Miss Andics go. We started a campaign against party bureaucrats. Julius Hay, the playwright, wrote a vitriolic article about a 'Mr. Kucsera', the archetype of the stupidly cruel party functionary. Some weeks later, quite accidentally, Geza Losonczy attacked the functionaries in a periodical on the same day that *Irodalmi Ujsag* published my leading article against them.

There were attacks against us in the party daily, and party headquarters accused us of inciting to revolt. Soon after this, on the seventeenth of September, 1956, there was the yearly general meeting of the Writers' Association. At this we staged the first democratic election by secret ballot in the country since 1945. The three hundred and seventy members of the association ousted unanimously the six party commissars who had directed the Writers' Association up till then. There was a majority vote against 'socialist realism'. The mood of the meeting was aggressive. Writer after writer got up to expose in no uncertain terms the political, moral, economic and cultural bankruptcy of the regime. It was clearly a revolt against party dictatorship. My contribution was comparatively mild. I said only these few sentences:

'Party headquarters accused me of inciting people against party functionaries. I am prepared to admit more. I have spoken and written against terrorism and injustice. Is that a crime? Even if it were, could I be punished in this country for it?

'General Farkas is a mass murderer – yet he is only cashiered and expelled from the party. You cannot cashier me, like Farkas, because I am not a general. You cannot expel me, because I am not a party member. If loss of rank or expulsion from the party is all you are willing to do against a murderer – even a mass murderer – what possible punishment can you threaten us writers with?'

Various scientists' and university students' associations were holding similar meetings. In the factories the workers were in an aggressive mood. The situation had changed to an unheard of degree. It was now the Security Police who feared the people instead of the other way around.

On the sixth of October Laszlo Rajk and three others were given a ceremonial reburial. Seven years earlier they had been hanged as archcriminals, imperialist spies and monstrous enemies of the working class. Now they were declared officially innocent together with hundreds of other corpses. More than a hundred thousand people turned out for the funeral. The entire country was again reminded of the mass murders committed in our midst.

The Undefeated

We – the group of writers around the *Irodalmi Ujsag* – had an uneasy day. We feared that Rajk's funeral would be turned into a bloody demonstration by some provocators. It was a relief when the funeral was over without any disturbances. It would have been awful – we thought at that time – if some rash act should lead to bloodshed. It would have meant brutal Soviet invasion.

On the twenty-first of October, 1956, Gomulka in Poland proclaimed everything we hoped and demanded for Hungary: socialist legality, the disbanding of Security Police, the end of terrorism. Everybody in Hungary was hopeful. The Poles – like us – fought for some more independence from the Kremlin rulers, for a general democratization, for the rule of law, for a kind of life which was almost worth living. They succeeded and Poland was not attacked by the Soviet Union. Surely we too should succeed if only we could get rid of the Stalinists in the Hungarian party executive.

The university students and the writers decided to hold a sympathy demonstration next day to express their admiration for the Poles and their determination to achieve the same liberties. It was decided to hold a meeting at the statue of our 1848 revolutionary hero Petöfi and from there to march through Budapest to the statue of the Polish General Bem, who was one of the great commanders of our War of Liberty in 1848.

On the morning of the twenty-third we had a meeting at the Writers' Association and agreed on a seven-point resolution, which remains good documentary evidence of how the writers felt a few hours before the demonstration started:

> *We have arrived at a historic turning point. We shall not be able to acquit ourselves well in this revolutionary situation unless the entire Hungarian working people rallies around us in discipline.* THE LEADERS OF THE PARTY AND THE STATE SO FAR HAVE FAILED TO PRESENT A WORKABLE PROGRAMME. *The people responsible for this are those who, instead of expanding socialist democracy, are obstinately organizing themselves with the aim of restoring the Stalin and Rakosi regime of terror in Hungary. We Hungarian writers have formulated the demands of the Hungarian nation in the following seven points.*
>
> *The main points were that there should be 'national independence;*

revision of international treaties on the basis of equality; that factories must be run by workers and experts; that peasants must be given the right to decide their own fate freely; that our electoral system must correspond to the demands of socialist democracy; that the people must elect their representatives in Parliament, in the Councils and in all autonomous organs of administrations freely, by secret ballot.'

A few minutes before one o'clock it was announced by Budapest Radio that the Minister of Interior prohibited all public demonstrations. We decided to march nevertheless and sent a delegation to the government to warn them that this last-minute prohibition might lead to bloodshed. The march had already started when the Ministry of Interior withdrew the ban an hour later. This was a momentous decision and a very grave one from the standpoint of the party leadership. In fact, a great public demonstration was to take place which was not planned and organized by the party. A dictatorship was too weak to crush the opposition. A dictatorship which for nearly a decade had forced organized public falsehood on a country now had to face the restoration of free public opinion and was forced to give way to popular demands. The terrorist regime which had punished even whispers of dissent by torture, prison and death had to give orders to its terrorist troops to stand by inactively while a great demonstration against terrorism took place.

The demonstration was essentially anti-Communist and anti-Russian, because without any previous planning, organizing or preparation it came to be held under the banner of the 1848–1849 War of Liberty that was crushed by Russian troops. The dreams and aims of the 1848 liberal revolution permeated everybody as we marched from the statue of Petöfi to that of General Bem. Without planning or conspiratorial preparation, a people atomized and turned against each other by the ideology of hate, intolerance and suspicion found now a common ideological platform – the great liberal heritage of 1848.

There was a mass meeting at the Petöfi statue. Our declaration was read. We chanted two lines from one of Petöfi's revolutionary poems:

'THIS WE SWEAR – THIS WE SWEAR:
SLAVES WE – NO MORE BE!'

And then the great march started. University students, writers, secondary school boys and girls, intellectuals, workers marched, and everywhere onlookers joined the demonstrators. In an hour there were three hundred thousand people marching.

We marched ten abreast, arm-in-arm. That march, that demonstration has often been described but never yet to my satisfaction. Here I can only describe my own mental and emotional state that afternoon. I would like to write an entire volume about that afternoon sometime. I was happy and worried and confused. It was wonderful to see and feel that in a city where for ten years suspicion and hopelessness had reigned supreme, where private feelings and public sentiments were in ugly discord, people marched arm-in-arm, trusting one another, fired by great hopes and a gay resolution.

But where would all this lead to? There must be no bloodshed, I thought. During the march I talked to several of my friends who during the next two days became leaders of our fight. They were in a similar frame of mind. The idea of an uprising did not enter our heads. One must be stark staring mad to think of ten million Hungarians fighting the Soviet Empire of more than two hundred million inhabitants. No – we thought and said – in the middle of the twentieth century, in the age of tanks, flame throwers and jet planes, armed revolutions are no longer possible.

But then why did we fight? Why did I – in my modest way – take part in the revolution? Because the fight had begun.

The Security Police fired on unarmed university students; the ordinary police was called out against us and instead joined the fight; the army was called out against us and they too joined us. The workers were fighting and so were the peasants. We were firing on the Security Police and Soviet troops. We turned against the Soviets. There was no way back.

A very rare thing in history had happened, something up till now seen only in the isolated cases of peasant rebellions: a whole nation rose spontaneously and in the turmoil of fighting found momentary leadership.

Knowing almost without exception all these later momentary leaders, I can state that none of them thought of or wanted an armed uprising, a Hungarian war against the Soviet Union.

But when the fight was on, we simply could not stop fighting. As isolated fighting groups mushroomed up every hour, a liaison organization had to be created to connect them. During the revolutionary days I too went on such liaison missions. They were dreary, very long and frightening walks though a huge city which had become a battlefield. And then the next issue of *Irodalmi Ujsag* had to be prepared. I fetched the manuscripts from my writer friends. For days and nights I roamed the streets to get together the material for the next issue. Each street crossing, each open space, was uncertain territory. The walls of houses, which gave one a sense of safety in normal times, now seemed pitifully weak. Bullets kept ricocheting in the narrow streets, distant cannonades echoed everywhere and great detonations reverberated for a long time in the avenues. One could never tell from which roof they would start to fire. For the lonely walker there was always the possibility of being fired at by his own people. I was often badly scared. It would have been stupid to be killed by a stray bullet. And what about the manuscripts? The weekly must be published.

But these private fears and worries were far less intensive than the impression given by my description. At the same time I was excited, exhilarated by the many wonderful things I saw. I was fired by great hopes.

What did I, what did we, hope for?

Our hopes, wishes and dreams varied according to the level of our information, according to our backgrounds and temperament. On the third and fourth day of our fight, when it seemed that we had a chance against Soviet tanks, I hoped that we could prove the possibility of national uprisings in the middle of the twentieth century. I hoped that the Hungarian people could prove that they were able to annihilate the Hungarian Communist dictatorship, *if it was backed only by six Soviet divisions*. I hoped that the pressure of world public opinion, that a really united UN's unanimous moral stand, the protest of great former colonial countries like India and Indonesia – that all this would force the Soviet Union to accord to Hungary a neutral-independent status similar to that of Austria or Finland.

Naturally I did not think all this out in a calm and orderly manner. Those were hectic days. We walked, we fought, we met, we talked for a bit, then rushed home to see if the family was safe, then we went down to queue up for bread or milk in a temporarily quiet district where heroic shopkeepers opened their shops. Everyone and everything was heroic in those days, even the corns on our feet after roaming all over the battlefield of the city.

I remember once thinking about the UN when some of us ran for cover because a Soviet tank showed up at the top of the street and turned its gun in our direction.

Once, about four o'clock in the morning, when I arrived at last in a quiet no man's land, I laughed aloud with joy because I thought: 'Thank God, Orwell was not right about the youth.' The twelve- to fourteen-year-old boys and girls who hurled petrol-filled bottles at Soviet tanks exploded the myth of indoctrination. Oh, no, I laughed, no, dear commissars, you did not brain-wash us after all. Hypno-pedagogics turned against you!

There were the groups of Teddy boys and girls who did some wonderful fighting. Before the revolution I had a very poor opinion of them. Ever since I think about them with respect.

And there were the children of 'Uncle Szabo'. He had hundreds of children. I must describe them to give some impression of those walks.

A dark square at the foot of a hill. On one side an abandoned work tower of the tube-builders. Distant cannonade, the faint pop-pop of shell-fire somewhere far away. One of the narrow streets leading up to the square echoes now the noise of approaching lorry engines. A dark shape on the work tower speaks into a megaphone:

'Children, attention. Security Police convoy is approaching.'

In a few seconds the first lorry – or is it a riot wagon? – enters the square and stops abruptly. At the last moment barrels are sent rolling from somewhere in front of the lorries. The entire convoy stops. In the next few seconds there is still silence but hundreds of small dark shapes jump out from the open doors of the houses on the two sides of the street and are already swarming on the lorries. Before the SP people have a chance to do anything, the children like little monkeys are all over their lorries, on top of the SP troopers. Dozens of little hands hold the SP men, wrench the automatics from their hands. By this time the street is lined with adults holding tommy guns. Some SP men escape, some are taken prisoner. Everything happens without a shot. Some adults board the lorries and drive them away. Now the megaphone is heard again from the work tower:

'Children, you may keep the automatics, but hand over the hand grenades to the adults.'

In a few minutes adults and children retire to their hideouts. Nothing happens for fifteen minutes. Then again approaching rumble and again the voice through the megaphone: 'Russki tanks ... three of them ... Barrels ready! Molotov cocktails ready! ... Now!' And now the square flares up. The boys and girls throw flaming Molotov cocktails at the tanks, the adults open up with their automatics. The first tank is soon aflame. The turret of the second opens, five or six Russians get out in a hurry and are mowed down by the automatics. The third turns round and retreats in great haste.

The megaphone speaks up: 'Good work! Thank you!'

The voice is that of 'Uncle Szabo', the group is that of the Szena Square in Buda.

On the seventh day of our fight, on the thirtieth of October, Moscow Radio broadcasted a Soviet government declaration that they had given orders to their Commander-in-Chief in Hungary to withdraw his troops from Budapest as soon as the Hungarian government so desired. The Soviet Union was furthermore ready to open discussions on the general position of Soviet troops in Hungary.

That morning I succeeded for the first time in going to the editorial offices of *Irodalmi Ujsag*, which was next door to a building held by Soviet troops. A phone call came. I was to go to the Kilian Barracks, the headquarters of Colonel Maleter. (He became a general in the evening.)

It turned out that the foundation meeting of the Central Council of the Revolutionary Armed Forces was to be held in the famous barracks. It was eleven o'clock in the morning when I succeeded in bypassing isolated fighting pockets and got near to the huge battle-scarred building. It was surrounded by burned-out Soviet tanks, skeletons of armed cars and rubbish heaps of collapsed buildings. The neighbourhood was guarded by the famous Corvin regiment of young workers. A group of them accompanied me to a side door from which a young soldier took me up to the first floor. There in a room the delegates of the various fighting groups, of the revolutionary committees and the representatives of the revolutionary police and army gathered to form the supreme command of the revolution.

Most of the delegates had their tommy guns flung on their shoulders. Each fighting group in Budapest and from most of the country had sent one or two delegates. University students, young girls, old and young workers, air force officers, army colonels, police sergeants, army privates, university professors, peasants and writers thronged the room. At the table of the presidium sat General Kiraly, recently released from prison, next to him Colonel Maleter, one of the heroes of the revolution and three workers, among them the eldest of the six Pongracz brothers, who was the commander of the Corvin regiment.

Colonel Maleter summarized the proposed resolution. The Council was to be the supreme organ of the National Guard – consisting of the former freedom fighters – and of the revolutionary army and police. With the exception of a few units and detachments, ninety-five per cent of the army and police accepted the authority of the Council. The Council was to command the army of the revolution. This army would keep order till after the election of a new government that could take over. Colonel Maleter then proposed, 'We won't give back factories, we won't give back the land.' All these proposals were unanimously accepted.

During the discussion a report came that in the Buda district a mob was besieging a block of flats where SP officers lived. Colonel Maleter asked, 'Who will volunteer to save those SP officers?' Many volunteered, but in the end Uncle Szabo, commander of the Szena Square battalion of children, was sent out. 'Bring them in,' Colonel Maleter said. 'They will stay under arrest till a proper court tries them in open trial.' Szabo fulfilled his mission. This was the fascist counter-revolutionary whom Kadar had hanged a few months later.

The question of foreign armed help was also discussed. Colonel Maleter reported that all the arsenals filled to the brim by Rakosi were at our disposal. We needed neither men nor arms. If on our Western frontiers foreign volunteers wanted to cross into Hungary, our front guards should politely ask them to turn back. 'We don't want a second Korea. We don't want a third world war.'

As Maleter, tall and slim, with a face hewn out of rock, spoke to us, I thought that in our crazy, spontaneous uprising the 'momentary leaders' were indeed most realistic. The newly formed Council unanimously decided against accepting foreign armed help. Without the consent of the Soviet Union – however reluctant – we could not preserve the fruits of our local victory. We had to be realistic. We intended to be realistic.

By November first we thought we were victorious. The Soviet high command started negotiations with General Maleter about the evacuation of Soviet troops. We proclaimed our independence and neutrality. We renounced the Warsaw pact, and the one-party system. The various parties started to organize. But they were realistic too. I spoke to many people belonging to the various parties during the days of our phony victory. All of them wanted a democratic socialist regime in Hungary. People who, had Hungary been in a different geographical situation – for instance between Norway and Sweden – would not hear of socialism, were realistic enough not to want to provoke the Soviet leaders more than necessary. They wanted a multi-party system, national independence and neutrality – *within the limits of the given situation.*

I had my misgivings. On the second of November the revolutionary issue of *Irodalmi Ujsag* was published. My leading article had the title: 'With arms at rest'. I concluded:

> *It is the task of present-day Hungarians to be tough, honest and true. At the end of an age in which filth poured from every direction, let us be purer than the purest. At the end of an age which wanted to reduce* man *to a frightened puppet, let us be more resolute than the most resolute ones of other ages.* AND LET US GUARD OUR FREEDOM WITH ARMS AT REST.

There was one more day of 'victory' and peace.

On the third of November, a Saturday, the people of Budapest thought they should have a quiet night's sleep after two weeks of facing death, two weeks of infernal noise and almost unbearable excitements.

The Undefeated

People moved up from cellars to their flats. Plans were made for a quiet Sunday.

The Sunday that never came.

It was still dark when with a terrific roar the city seemed to explode. The alarm clocks of death chased us out of beds, still drunk with sleep, knowing full well that the end had come. The Kremlin leaders had decided to crush us.

We rushed to our wireless sets. With sinking hearts we heard the majestic sadness of our National Anthem.

'God bless us Hungarians.' The radio has nothing to tell the people. Just the National Anthem. It seems so sad now. So infinitely sad. And then the Song of the Nation – Szozat. Only the orchestra plays but everyone knows the words: 'It cannot be that so many hearts shed their blood in vain.' A hundred years passed and we again have to sing: 'It cannot be ...'

Can it be?

What now?

Drunk and numb from sleep and despair, I struggled to wade through the black waves of the vile nightmare which was our life during the coming days and weeks. In a world which had started to blur, in which everything was out of focus, I hoped that my head would clear, that I should see the way, that I should be able to rush ... rush where to? ... It is urgent ... terribly urgent ... But what? ... Save, save, save! What? Is there anything to save? Is there anything to hold on? Why life? What was the point in our lives? Was it worth while to go through my tortuous life?

But it was urgent. With trembling fingers I turned the dial, to the accompanying music of our National Anthem and the din of cannonade. In the hostile dawn under the neutral black clouds we all felt like ants in an antheap a few seconds before a giant boot annihilates them with an absent-minded step.

The very ferocity of the attack showed that the Soviet command intended to bludgeon, batter and smite down the people of Budapest to submission. While hundreds of heavy guns, mine throwers and tanks were pounding the city, jet bombers appeared in the sky. Would they bomb us?

Free Kossuth Radio – free for how many days? – had nothing to say. Not wanting to mislead anyone, they played alternatively the National Anthem and the National Song.

At four-twenty a.m. we heard the voice of Imre Nagy. His first message that morning – to be repeated in English, French and German – had the following text:

> *This is Imre Nagy speaking, Chairman of the Council of Ministers of the Hungarian People's Republic. In the early hours of dawn Soviet troops launched an attack against our capital with the obvious purpose of overthrowing the legal Hungarian government. Our troops are fighting. The government is in its place. I want to inform the people of our country and of the world of these facts.*

And then again the National Anthem.

Meanwhile quick telephone conversations. The outlines of the nightmare cleared up a little. There were already decisions. The Hungarian Army units which faced the steel ring of the Soviet tanks were putting up only a token resistance. Already the entire Soviet Union was waging war on us. No point in resisting from street to street, from house to house. The freedom-fighter units had to be told not to open fire on the entering Russians in order to save the population from a senseless massacre. Liaisoning, alas, was now easy. During our 'victory' days, the telephone lines were put in order. No walk now, just dial away.

I dialed the number of the flat in which the commander of the Corvin regiment had his headquarters. Long, long ringing. At last a deputy commander answered the phone. His voice was curiously calm:

'Yes, we realized that we should not open fire. But the Soviets did. They took up position around our block and opened up on us with everything they had. The cellars are filled up already with more than two hundred wounded and dead. We shall fight to the last man. There is no choice. But inform Premier Nagy that we did not start the firing.'

No, none of the groups started to fire. But the houses from which they fought during the first phase of the fight were cannoned to smithereens.

Dial away, dial, do something! … Premier Nagy cannot be found. What to do now?

The Undefeated

The din of cannonade; the radio playing the National Anthem; Soviet tanks streaming into Budapest, a holocaust of vicious armour – and then the last message of Free Kossuth Radio: the appeal of the Hungarian Writers' Association:

> *We ask for the help of every writer and scientist of the world, of every writers' association, of every academy, of all intellectual leaders. Time is short! You know the facts, we do not have to tell you these. Help Hungary! Help the Hungarian people! Help the Hungarian writers, scientists, workers, peasants and intelligentsia. Help! Help! Help!*

This was read in all civilized languages. 'Help! Help! Help!' – and then silence. The free radio of Budapest went dead.

The 'second phase' ... how should I describe the meaning these two words had for us? In the first phase, there was hope. In the second, Budapest became the dark city of blood, the graveyard of a revolution, the graveyard of our hopes.

The city fought on for eight days. The Soviets bombarded to rubble every house from which a single shot was fired. Why go on with the hopeless fight? Just to destroy our city? Just to have our children killed?

Then there was the general strike. That had to be stopped too if we did not want to commit national suicide.

Then the hideous slogans and stupid lies returned. Deportations and arrests were started again. By the end of November the Nausea was in full swing. Imre Nagy was given written safe-conduct, then kidnaped. There was a promise to set free the arrested people, and then further arrests.

The violated city is unclean. Rubble still sprawls across the streets. Big block of flats expose their ripped-up bowels. Boarded-up windows are blind, empty eyes. People live on borrowed time. There is not much to wake up for; there is not much point in doing anything. True, one has to queue up for milk and bread and meat – if one still has the money. But how long will the food last – or the money?

In the bleak mornings in the big block of flats neighbours get together to find out who has been arrested during the night, or which of the flats was left by people trying to escape. The people who lost their homes during the fight live by now in flats left by fugitives. The bombed-out families move into fully furnished flats with wardrobes full of clothes. There is a full larder; there may be toys on the floor. The original tenants are now in refugee camps somewhere in the West, a concentration camp somewhere in the East – or they may be lying dead on a muddy field near the frontier.

Fifty thousand people have left already but there are still a million and a half refugee candidates – for most of the city thinks about nothing else but escape. It is not the danger that deters so many – it is sheer lack of energy.

But I have to have energy. There is no point in staying. Why go back to prison again?

So for the second time in my life, I began preparations to escape from 'my' country. A fur sack for the baby. A rucksack filled with baby food, nappies and manuscripts. I called up a doctor. We had to have medicine for the baby to make him sleep during the long frontier passage.

The frontier was already crammed with Russian tanks and SP monsters. I could not risk challenge by Russian or SP guards on the route. We had to choose a swampy region of the frontier where even the Russians would not like to wade about.

It was a stormy night when a group – there were thirty-three of us – entered the swampy frontier region. We waded knee-deep in mud and water. The Russians kept sending up flares. Machine guns rattled in the distance. Each step was an enormous physical effort.

With my son asleep on my shoulder, and Agi at my side, we struggled on for hours. At one point all our strength was gone and we lay down on a drier piece of land where the mud was only ankle-deep. There I lay, holding my little son in my arms and looking up at the stormy sky in despair.

After an hour or so, we gathered enough strength to start wading again. By now we were alone in no man's land. Then we saw swiftly moving shadows: another group of escapees. They helped us on. We struggled with the swamp for another two hours. Then at last an Austrian flag – and a haystack! We collapsed.

The Undefeated

When I returned to consciousness, I looked at my watch. It was just midnight. It was my son's first birthday.

The obsession was burned out in me. I am a stateless person now without fanatical convictions. I have come to suspect that fanaticism is the original sin. I am confused and believe in simple things like common sense and common decency.

Maybe the time will come when I shall know the meaning of my life. Meanwhile I am grateful for having survived up till now, and hope to write stories, not to live them.

Afterword

WHEN BOBBY WAS IN CAIRO at the end of the War, he started to write a novel in English. The manuscript was to have a curious history. He brought it back with him to London and, later, to Hungary. He lent it to me during our brief courtship. When he was arrested it was therefore the only possession which survived from his home. It became, more or less unchanged, the first draft of *The Undefeated*. The original title was *The Survivor*.

When we fled Hungary in November 1956, the manuscript was the most precious item that Bobby put in his knapsack. He lost his shoes in the swamplands of the Austrian border, but the book survived. When we reached Andau, the first Austrian village, it was filled to the brim with thousands of refugees, a number considerably greater than its entire population. Red Cross vans served coffee and tea; warm clothing was available by the ton; nurses and ambulances were at the ready and the High Street was lit up like a Christmas tree. Jeeps, lorries and innumerable private cars caused traffic jams. We heard German, English, French voices; signs in Hungarian and German pointed towards the school building where mattresses and showers were available. To say that we were made welcome is the understatement of the century.

As we stood around dazed at the sight, not quite knowing where to start, a tall man in a khaki overcoat with a gigantic RAF-style moustache detached himself from the crowd and walked resolutely towards us. 'Do you understand English?' he bellowed. Seeming greatly relieved by our 'yes', he took Bobby resolutely by the arm, and waved at me to follow. Bobby was shoeless, and I was clutching the baby, but we happily waded through the snow towards a Nissen-hut.

The Undefeated

'I know exactly what you need,' he announced as we entered the dimly lit hut. Oh yes, yes, I wanted to say and looked around, but saw no shoes – just a camp-bed, chairs, a small table with some cigarettes, and a silvery shimmering large object placed on it. The two men were already in swift conversation. I collapsed on the bed with the baby in my arms. The moustachioed apparition smiled, picked up the silver object, waved his arms like a magician and shook it vigorously for a few minutes. Then he conjured up some glasses out of nowhere and poured out a large dry martini, adding: 'No olives, I'm afraid. Welcome to the West.'

We soon left by train for Britain. Bobby was ecstatically happy; he couldn't sleep, he couldn't sit still and he couldn't stop talking. The train, full of Hungarian refugees, stopped at every station where a speech was made by the burgomeister, usually followed by a brass band playing the Hungarian National Anthem; then we were given generous gifts. In one way, almost too generous; schnapps was included, so it was a spirited journey in every sense of the word.

The Channel crossing to Dover sobered up even the merriest. Bobby and I started to view our future with some trepidation. But if you start from scratch, there is only one way to go: up. On arrival at the clean and empty military camp, we had only one battered suitcase, several large plastic bags full of the discarded junk of West Germans, baby gear, and about £5 worth of Austrian schillings. A young private found a cot for Georgie, and we had a telegram from one of Bobby's old friends who, as it later turned out, sent the same message to every port in the UK where Hungarians were expected to land. I still have it. 'If Hungarian refugee named Paloczi-Horvath arrived continent tonight please ask him to telephone etc.' Bless him, wherever he is.

The camp was fine. Except the food. Within 48 hours, a deputation was sent to the commandant with the message: please can we have Hungarian food. The commandant turned out to be a very wise man. He gave a chit to a delicatessen in Dover, bought a few pounds of paprika, and told the Hungarians to do their own cooking.

The 1956 Hungarian exodus was the greatest proof – if proof be needed – of how whole countries can react to the desperate plight of the unfortunate. We experienced enormous generosity, kindness – an open heart all the way. The welcome we received was completely unlike that given to others in later, less generous, times. At our first Christmas, after we had moved to Kingston, a total stranger turned up at our doorstep, told me that she was a neighbour in the same street and gave me a cake she baked herself. I just cried.

Bobby was blooming, he was at home. I never felt a refugee, I was accepted and made welcome from the first day. We stayed in Richmond with friends of friends in a beautiful house right on the top of the hill which looked down on the river. My hostess, Joan Kaplan, was goodness itself. She showed us to our room, offered me yet more clothes. After we had settled, Joan asked me to tell her honestly what were my most urgent needs.

'A hairdresser,' I replied.

'A what?' she asked incredulously.

'Well, I just can't manage to wash my hair,' I admitted lamely. 'I've done it twice since we left. The result is disastrous. Where is the nearest hairdresser?'

'What did you do in Hungary?' Joan asked.

'Went to the hairdressers.'

'Always?'

'Yes. Why? Doesn't everybody?'

'Not here. Not quite. Were you terribly rich?'

'No, not at all.'

Communism is a strange economic system, not easily comprehensible to an English barrister's wife from Richmond Hill. She must have thought: 'Here is this strange young woman in her ghastly clothes, no earthly possessions, no money, no home and she wants a hairdresser.'

Bobby added to the confusion by going off to Fleet Street on our first day in London and returned wearing at last a clean new shirt, carrying a portable typewriter, and a large bunch of red roses. I reached out longingly for the flowers and got a rap on the knuckle. 'The roses are for Joan, naturally. The typewriter – well, that's the first thing I always buy when I arrive somewhere without anything. I must write some articles quickly. The Daily Herald gave me an advance in cash; it wasn't that easy, their accountants have never met anyone

without a bank account. So, here is some money, Agika, go and get
some clothes, you look simply awful in those hand-me-downs. Then
we must find somewhere to live. Furnished, I guess, as we are not likely
to have any furniture for some time.'

Joan forbore from mentioning that this, indeed, would be the case
if he kept buying bunches of flowers for his hostess and urging his wife
to get some clothes. In fact, she picked up the vibes pretty fast and,
when I told her that Bobby had given me £25, she said 'What the hell.
Go to Jaeger, I'll show you on the map how to get there.'

Georgie was farmed out for a fortnight, as we really did need some
sleep. Some wonderful family connected to the PEN Club offered to
take in a Hungarian child for a while. They lived nearby in Putney and
had five or six kids of their own. It made no difference at all; one extra
boisterous toddler was barely noticed in their large kitchen. We visited
him daily. He ate cornflakes, seemed blissfully happy and didn't miss
us at all. (Coming from backward Eastern Europe, we didn't know
about Dr Spock and bonding and such things. A baby was a baby and
whoever was passing by in that large kitchen fed him, while we were
only too happy to have a little rest for a change.)

The furnished house was in Kingston, five minutes from the river.
It was dark, dingy, sparsely furnished and – as I discovered only later
– had almost no heating, apart from a fireplace in the 'parlour' which
neither of us ever managed to light without creating clouds of smoke.
We went to Bentalls department store and bought two portable electric
heaters, some paprika, and Christmas decorations. I decided to try to
reciprocate the hospitality of Joan and her husband. We served them
a dinner in the ice-cold dining room, ate sardines on toast, bully-beef,
and a sponge cake without any filling.

And yet underneath all the hysteria and delight there was unre-
solved and suppressed stress. Homesickness, and guilt about those left
behind, and lots of fear. I had a recurring dream (which I later discovered was shared by almost all Hungarian refugees): I dreamt that I was
back in Budapest and was desperate to get out. I couldn't fathom why
I had returned. Had I been kidnapped? Had I returned deliberately?
Whatever the reason, I knew that I wanted out, that I was scared to
death. I would wake up screaming.

It took years to get rid of that dream. It finally disappeared when I started to dream in English and began to solve at least some of the deep undercurrent of pain.

During the first few months Bobby was often away, giving lectures about the Hungarian revolution. When home, he was pounding the typewriter. We needed the money.

The news from Hungary was grim. It was back to the old Stalinist model with monotonous news about arrests and executions; the unanimous uprising of a whole country was labelled a counter-revolution staged 'by a handful of agents of Western imperialism' and so on. I still have a copy of a letter which Bobby greatly treasured. It was smuggled out through Vienna:

> ... *Then you left. We rang up people and there was no answer. We knocked at doors, but only strangers appeared. Budapest for us became like a theatre after the performance was ended, when the actors have all gone home, lights were turned off and only the blank scenery stares into the void. We continued to live, for we could do nothing else.*
>
> *And how we live. Dreariness, nausea, disgust and danger from morning till night. Compulsory rejoicing and voluntary treacheries. The resurrection of the most worn-out propaganda-phrases; the commissars back in the saddle. Martial law, deportations and official slaughter.*
>
> *Now you are emigrés. But it is we who are the exiles in our own land. A double exile. Exiles from the outside free world and locking ourselves away from reality into the privacy of our thoughts. Your letters have an undercurrent of homesickness. We smile. We envy you your homesickness ...*

I asked the newsagent in Kingston whether she knew someone who would look after Georgie. Years later 'Auntie', who effectively became Georgie's surrogate grandmother, told me that she couldn't make head or tail of us. When she mentioned references, I never bothered with such mysteries. She had such a kind face with a warm smile. I felt sure it would work and of course it did. Georgie's first words were in English.

Did we mind that Georgie didn't speak Hungarian? Now that's a bit complicated. Yes and no. But mostly no. Bobby, despite his strong and painful links with language and homeland, didn't want to bring up his son as an outsider with an identity problem. As time passed we, too, spoke a mixture of Hungarian and English at home, so his 'mother-tongue' whatever that meant in his case, became English. He could understand some Hungarian and could manage if he had to, which wasn't necessary until thirty years later when he ordered a glutinous Chicken Paprika in the Café New York in Budapest. His roots were Richmond Park (where Auntie took him to feed the ducks), Robin Hood (on the telly), and Marmite on toast.

Though Bobby kept in close touch with the 1956 Hungarian emigré friends, and though he also worked for an influential Hungarian magazine called 'Literary Gazette' he decided not to get in touch with his own family in Hungary. 'It would cause trouble, a lot of trouble. *They* would take their revenge till the seventh generation. I know *them.*'

However, it never occurred to me not to keep in close touch with my own parents. My father was a light-music composer: jazz and blues. He never had anything to do with politics, was no member of any party. When they decided to emigrate and follow us to London, we were delighted. Come and start a new life, it's never too late. They applied for a passport.

After some months' delay the passport was granted together with an exit permit. They sold everything, packed four large trunks with 'emotional luggage' such as records, china, sheet music, photographs, and 3000 Hungarian books. This was duly inspected and sealed by Customs Officers, and despatched on its slow way to London.

In the June of 1957 my parents were to spend their last night in their home in Budapest. It was bare, save for some mattresses and a couple of chairs. The train to Calais was due to leave next morning. They had two small overnight suitcases and about 50 dollars allowance of foreign currency. Nothing else.

The telegram came when I returned from shopping for the festive meal I had planned for my parents' arrival. The two civilian employees of the Ministry of the Interior who took away my parents passports were polite. Permission to emigrate has been revoked. No reason was given. Bobby didn't seem surprised, but I broke down. I didn't see my parents for ten years.

Bobby's caution was well-founded but it didn't always make a difference. After we left, his brother lost his job from one day to the next; his nephew, Adam, whom he barely knew was refused a place at university for five years – just because he bore the name Paloczi-Horvath.

Bobby died in 1973 of a heart-attack. No pain, no long illness – the Gods repaid the debt they owed. Our son was 17 years old. In the morning of that same day Bobby put the finishing touches to a BBC Television documentary script about Stalin. He was pleased. It was work well done.

His life since 1956 had been happy, buoyant, and professionally fulfilling. By the spring of 1957 Bobby gave up lecturing and began to work full time as a freelance journalist and writer. In March he wrote a series of articles for the Sunday Times about the Hungarian Communist leadership, past and present, entitled 'Sinister Profiles'. It was very successful and more commissions followed. With Hungarian emigrés the belief in miracles seems to be an endemic disease, and Bobby was an unrepentant believer. His infectious optimism permeated our whole life; though we were often broke, the ups and downs of freelance existence never much bothered him. There was always tomorrow. Happily we had more good news than rejections.

He also worked maniacally re-writing *The Undefeated* into a full-length autobiography. Supportive encouragement came from his friends and his literary agent. In 1958 Secker & Warburg accepted it for British publication.

Returning home from a dinner party in October, we found a note from Auntie. 'Please ring James McGibbon at his home, no matter how late.' James was our agent at Curtis Brown. I listened to Bobbie, while he telephoned. 'Please, dictate me the telegram,' he said quietly to James. As he wrote it down, I read it together with him: 'By unanimous vote Atlantic Editors award Non-Fiction Prize to *The Undefeated*.' The

Prix de la Liberté in Paris followed a year later. The book was eventually published in ten languages.

In its first chapter Bobby had related how a cellmate had said to him, 'What a wonderful thing it would be if we could put our messages in bottles and let the waves carry them to the shores of free countries!' Now one of the bottles had at last arrived.